Mark Twain & the South

Arthur G. Pettit

Mark Twain & the South

The University Press
of Kentucky

for Kenneth M. Stampp

Contents

Acknowledgments

IN THE course of this study I have contracted intellectual debts that I shall never be able to repay and cannot even fully acknowledge. I have benefited greatly from the works of Walter Blair, Louis Budd, James M. Cox, John Hope Franklin, Winthrop D. Jordan, Justin Kaplan, Lewis Leary, Kenneth Lynn, Louis D. Rubin, Jr., Henry Nash Smith, Kenneth M. Stampp, William R. Taylor, and C. Vann Woodward. David Bertelson, Henry Nash Smith, and Kenneth M. Stampp at the University of California at Berkeley read the manuscript in an earlier form with their usual wisdom and patience. My colleagues Louis G. Geiger, Tom Mauch, Dennis Showalter, and Mark Stavig, and my former student Timothy Jacobson, read later stages and offered many helpful suggestions. Three grants from the Ford Humanities Committee at The Colorado College provided funds for travel, research, and typing. Ralph Gregory in the Mark Twain Library at Florida, Missouri, provided most of the data for chapter 1 and several statistics for chapter 9. Frederick Anderson, editor of the Mark Twain Papers at Berkeley, read the entire manuscript, and saved me from a number of serious errors. When I was floundering more than usual, my colleague Ruth Barton gave the manuscript a new direction and tried to remind me that even in literature so directly autobiographical as that of Mark Twain, the historian must constantly remind himself that he is dealing not with history but with fiction. My deepest gratitude goes to Thomas S. Schrock at the University of California at Santa Barbara, who read and criticized the manuscript so many times, always with competence and restraint, that it became in essence a collaborative work. Any bad art, faulty judgments, or factual errors that survive the labor of these friends are mine alone.

The person to whom I owe most is my wife Lynn, who read the work and kept the faith under conditions that lasted far too long. Together we dedicate this book to a man of uncommon compassion and understanding who has been my richest source of personal and professional inspiration. Kenneth M. Stampp has influenced my views of history and of myself more than he can ever know.

Acknowledgments

I wish to thank the editors of the following journals for permission to reprint material that first appeared in their pages: *Journal of Negro History* 41 (Spring 1971), copyright 1971 by the Association for the Study of Negro Life and History, Washington, D.C.; *Rocky Mountain Social Science Journal* 7 (April 1970), copyright 1970 by the Robinson-Warfield Company, Fort Collins, Colorado; *Southern Literary Journal* 4 (Fall 1971), copyright 1971 by the Department of English, University of North Carolina at Chapel Hill; and *Western Historical Quarterly* 1 (January 1970), copyright 1970 by the Western Historical Association, Utah State University, Logan, Utah.

I warn the reader that if he leaves out of the account an indignant sense of right and wrong, a scorn of all affectation and pretense, an ardent hate of meanness and injustice, he will come infinitely short of knowing Mark Twain.

William Dean Howells,
Century Magazine (September 1882)

It is by the goodness of God that in our country we have those three unspeakably precious things: freedom of speech, freedom of conscience, and the prudence never to practise either of them.

Pudd'nhead Wilson's New Calendar (1897)

Introduction

Every man's work, whether it be literature or music
or pictures or architecture or anything else,
is always a portrait of himself, and the more he tries
to conceal himself the more clearly will his
character appear in spite of him.
Samuel Butler,
The Way of All Flesh

We are so much in the habit of wearing disguises
that we end by failing to recognize ourselves.
La Rochefoucauld,
Maxims[1]

MARK TWAIN is an enigma. Like his creator Samuel Clemens and the South which nurtured him, he is a great tangle of tensions and dualities. If Southern historians have had trouble separating Southern fact from Southern fiction, the student of Mark Twain has a similar problem, for the man was caught up in virtually the same mixture of fascinations, myths, and half-truths that bemused and tormented the South. Southerners were supposed to be intrigued by Ancestry and by Cavalier origins. So too was Mark Twain. Southerners were supposed to be plagued by the Past, to be haunted by memories of slavery, the War, and Reconstruction. So was Mark Twain. Above all, Southerners were supposed to be consumed with shame and guilt over their treatment of the black race. And so was Mark Twain.

If Southerners were obsessed with Time and Place, Defeat and Deprivation, Race and Guilt, it is not surprising that spokesmen for the South have struggled for the better part of two centuries trying to explain their special situation. Nor is it surprising that in trying to explain the Burden they have added to it. The variety of symbols and shibboleths adduced by commentators has proved as bewildering as "the reality" itself. Out of a melange of myths, images, and theories, historians have come up with an impressive assortment of phrases to distinguish the Southern from the general American Way: the Southern Burden, the Southern Curse, the Southern Enigma, the Southern Irony, the Southern Riddle, the Southern Tragedy.[2] And so again with Mark Twain—errant son of the South, disloyal and disinherited, but still heir to the Burden and the Tragedy, and himself enigmatic and cursed.

Whether the historian's slogan or rubric refers to historical fact or to myth is not the chief question for the student of Southern literature or of Mark Twain. For it was the South *as* a series of images and myths,[3] the South as memory and feeling, which most concerned Mark Twain. If ambivalence characterized the South he wrote about, profound ambivalence characterized Mark Twain's approach to the South. Indeed any list of paired Southern affinities and antipathies reads like a catalog of Clemens's own attitudes and affects: leanings toward aristocracy and toward democracy, love of past and lust for progress, devotion to region and allegiance to nation. And, more than anything, ambivalence toward blacks: affection and distaste, defense and abuse, compassion and callous-

5

ness. It is true that other Americans had these mixed feelings, but they were the raw nerves of the South. And if the South was acutely distressed by being of so many minds and moods, so too was Mark Twain.

Consider the man's astounding personal and ideological incoherence. It is well known that Samuel Clemens was a man of many faces who never achieved a unified personality; critics call it the Mark Twain Problem. Though probably the most colorful and conspicuous American of his time, he felt the need to search out lesser figures to admire and emulate. He was vain, but he acknowledged his vanity with a childlike innocence that became a vital part of his appeal. He could be both kind and cruel: a clergyman acquaintance called him "the worst man I ever knew. And the *best*." A self-dramatized misanthrope who ranted tirelessly against the damned human race, he also loved a few people with an intensity that was downright discomfiting. A master of invective who spewed forth a great stream of venom and hatred,[4] he also followed up many of his public and private scurrilities with deep remorse and prolonged self-flagellation. Proud of his reputation as a liar, he may have been the most completely honest man of his time and was surely his own most severe moral critic, censor, and tormentor.

As a thinker and as a man of action Clemens showed much the same confusion. Fancying himself a level-headed philosopher, he usually relied on snap judgments, to be abandoned later if they didn't hold up under criticism or if the initial enthusiasm wore off. Fascinated by determinist logic, he reached most conclusions by impulse, argued in support of self-evident propositions, and showed little patience for sustained inquiry. Untroubled by inconsistencies, he was, from moment to moment, a realist or an idealist, a pessimist or an optimist. His affections oscillated between Europe and America, East and West, North and South, the past and the present, aristocracy and democracy, solitude and society, indolence and industry, the intellect and the heart, dream as reality and reality as dream. Out of patience with his times, he nonetheless enthusiastically embraced the "sivilization" that Huck Finn lit out from. Fond of imagining a day when Americans were not mad about money, he wanted to be rich: he had lofty conceptions about the simple life but no gift for living it. Deeply distraught over the business ethics and machine madness of the Gilded Age, he patented at least four inventions, considered some shady business enterprises,[5] and, throughout his life, tended to humanize machines and to mechanize people. He was alternately an eccentric and a conformist, a Christian and an atheist, an imperialist and an isolationist, an outspoken patriot and a disillusioned expatriate who spent a quarter of his adult life abroad. At once the idol of the common man and the pet and protege of the plutocracy, he championed labor unions and hobnobbed with Standard Oil moguls, endorsed the Russian Revolution and accepted barrels of Scotch whiskey from Andrew Carnegie.

The same doubleness characterized Mark Twain's career as a writer. He called himself the people's author, deliberately catering to "the belly and the members" rather than to "the head," but he was pleased when he cracked that bastion of intellectual respectability, the *Atlantic*. He wrote about the Far West and the Mississippi Valley with a freshness altogether new in polished American letters; yet he sometimes thought more highly of his trite tales of the Old World written in tired Victorian prose. He patched and padded some of his books unashamedly and insisted on at least one occasion that he would not write a book unless it would *"sell";* yet he wrote *The Prince and the Pauper* and *Joan of Arc* for love, not money. At the peak of his powers he turned himself almost exclusively into a summertime writer, spending the rest of each year as entrepreneur, impresario, traveler, lecturer, inventor, publisher, dramatist, and entertainer. Later, when his creativity was on the wane, he wrote year round, leaving more unpublished than published manuscripts. Even his most ardent admirers admit that he wrote his share of bad literature and squandered his talent by commercializing himself—allowing the performer to eclipse the writer. Still he gave us one of the world's great prose styles, a half-dozen books of lasting fame, and one of the few acknowledged masterpieces of American literature.

Clemens's double nature was not merely implicit: all his life he was disturbed by a dream self that seemed to lead a separate existence and to give him the feeling of being a twice-born man. Actually his personality was not so much split as splintered. His writings spill over with disguises, dissimulations, deceptions, twin personalities, double creatures, fakes, frauds, impostors, and pretenders. In his last coma he spoke of Dr. Jekyll and Mr. Hyde—and we are reminded of the prince and the pauper, the Siamese twins, the Huck Finn he admired and the Tom Sawyer he resembled, the American who pretends to be an earl and the earl who pretends to be an American, the white and mulatto babies who look alike and are switched, Hellsfire Hotchkiss passing as a man and Wapping Alice passing as a woman. There are also those personal aliases: Samuel Langhorne, J. B. Smith, J. P. Jones, C. L. Samuel, S.L.C., Sam, Mark, Youth, Child, Little Man, Colonel, and King.[6] But surely Clemens's most devious and enigmatic creation was Mark Twain[7]—a legend in his lifetime, a protagonist of the American experience who took on the air of a national institution, a common cultural property of the country who was expected to record, and to reflect, certain widely held opinions of his time.

No one understood the awesome power and precariousness of his position better than Mark Twain himself. In an era of colorless presidents and shadowy business figures he was the Most Conspicuous American, with a consummate knack for playing at the edge of public opinion. As jester to his generation he held a one-man post of criticism, privileged to twit whomever and whatever he chose, taking liberties few others were allowed. As the country's foremost showman he finally towered over his creator—became more real and more representative of his times than Clemens. But even after he enlarged on his claim as the nation's Representative Man by appointing himself Ambassador at Large for the Human Race, Mark Twain still remained uncertain about who he was and whether he was, indeed, the representative man. Sometimes he thought of himself as a prodigy of nature—an unaccountable freak like Halley's comet, which had blazed over his birth in 1835 and which he expected to oversee his death. At other times he thought of himself as the archetypal man. His boast that he was "the whole human race compacted and crammed into a single suit of clothes"—a man housing in his person "every quality and every defect that is findable in the mass of the race"—was not altogether a joke.

So in justice to the man's genius, which was grounded in ambivalence and confusion, we should shun the temptation to search out patterns of consistency where they do not exist. Any attempt to discover order in, or to impose it upon, Mark Twain's jumbled response to the issues of his time would distort the man and his achievement. He did not place tidy thought very high on his list of desiderata. Yet it is precisely in his response to black people and to the South that we find order emerging where we expected chaos. Having learned about the man's protean personality, we find that his feelings on race and region move in an intelligible direction: from Southerner to anti-Southerner to one who longed for a South he finally realized had never existed; from conscious bigot to unconscious bigot to one who became fully aware of his bigotry, fought it, and largely overcame it. For all the backing and filling that attended the Reconstruction of this Southerner, there is a clearly traceable movement away from the white South and toward the black race.

The movement did not begin until Clemens was well into his thirties. Born to a poor but proud border Southern family, he was raised on the notion that all Clemenses were descended from Virginia bluebloods and that his native state (which he sometimes called the South, sometimes the West)[8] stood directly on the line of friction between North and South—its predominant Southernness salted down by the presence of a sizable contingent of Yankees. It was this mixed society that provoked Mark Twain's best writing. And it was this mixed society to which Samuel Clemens owed so much of the intense intellectual and emotional confusion he experienced on his way toward a reconstructed view of his native South.

The confusion was intensified by the fact that the Clemens family, like most Missourians and other Americans, held "niggers" to be vastly inferior to whites. Unlike most Missourians or other Americans, the Clemenses sometimes owned a few slaves, and Clemens himself accepted the South's peculiar institution well into his twenties. His early notebooks and journals are liberally sprinkled with jokes about black body odor, fried nigger steaks, black sexual promiscuity, and the evils of miscegenation. Yet he eventually married into an abolitionist family, befriended Frederick Douglass, financed a black artist's apprenticeship in Paris, and supported several black students through Yale Law School. As Mark Twain he lectured in all-black churches, championed the cause of Booker T. Washington, wrote blistering essays about atrocities committed against blacks, and gave large doses of dignity and power to three of the outstanding black characters in nineteenth-century literature. He began his career as a segregationist, turned himself into a champion of interracial brotherhood, and ended his life as a prophet of racial war.

It is precisely this "reconstruction" that makes the career of Mark Twain as a Southerner worth studying. This man belongs in the distinguished company of a long line of Southern writers who have tried to transcend their heritage without disclaiming it. Like so many Southerners whose principles pushed one way and memories pulled another, Mark Twain was torn between passionate loyalty to the South and bitter alienation from it. Almost to the end he remained of two minds about the South—the South as Eden and the South as Wasteland. From *Huckleberry Finn* on he wrote out of a tension shaped by concurrent attraction and aversion for the South. And, as he grew older, the impulses that informed his inquiry into his own Southern past were his love—and fear—of the black man.

Toward the end of his life, while the fan of racial friction spread northward, Mark Twain began to question the justice of Southerners' bearing the stigma of a national aberration. In his last years he increasingly viewed the South less as a regional freak and more as a symbol of an impending nationwide racial holocaust: the Crisis of the South was becoming all-American. If Mark Twain saw lights going out across Dixie a bit earlier than elsewhere, it was only because to him Southerners were, after all, like everyone else only a little more so, and that as the South goes so too will go the Nation. Either Americans were becoming more Southern or Southerners more American—by the turn of the century it really didn't matter which. For Mark Twain, in the twilight of his life, Southern history had become a parable of man's tragic but richly deserved lot. The South was simply America, if not the world, in microcosm.

In the last thirty years of his life he was by no means alone in his thinking. The Gilded Age had its prophets of doom as well as its preachers of progress—and Mark Twain served in both camps. For all his savage criticism of the era that bears the abusive title he gave it, his distress was brought on by his participation as well as his criticism. This man deserves the close study of the social historian because his divided personality, and his inimitable way of saying things, reflected and expressed some of the most advanced thoughts and entrenched prejudices of his time. To trace his attitudes toward the South and the black race is to glimpse the evolving opinions of a good many Americans during a half-century of unprecedented social change. That he was as complex as the age he named and satirized—and as tortured and confused as the South herself—enlarges his importance. For Mark Twain came to look upon his personal lot and that of the country, especially that of the South, as similar and tragic.

1

Convinced & Content:
The Missouri Years

I had seen and known negroes since I could
remember. I just looked at them as I did at rain, or
furniture, or food or sleep. But . . . [now] I
seemed to see them for the first time not as
people, but as a thing, a shadow in which I lived,
we lived, all white people. . . . I thought of all
the children coming forever and ever into the world,
white, with the black shadow already falling upon
them . . . in the shape of a cross . . . as if they
were nailed to the cross . . . a long line of them
with their arms spread, on the black crosses.

William Faulkner,
Light in August

There isn't anything you can't stand, if you are only
born and bred to it.

A Connecticut Yankee
in King Arthur's Court[1]

MARK TWAIN's confusion over the South and over his relationship to her was grounded in his ancestry and in his first seventeen years in Missouri. Though he liked to claim that his roots went deep into the egalitarian soil of the valley of American democracy, neither Samuel Clemens nor his forebears really saw themselves that way. Both sides of the Clemens family believed they sprang from cavalier stock. His mother boasted a wondrously exiguous connection with the earls of Durham; his father claimed a more credible link with a Roundhead judge named Gregory Clemens, who lost his head for conspiring to remove that of King Charles I.[2]

In his *Autobiography*, that piece of near-fiction he thought of as the most unvarnished personal history ever written, Mark Twain remembered his mother, Jane Lampton Clemens, as a fiery-tempered Kentuckian who had traced her ancestry, to her personal satisfaction, through nine hundred years worth of connections with feudal lords in England and into lofty new world lineage as well. Although the Lampton legacy was deflated to the point that she could offer only two or three slaves as a dowry when she married John Marshall Clemens, Jane Clemens was fond of reminding her children that her father had been a substantial slaveowner in the Virginia piedmont before the Revolution. After her two grown sons married into Northern families, she continued to act like a Southern aristocrat by breeding and by instinct, a diehard Missourian who disliked, distrusted, and despised Yankees "with a splendid energy."[3]

Clemens's father, John Marshall Clemens, was a dignified and austere Whig descended from a long line of Virginia landowners and slaveholders.[4] Though an unsuccessful lawyer, merchant, and farmer and hardly a blue-stocking, Judge Clemens—so titled because he served briefly as justice of the peace—considered himself an authentic throwback to the ethos of a previous generation, a leftover Jeffersonian stranded in the backwash of the Mississippi frontier.[5] During his short life (he died of pneumonia when Sam Clemens was eleven) John Marshall Clemens managed to persuade his family that they should take just as much pride in their "fine Virginia stock" as in the seventy thousand acres of undeveloped land he purchased and left for them in Tennessee.[6] For these two reasons, worthless land and worthy blood, the Clemens family—shabby but respectable, poor now but with high hopes—was ex-

13

pected to live up to that aristocratic taint that Mark Twain remembered as percolating through Missouri's upper class.

The family was also qualified for membership in Missouri's social elite by way of the sometime ownership of slaves. Before Sam Clemens was born his father owned a slave or two in Tennessee, and he also owned and rented a few slaves in the backwoods village of Florida, Missouri, where Sam was born.[7] When the family moved to Hannibal in 1839, Marshall Clemens owned slaves as he could afford them. Though closer to Keokuk, Iowa, than to St. Louis, Hannibal was linked to the lower South by the Mississippi and was settled largely by Southerners, who brought their slaves with them. By 1850, when Sam was fourteen, the town numbered about 2,000 whites and 300 slaves.[8]

Like many border Southerners, Mark Twain had trouble remembering whether slavery was brutal or benevolent. At a distance of some forty years from the institution he was certain that most slaves in Missouri were "convinced and content" and that "cruelties were very rare, and exceedingly and wholesomely unpopular." Yet two paragraphs later he admitted that slavery stupified the white man's sense of humanity[9] and that to admit it existed *anywhere* was "to admit that you may describe any form of brutal treatment which you can imagine and go there and find it . . . applied." He also remembered that everyone in Hannibal loathed the town's chief slave trader, William Beebe, but that everyone also got used to the way Beebe made his living.[10] Clemens's own father had long and complicated business dealings with Beebe, and Mark Twain vividly recalled as a boy seeing gangs of slaves chained together on Hannibal's cobblestone wharf, waiting to be shipped down the river.

Like many Southerners, too, Mark Twain was upset over the damage wrought by slavery on whites as well as blacks. In an unpublished essay written in the 1880s he recalled that the "wise & the good & the holy" all agreed that slavery was "right, righteous, sacred, the peculiar pet of the Deity, & a condition which the slave himself ought to be daily & nightly thankful for." Skeptics need only look in the Bible to settle their minds about that, and Bible texts were read aloud to congregations on Sunday morning to make the matter sure. In point of fact Hannibal's churches did serve as bulletin boards for announcements of forthcoming slave auctions, and Mark Twain remembered one Methodist minister in Hannibal who sold a black child to another clergyman, who in turn took the child down the river to be sold in the lower South.[11]

For a man who thought slave cruelties in Missouri were rare, Mark Twain remembered quite a few of them. In the last decade of his life he told his biographer, Albert Bigelow Paine, that as a four-year-old child in Florida, Missouri, he had tossed and turned in his bed one night while he listened to the groans of a captured runaway slave who had been tied and beaten in a shack near the Clemens home. In 1845, when he was nine, Clemens was an eye witness to a shattering incident. Standing on one of Hannibal's main streets, he watched a white overseer strike and kill a slave with a slag of ore. A half-century later, in a passage dictated for his autobiography but deleted from the published version by Paine, Mark Twain added: "I knew the man had a right to kill his slave if he wanted to, & yet it seemed a pitiful thing & somehow wrong, though why wrong I was not deep enough to explain. . . . Nobody in the village approved of that murder, but of course no one said much about it. . . . Everybody seemed indifferent about it—as regarded the slave—though considerable sympathy was felt for the slave's owner, who had been bereft of valuable property by a worthless person who was not able to pay for it."[12]

Fifty years after leaving Hannibal and halfway around the world in Bombay, Mark Twain watched a German hotel manager strike an Indian servant. The incident carried him back at once to the antebellum South and revived his deep sense of guilt and remorse. "I was able to remember that the method seemed right and natural to me in those days," he wrote, "I being born to it and unaware that elsewhere there were other methods; but I was also able to remember that those unresented cuffings made me sorry for the victim and ashamed for the punisher."[13]

The incident that left the deepest impression on young Clemens took place in 1847, when he was eleven. A runaway slave named Merian Todd swam the half-mile of river separating Missouri from the "free" state of Illinois and hid in the Illinois bottoms. A ne'er-do-well Hannibalian named Benson Blankenship, whose younger brother became the model for Huck Finn, found the slave in the swamp thickets. Ignoring the fifty-dollar reward and the Illinois law requiring that runaways be returned to their owners, Blankenship fed and concealed the black man for several weeks. Word eventually leaked out and a band of woodcutters chased Todd into a swamp, where he drowned. According to a local newspaper the slave's body was "much mutilated" by the woodcutters. A few days later, while rowing around the foot of an island with some friends, Clemens watched the slave's mangled body rise to the surface of the water after being jarred loose from some debris.[14]

In a slave society there was no guarantee that violence would stay on one side of the color line. On November 8, 1849, the *Hannibal Courier,* with thirteen-year-old Clemens on its staff as printer's apprentice, carried the most spectacular story of the year under the headline "ATROCIOUS MURDER AND RAPE." A young slave known locally as Glasscock's Ben was accused of killing a ten-year-old white boy with a rock, raping the boy's sister, and slitting her throat. A "thrill of horror," cried the *Courier,* swept "our whole country." The slave, who thought he would escape hanging because he was worth a thousand dollars, was threatened with mob action but survived to be on hand for the first legal hanging in the history of Marion County, before one of the largest crowds ever assembled for a social function in Hannibal.[15] Fifty-two years later, in 1901, Clemens still remembered the hanging. In a letter to his publisher about the possibility of writing a book on lynching he wrote: "The negro raped a young girl and clubbed her and her young brother to death. . . . I remember all about it. It came out that his owner smuggled him out of Virginia because he had raped three white women there and his commercial value was deteriorating."[16] Small wonder that some of Clemens's more disturbing dreams in later years included the very cruelties of slavery, committed by white on black and black on white, that Mark Twain alternately admitted and denied as part of antebellum life in Missouri.

Samuel Clemens's earliest and strongest impressions about slavery and black people were formed in his own home. John Marshall Clemens was a chronic business failure, but he sometimes managed to keep a household servant or two on hand. Since only one in eight white families in Missouri owned any slaves at all,[17] Judge Clemens came fairly close in this respect to the elite position he sought.

Relatives later insisted that slavery was practiced benevolently in the Clemens household and that the word nigger was rigidly forbidden. But family correspondence during these years suggests that this common expression was more a household habit than a forbidden word,[18] and Marshall Clemens did not always practice slavery benevolently. In 1823 he sold a seventeen-year-old boy for $250 to a man in Mississippi, where slavery was widely viewed by border Southerners as hell on earth. He also rented slaves, a common practice in the border South. According to Mark Twain's later testimony one of the family slaves, a boy named Lewis, was "commonly cuffed" by his father for "any little blunder or awkwardness" and given "a lashing now & then, which terrified the poor thing nearly out of his wits." Although Mark Twain was quick to add that his father's punishment of slaves "proceeded from the custom of the time" rather than "from his nature," the custom of the time was upheld in the Clemens household. When a young slave woman named Jenny snatched a whip from Jane Clemens, who was about to beat her, Judge Clemens rushed home, tied the black woman's wrists together, and flogged her with a cowhide whip. Later, like Roxana in *Pudd'nhead Wilson,* Jenny was sold down the river.[19]

The history of another family slave tells much about Marshall Clemens. In November 1840 the judge acquired an elderly black man named Charley in the settlement of a long-standing debt. Slightly more than a year later, in January 1842, he took Charley with him on a business trip to Tennessee and Mississippi, hoping to sell the slave farther South for a higher price than he had paid for him. Somewhere in Mississippi, Marshall Clemens found the financial misfortunes of a white man who owed him $470 so tragic that he "could not have the conscience," as he wrote his wife, to collect the debt. But he was less concerned about Charley. Although the slave's fate is not certain, a promissory note given Judge Clemens by one Abner Phillips in Natchez "for value received the 24th day of January 1842" suggests that Charley was turned in for ten barrels of tar worth forty dollars. Forty-two years later Nigger Jim would be sold by the King and the Duke for "forty dirty dollars."[20]

And forty-five years later Mark Twain saw something terribly wrong with his father's behavior. In an unpublished tribute to his mother written in 1890 or 1891 he observed that his father had made a "hard & tedious journey" in midwinter, "plowing through ice & snow, horseback & per steamboat for six weeks" to collect a sizeable debt that few men "wouldn't have collected, & the man's scalp along with it." Yet "poor Charley's approaching eternal exile from his home, & his mother, & his friends, & all things & creatures that make life dear & the heart to sing for joy" troubled his father not at all. Selling a slave affected Marshall Clemens "no more than if this humble comrade of his long pilgrimage had been an ox—& somebody else's ox." Though Mark Twain "thank[ed] God" that he had "no recollection of him as [a] house servant of ours," he did not forget either Charley or his father's behavior. In 1892, in an early draft of *Pudd'nhead Wilson,* he introduced a Missouri slaveowner named Percy Driscoll, who is patterned closely after Marshall Clemens. To stave off financial disaster from unsuccessful speculation (a chronic disability of Marshall Clemens's), Driscoll takes a slave named Jim on a long horseback ride in the wet and cold of winter to Tennessee, where he hopes to sell Jim and to collect a debt of four hundred dollars from a Tennessee planter. Finding the planter in desperate circumstances, Driscoll writes home to his wife that he "had no heart" to press the issue and had cancelled the debt, but that he hoped to make up for the loss by selling Jim. "It never occurred to him," Mark Twain says of Driscoll, that Jim "had a heart in his bosom to break, & left hearts behind him that could break also."[21]

Mark Twain sometimes thought he was too harsh on his father; but Marshall Clemens was, after all, a pillar of the community and was expected to uphold popular attitudes toward slavery and toward abolitionists, and he did. In September 1841, when Sam Clemens was five, his father was foreman of a county jury that sent three abolitionists to prison for capturing five slaves and taking them across the river into Illinois. In an action filled with irony, the slaves returned to Missouri, captured their benefactors, and turned them in to the sheriff. Faced with lack of witnesses for the prosecution, the court waived the South's usual rule forbidding black testimony against whites and allowed the slaves to enter evidence against the abolitionists in court. The citizens of Hannibal, who favored hanging the abolitionists, finally accepted with "considerable applause" the twelve-year sentences of hard labor handed down by the Clemens court. Mark Twain later remembered how proud the town was of his father's leadership in the case.[22]

Young Clemens gained his most intimate acquaintance with slaves during several summers spent on his Uncle John Quarles's farm near Florida, Missouri. Quarles owned perhaps a dozen slaves.[23] With the exception of Aunt Hannah all were one family, which may explain the sense of closeness between slaves, and between slaves and slaveowners, that Mark Twain remembered as part of slave life in Missouri. One of the Quarles slaves, Aunt Hannah, was an ancient invalid "cooness" "upward of a thousand years old" with a bald spot on the top of her head from the horror of seeing a pharaoh drown. Mark Twain remembered that "whenever witches were around she tied up the remnant of her wool in little tufts, with white thread, and this promptly made the witches impotent." Thirteen years after leaving Missouri, Clemens reminded himself that "niggers tie [their] wool up with thread, to keep witches from riding them." Sixteen years after that notebook entry, and thirty-eight years after the end of Clemens's personal experience with slavery, Nigger Jim would be ridden by witches in *Huckleberry Finn* and one of Silas Phelps's Arkansas slaves would tie up his "wool" with thread.[24]

The slave who left the strongest impression on Clemens was Uncle Daniel, the middle-aged head of the Quarles slave family, described by his owner in 1855 as "my old and faithful servant Dann who is now in the fiftieth year of his age about Six feet high Complexion black, big mouth and thick lips."[25] Sixty years after seeing Daniel for the last time, Mark Twain remembered him as a "faithful and affectionate good friend, ally and adviser" who had the most level head "in the negro quarter" and possessed the qualities of "patience and friendliness and loyalty" that Mark Twain transferred intact to Nigger Jim. Daniel also told frightful ghost stories:

I can see the white and black children grouped on the hearth . . . and I can feel again the creepy joy which quivered through me when the time for the ghost story was reached. . . . We would huddle close about the old man, & begin to shudder . . . & under the spell of his impressive delivery we always fell a prey to that climax at the end when the rigid black shape in the twilight sprang at us with a shout.[26]

Yet if Clemens enjoyed ghost stories, and even enjoyed setting himself up as "a person of low-down tastes" who preferred "the company of the niggers . . . to that of the elect," Mark Twain also recognized that too many terms and conditions were imposed on both races to permit the degree of intimacy he sometimes wished to remember. When wills or tempers crossed, the black had to yield. "All the negroes were friends of ours," he wrote late in life, "and with those of our own age we were . . . comrades, and yet not comrades; color and condition interposed a subtle line which both parties were conscious of and which rendered complete fusion impossible."[27]

Everything we know about Clemens's early life supports this remark, especially the atmosphere of his own home. Mark Twain later wrote that his mother was distressed by the mistreatment of slaves, as she was distressed by the mistreatment of cats and other "creatures," but Jane Clemens never spoke out against slavery as a social institution. John Marshall Clemens may have pondered the moral and philosophical shortcoming of slavery, but he owned slaves when he could afford them. And Samuel Langhorne Clemens apparently gave little thought or feeling of any kind to the institution that was tearing families, states, and the union apart. He was, after all, in his late teens and early twenties when his older brother Orion split the family in fairly common Missouri fashion by becoming an abolitionist.[28] Yet even after he began to contribute occasional columns—some serious, some frivolous—to his brother's Whig newspaper in Hannibal, Sam Clemens remained silent on the whole business of slavery.

For all Mark Twain's later remarks on the position of blacks and the condition of slavery in his native state, we know next to nothing about how young Clemens felt. That we have to go forward a half-century to learn about Missouri slavery through Mark Twain is perhaps inevitable. He was always his own biographer. But Clemens's silence during the 1850s suggests that he probably viewed the peculiar institution the way most Missourians viewed it: as a customary (though by no means unquestioned) part of life in the border South. Not until he left Missouri in 1853 did Clemens begin to open himself up about slavery. When he did he spoke in very general terms. But his outpourings against blacks *as* blacks became very specific indeed.

2

The Most Conceited Ass
in the Territory

I can picture myself as I was 22 years
ago . . . a callow fool, a self-sufficient ass, a mere
human tumble-bug, stern in air, heaving at
his bit of dung & imagining he is re-modeling the
world & is entirely capable of doing it right.
S. L. Clemens to J. H. Burrough (1876)[1]

WHEN Sam Clemens left Hannibal in May 1853 to begin eight years of knocking about in the East as an itinerant typesetter and then in the South as a river pilot, his letters home reveal, for the first time, the extent to which he had accepted Missouri prejudices against "fat, lazy 'niggers.' " From the Crystal Palace Fair in New York he wrote his mother that he found the town of Syracuse especially interesting, because the court house had once been "surrounded with chains and companies of soldiers, to prevent the rescue of McReynold's niggers, by the infernal abolitionists." Clemens was annoyed to see at first hand the degree of freedom enjoyed by blacks in the North. "I reckon I had better black my face," he added in the same letter, "for in these Eastern States niggers are [judged] considerably better than white people." In another letter to his mother he complained that he had to pass by a motley assortment of humanity on his way to dinner in the evening, including "niggers, mulattoes, quadroons, Chinese, and some the Lord no doubt originally intended to be white, but the dirt on whose faces leaves one uncertain as to that fact." To be compelled to walk within smelling distance of this "mass of human vermin" would anger the "most patient person that ever lived." From Philadelphia Clemens asked his brother Orion how he liked the foolish "free soil" arguments of the North and expressed a homesick longing to see a "good, old-fashioned negro" slave again.[2]

When his ambition to set up a coca plantation in South America was dashed by the fact that no ship was expected to leave for that part of the world "during that century," Clemens became a cub apprentice and then a pilot on the lower half of the Mississippi. Awed by the regal life of the gold-leaf, kid-glove, diamond breast-pin pilots who were the nearest thing to an aristocracy on the river, he drank his coffee with burnt brandy, danced the schottische on the hurricane deck, and sported ruffled shirts and muttonchop whiskers. Off duty in New Orleans he praised the Mardi Gras extravagantly, splurged on ten-dollar dinners in the French quarter, walked the Vieux Carre, and boated with Southern belles on Lake Pontchartrain. His single literary effort between 1857 and 1862 was a callous burlesque that referred, among other things, to the hundreds of slaves who were slaughtered up and down the Mississippi valley after an abortive uprising in 1813.[3]

Two decades later Clemens looked back on his behavior in the

1850s and pronounced harsh judgment: "Ignorance, intolerance, egotism, self-assertion, opaque perception, dense & pitiful chuckle-headedness—and an almost pathetic unconsciousness of it all" was what he had been when he was twenty, and it was "what the average Southerner is at 60 to-day." But in the late 1850s Clemens had not yet reached this level of perception. On the eve of the Civil War he flirted with Know-Nothingism, then joined the coalition of ex-Whigs who called themselves Constitutional Unionists, supported the Dred Scott decision, and carried most of the border South in the election of 1860. While his brother voted for Lincoln, Sam Clemens rejected even the moderate Democratic candidate, Stephen Douglas, who carried Clemens's own state.[4]

Clemens's Southernism, in other words, was a matter of conscious choice as well as regional background. Although he supported the Whig ideal of Union *and* slavery in 1860, he had no constitutional scruples about the South's right to secede. A cryptic notebook entry made a half-century later still evokes the wild secessionist fever that spread through Clemens as well as the South when the states through which he was piloting began to leave the Union. "Jan. 26—'61:, La. went out," Clemens wrote in 1905. "Great rejoicing. Flags, Dixie, soldiers." In February of 1861, while his boat was docked in New Orleans, he wrote Orion that his Southern allegiance had just been confirmed by a visit to a notoriously accurate fortune teller. In an effort to shock his Unionist-abolitionist brother Clemens reported that "Madame Caprell" had just told him that he was Southern to the core, that he would "finally live in the South," and that he would always remain loyal to Southern values and ideals. His Missouri niece, who knew him well at the time, upheld Clemens's self-prophecy by claiming that he was a Southerner and that "his sympathies were with the South."[5]

Actually there was some doubt about how tenaciously Clemens would cling to his Southern sympathies if he had to fight to uphold them. It was one thing for him to defend the right to secede in the abstract, quite another for him to *do* it. When President Lincoln warned that pilots who stayed on the river might be drafted to serve on Union gunboats and that they certainly could expect to be fired upon by both sides, Clemens perceived that it made good sense to leave the river for the few months it might take for the skirmish to die out. His niece later recalled that Clemens "was obsessed with the fear that he might be arrested by government agents and forced to act as pilot on a government gunboat while a man stood by with a pistol ready to shoot him if he showed the least sign of a false move." Clemens himself later described the misfortunes of pilots who chose to stay at the wheel and were sometimes shot out of their glass perches for their trouble: "Pilots used to hold up a spittoon or a caneseat chair to protect their heads & hide behind a bit of canvass or lie down on the floor. One in white linen held a spittoon to his head, with the breaking glass rattling around him; the content spilt on his clothes & when he saw it he said 'O God, I'm shot!' and fainted."

Understandably reluctant to remain in such a vulnerable position, Clemens made his way home to Hannibal quickly.[6] Sometime that summer he got together at night, Tom Sawyer style, with some of the "boys" (Clemens was twenty-four) he had played with fifteen years earlier and swore allegiance to the Ralls County Rangers. For lack of a better choice, as he said later, he was appointed second lieutenant. Since the state they were defending from Union invaders was primarily in Union hands, the rangers first drilled secretly near Hannibal, then retreated to a position farther away from the enemy. After two weeks of hiding in corncribs by day and retreating "like a rat" through mud by night, it occurred to Clemens that this was not what he had had in mind when he joined. "My splendid Kipling himself," he wrote in 1891, "hasn't a more burnt-in, hard-baked, and unforgetable familiarity with that death-on-the-pale-horse-with-hell-following-after, which is a raw soldier's first fortnight in the field."[7]

For Clemens one fortnight was enough. Although his decision to "resign" was due more to weather conditions and a swollen ankle (sprained when he fell from a burning hayloft where he was resting from his latest retreat) than to any ideological change of heart, like Huck Finn he found it easier to light out for the territory than to be at once a disloyal Northerner and a treasonous Southerner. Consequently when the incurably penniless Orion needed money to travel to Nevada in the summer of 1861 to assume his appointment by President Lincoln as Republican secretary of the new territory, Sam Clemens, ex-Confederate seeking political asylum but still a Southern sympathizer, was quick to offer his company as well as his money.[8]

In Nevada, Clemens did not modify his Southern convictions at once. Though there were more Northerners than Southerners in the territory,[9] the Southern minority was loud and well organized.

Clemens's permanent place of residence, Virginia City in Humboldt County, was named by Southerners and was a stronghold of secessionist sentiment. When the territory at large emphatically rejected a statehood proposal, in part because it would permit free blacks to enter the new state, Humboldt County polled the largest negative percentage in the territory. Local secessionist newspapers claimed credit for defeating the statehood bill, declaring that "our folks put it up to help slaughter that free nigger Constitution, and may be they didn't succeed! Oh, no!"[10]

Nevertheless, even though Southerners could express themselves freely in the territory in 1861 and early in 1862, Clemens managed to overstep himself. Shortly after he arrived in Virginia City he apparently boasted that he had been a first lieutenant in the regular Confederate Army, which offended Northerners. Later, when it was learned that this Southern hotspur had actually been a second lieutenant of Missouri farm boys who spent most of their time retreating, Clemens suffered considerable personal embarrassment and managed to offend Southern sympathizers. James Nye, the Union territorial governor, called Clemens a "damned secessionist" and Judge G. T. Sewall of the Virginia City circuit court swore an oath to whip Clemens "on sight" for his Southern sentiments. "Now what would you advise a fellow to do?" Clemens asked his friend William Clagett, "take a thrashing from the son-of-a-bitch or bind him over to keep the peace? I don't see why he should dislike *me*. He is a Yankee, and I naturally love a Yankee." In another letter to Clagett he referred to Union troops in the East as "they," and complained bitterly that "our Missourians" had just been "thrashed" by the enemy. "Now, when I was on the Sacred Soil," Clemens assured Clagett, "I used to be terrible as an army with banners."[11]

Given this rakish behavior, it is not surprising that when Clemens described himself in a letter home as "the most conceited ass in the Territory"[12] he echoed an opinion widely held in Nevada. It was especially distressing for Orion Clemens, as acting governor of the territory when Nye was in Washington, to tolerate an upstart brother who carried the official title of assistant secretary of state of the Territory of Nevada but who spent too much time in saloons and was widely known as a disloyal and disreputable troublemaker.

Then, quite suddenly in the early part of 1862, Clemens began to realign himself. Clearly unhinged by the rapid growth of Union sentiment in the territory, he first hedged about his Southern convictions, then threw them away altogether. Within a few weeks his cautious retreat became a pell-mell rout as he hastened to discard his Southernism and to cast himself in the role of a converted Yankee. By September 1862, just six months after his letter to Clagett about "our Missourians," Clemens was referring to the Northern armies as "we"! In another letter to Clagett he declared that "the very *existence* of the United States" was threatened, and that the mortal danger of the Union now concerned him very much:

I am afraid we have been playing the game of brag about as recklessly as I have ever seen it played. . . . D—n it! only to think of this sickening boasting—these miserable self-complacent remarks about "twenty-four hours more will seal the fate of the bastard confederacy—twenty-four hours more will behold the United States dictating terms to submissive and groveling rebeldom!" Great God! and at that very moment the national army were inaugurating a series of retreats more disastrous than bloody defeats on the battlefield!

Couching his conversion in sarcastic terms, Clemens managed to convey the idea that, as a recent convert, he had the right to be put out over the North's shabby military performance. "Last week," he wrote Clagett, "the nation were blowing like school-boys." This week they are "trembling in their boots and whining and sniveling like threatened puppies—absolutely frantic with fear. God! what we were going to do!" Now the military situation was completely out of control: "The rebel hosts march through Kentucky and occupy city after city without firing a gun; Nashville is threatened; Memphis is threatened; Louisville quakes like an aspen; Cincinnati is stricken as with a palsy; Baltimore holds her breath and listens for the tread of the forty thousand; Pennsylvania shivers with a panic! Oh Christ!"[13]

Easterners were not the only ones shivering with a panic by the fall of 1862. Clemens's voluminous scrapbooks of the period show that he too felt the pressure—not of the Southern armies but of his brother's Union appointment and of the shifting sentiment in the territory. Earlier in the year he had filled his scrapbook with newspaper articles praising secessionist sentiment in the West. Now, late in the same year, Clemens began to paste in editorials written by prominent citizens who reminded Orion Clemens that his duty as acting Union governor was to remove all Southern sympathizers still in the government. One article in Clemens's scrapbook shows that Orion did in fact remove the probate judge of Lander County for disloyalty. Another article clipped and saved by Sam shows that Orion fired a certain notary public on the grounds that the man was not only a Copperhead but an especially loud mouthed one.[14]

None of this was lost on Clemens, who had a reasonably good feel for the pulse of public opinion. The past was pursuing him and he felt offbalance and defensive. Through the last quarter of 1862 and into 1863 he became, according to his biographer Paine, increasingly contentious and neurotic, restive and resentful. His letters home are punctuated with accounts of real or imagined insults. He moped about rejection and snubbing and "took the waters" at several Western spas to relieve disorders that were, according to Paine, mostly psychosomatic.[15] Throughout this period Clemens continued to fill his scrapbooks with newspaper pieces about what happened to citizens foolish enough to express the same Southern views that had been perfectly safe a year earlier. He also saved such flowery samples of Northern battle rhetoric as "Rebel Troubles," "Stand by the Union, and fight till we die," "The Star Spangled Banner," "God Save the Union," "Crush Treason's great delusion," "Chastise All Traitors," and "The Union Train" that was going south to "clear the track" of all "rebel ruffians." In less than two years Clemens crammed more than seventy-five articles and editorials about the war into his ballooning scrapbooks, a hobby which suggests that his boast that he took little interest in Eastern war news was an exaggeration.[16]

By mid-1863 Clemens was ready to make his conversion public. On July 31 "Mark Twain,"[17] reporter for the *Virginia City Territorial Enterprise,* sat down to record an event of irresistible symbolism for Union patriots. Earlier in the war Northern sympathizers, aware that Southern sentiment was strong in Virginia City, had planted a Union flag on top of nearby Mt. Davidson by way of provocation. On the last day of the siege at Gettysburg, an unusual electrical storm drew large crowds to Virginia City's streets. As the people watched the storm and awaited battle news from the East, Mark Twain went back to his desk and added to the suspense by pointedly comparing Northern chances for victory to the beleaguered flag on Mt. Davidson. When the flag emerged from the storm still flying in all its Union glory, Mark Twain did what he could to help the symbolism along: "*It was the flag!* . . . a mysterious messenger of good tidings. . . . It was the nation's emblem transfigured by the departing rays of the sun. . . . The superstition grew apace that this was a mystic courier come with great news from the war. . . . Vicksburg fallen, and the Union arms victorious at Gettysburg!" Winding up with the usual Western way of announcing good news, Mark Twain added that "every man that had any respect for himself . . . got drunk."[18]

Yet Mark Twain's interest in happenings in the East reached an even higher pitch if they had some connection with Clemens's war record. As a reporter covering the Nevada constitutional convention in 1863, he fretted over one clause in the statehood proposal that would disfranchise all persons who had voluntarily borne arms for the South. When the clause passed, Mark Twain came to his own defense. In an article entitled "True Son of the Union" he denounced the jingoism of super-Unionists who indulged in the same kind of "flag-flying and gin-soaking" patriotism that Mark Twain had used himself in his ode to the storm-tossed flag flapping atop Mt. Davidson. Throughout the "True Son" article the implication is that beneath the surface of Mark Twain's earlier superficial disloyalty ran a strong current of submerged affection for the Union—a current that may have gone underground for a while but had emerged far more powerful than the shallow boasts of the super-Unionists. Then, having beat his breast in public, Clemens turned around and privately pasted still another article into his scrapbook, this one urging "Generosity," "Justice," and "relief for the suffering people" of the South that probably provided some vicarious relief for Clemens as well.[19]

Meanwhile Mark Twain continued to use the reporter's desk to disengage himself from a cause he no longer wished to embrace or to defend. In September 1864 he gleefully reported that all the lights in the hall of a Copperhead meeting in San Francisco suddenly went out—clearly an ill omen for Southern sympathizers. Indeed one speaker at the meeting was so out of line that Mark Twain halted his anti-Copperhead diatribe in mid-sentence to insert the two damning words—A SECESSIONIST—in bold type before adding that the speaker had "openly avowed himself a Southerner" and had said "things savoring strongly of what opens the gates of Alcatraz." Actually the Copperhead in question spoke no differently than had Clemens himself during the first six months of his stay in the West.[20]

If Clemens's switch to the winning side had a sense of suddenness about it, a feeling that he struck a clandestine bargain with his former Southern values, we should avoid confusing his Southern with his Confederate values. When loyalty to the Confederacy proved a handicap in the face of shifting Western opinion—especially when it began to interfere with Clemens's main business in the West, which was to make money—it did not take him long to decide that dropping the Confederate South was indeed a small price to pay. As prospector, speculator, and hobnobber with some of the territory's foremost political and financial figures, Clemens was hardly the neophyte he made himself out to be in *Roughing It*. When the North-South issue got swept under by the silver fever, Clemens's ardent Southernism went under with it. Caught up in the flush times of Western boosterism, he simply found that "conversion" paid off.

He was probably relieved to learn that coming down on the winning side did not require revision of his views about black people. Nevada Territory, like most of the West and the North, was anti-black as well as antislavery and enjoyed the usual nigger jokes. With his Southern background, vernacular skill, and tendency to search out off-color subject matter, Mark Twain was quickly attracted to this kind of humor. Occasionally the results were more than he bargained for. The most notorious example was the so-called Sanitary Fund episode, probably the most damaging incident of Mark Twain's Western career.

In May 1864 a group of Virginia City's feminine elite decided to put on a masquerade ball to raise money for the U.S. Sanitary Commission, a national charity organization. After the ball, however, the ladies decided to put the money to another, unspecified use. Clemens, while drunk, volunteered his notion of what that use was. The sanitary funds, he wrote late at night in the *Enterprise* office, had been diverted from their proper destination and were now on their way to "aid a Miscegenation Society somewhere in the East." He read the squib to editor Joe Goodman, who warned strongly against its publication. In a stupor Clemens left the copy on his desk, where it was taken up by the night foreman and splashed across the front page of the *Enterprise* the following morning.

Probably no accusation could have generated more controversy in the 1860s in any city in the country. Almost before the ink was dry the offended ladies, easily guessing who the author was (Clemens had been sober enough not to sign the editorial), forced him to make a halfhearted, unsigned apology, which he pasted into his scrapbook alongside four irate letters requesting separate appointments on the field of honor. In a letter to his sister-in-law—one of the offended ladies as well as the wife of the acting governor of the territory—Clemens complained that the pious and pettifogging ladies of Virginia City had made far too much out of a mere journalistic caper, but he promised that he would not get drunk again.[21]

The community, however, was not ready to let the matter drop. When James Laird, editor of the rival newspaper, upbraided Clemens for his unseemly behavior, Mark Twain, fully exposed by both Laird and the ladies, finally dropped his mask of anonymity. Labelling Laird a "putrid, . . . groveling, vulgar liar" and an "ass," both "on general principles" and from "maternal instinct," he demanded an immediate apology from Laird's "craven carcass" or "the satisfaction due to a gentleman." Laird, goaded into further reply, held his ground. Blast provoked counterblast and the two covered themselves with so much obloquy that it appeared that a duel, carefully avoided by each party up to this point, would actually occur.[22]

Yet in the end neither side seemed willing to go beyond lip service to the chivalric code. Although Laird reaffirmed that Clemens was indeed a colossal humbug, "a liar, a poltroon, and a puppy" and insinuated that his war conduct was scarcely honorable, Clemens faced the miscegenist crisis in characteristic fashion. Like Huck Finn he lit out. Warning his brother that he was prepared to leave the territory for good to avoid damaging his own (but not a word about his brother's) reputation, Clemens fled both Nevada and his opponent for the more congenial atmosphere of San Francisco. Before he left, however, he advised the acting governor of the Nevada Territory to have nothing more to do with ladies aid societies.[23]

It is not likely that Mark Twain ever noticed the striking resemblance between his own rhetoric and conduct in Nevada in 1864 and that of the loud and eccentric Southern editor he caricatured in "Journalism in Tennessee" just five years later. Nor did he see any need at the time to change his ways. He had not been in the Bay City long before he began to repeat the pattern of behavior that hastened his departure from Nevada. Thrown in jail for slurring the San Francisco police once too often, he jumped bail and fled to a mining claim on Jackass Hill, where he wrote a "villainous backwoods sketch" called "Jim Smiley and His Jumping

Frog." Back in San Francisco, he was described by a local editor as a mountebank, a hypocrite, a jailbird, a bailjumper, a deadbeat, and an alcoholic who, the editor insinuated, had recently been rolled in a whorehouse and probably had a venereal disease.[24] Whether the charges were half-true or totally false, Mark Twain's general deportment in California was not much different from what it had been in Nevada—including a few irreverent references to niggers[25] which suggested he had not learned much from the Sanitary Fund episode.

Yet when he left San Francisco for the Sandwich Islands in the spring of 1866 to "work up" island life for the *Sacramento Union*, Mark Twain ran into an entirely new racial situation that came closer to unseating his established convictions about dark-skinned people (he insisted on calling the Kanaka natives niggers) than any event during his years in the West. Although the high rate of illegitimacy and miscegenation on the islands horrified him, it also titillated him. Privately Clemens jotted flippant notes about Kanaka children who were one-half nigger, one-half white, and two halves illegitimate, and noted bluntly enough that the two principal activities of the Kanakas were stealing and fornicating: no matter what else they might do for recreation, "Kanakas *will* have horses . . . & the women *will* fornicate."[26] Yet he also admitted that he was strongly attracted to the "dark, gingerbread colored beauties" of the islands—so much so that the safest way to handle them was to burlesque them. So in *Roughing It,* when Mark Twain comes upon some native women taking their baths, he sits down on their clothes on the riverbank and invites them to come out before they catch cold. Some months later, on his way East, he decided that the dark, large-breasted, and comely girls of Nicaragua were virtuous according to their own lights, but that their lights were "a little dim."[27] Not until much later, in some notebook scribblings about sex, dreams, and black women, did Clemens begin to explore *why* he may have been attracted to persons of dark skin.

Notwithstanding his later remorse over his behavior in the 1860s, Clemens seemed pleased that he had managed one major change in ideological direction. During the five and a half years that he spent in the Far West he reached and passed beyond the peak of his wartime commitment to the political and social values of the South. Fleeing from a dangerous and disruptive war, he found the West an ideal locale in which to escape accountability for his

Confederate desertion and to switch sides with a minimum of permanent embarrassment.[28] Given a choice Clemens doubtless would have changed his Southern colors more slowly. The moment of reckoning was forced upon him with what he regarded as unseemly haste. Yet when the time came his conversion seemed less a violent wrenching away from cherished Southern beliefs than a carefully calculated change in direction, a recasting of his role within *Western* society. Although the shift to Yankee patriot demanded some concentrated mental gymnastics, it probably caused Clemens very little moral anguish.

During his stay in the West, he learned too that his inherited convictions about black people could easily outlast his desertion of the Confederate cause. Embracing the Union clearly did not require embracing the black man. Indeed it did not take Mark Twain—and a host of other humorists—long to learn that emancipation, and the relief from national guilt that came with it, actually broadened the appeal of nigger jokes. It was all in the manner of telling: when presented frivolously, jokes about blacks were engaging; when presented with an undercurrent of maliciousness, they were not. Handled delicately, with the peculiar combination of feigned innocence and outrageous exaggeration which became Mark Twain's trademark, they usually moved his readers or listeners to laughter. This was, after all, the function of Mark Twain's humor. It was also why we should not take such jokes too seriously. As part of Mark Twain's humorous stock-in-trade, they were both useful and harmless: jokes first, prejudice second. Only when he crossed into forbidden territory, as in the Sanitary Fund fiasco, did Mark Twain seriously miscalculate the mood of his audience.[29]

That he rarely did so after the mid-1860s was due largely to his rising success and self-esteem as author and lecturer. Diffidently and erratically, already well past the age when most have chosen their vocation,[30] Mark Twain was beginning to map out a professional area bounded by journalism, popular literature, and the popular lecture. During the autumn of 1866 he gave his first public lecture in San Francisco on the subject of the Sandwich Islands. After a seizure of stage fright so intense that he thought he saw the face of death, he found he had struck a new vein of triumph. He could mesmerize his audience, control it, move it to laughter, tears, or self-righteous indignation. With his shuffling walk, shaggy hair, poker face, and drawling delivery he showed his debt to Artemus Ward, the top platform entertainer of the day. But even

33

before Ward died in England in 1867 from tuberculosis and drink, Mark Twain was the master of a style of ballyhoo and self-promotion that captivated audiences throughout the gold country.

By the time Clemens left the West in 1866, just turned thirty-one, he faced eastward toward the lasting commitments of his life. He left behind for good[31] the frontiers which had nurtured him and which Mark Twain celebrated and eventually symbolized. He also left behind the rebel convictions that he had brought with him in 1861. When Clemens went East he bore peace and good will toward the Union and the Yankee. But on the subject of blacks he was essentially the same man when he left the West as he had been when he left the South thirteen years earlier.

3

Bless You, I'm Reconstructed

We are chameleons, and our partialities and
prejudices change places with an easy and blessed
facility, and we are soon wonted to the change
and happy in it.
Speeches (1906)[1]

BETWEEN 1867 and 1874 Clemens's life took a sharp and spectacular turn. Within eight years he married into Eastern respectability and a quarter-million dollars, built a lavish mansion in Hartford, Connecticut, and in general installed himself as "an immovable fixture among the other rocks of New England."[2] In part through the good offices of others but primarily through luck, talent, and shrewdness in stage-managing his own affairs, Mark Twain rose spectacularly in financial, social, and literary status—altogether an intoxicating experience that left Clemens himself a little giddy.

In this brief span of time the still plastic persona called Mark Twain continued to experiment with a wide range of moods: to test audience psychology, to feel the public pulse, and increasingly to manipulate it at his will. As Mark Twain became a more confident persona, Clemens put him to the task of dealing with the painful material of his own Southern past. Indeed it was through Mark Twain that Clemens accomplished his near-complete and dramatic rejection of the postbellum South. It was also through his persona that he began to make his first tentative shift in attitudes toward the black race.

Clemens's reformation (and he regarded it as such) did not get under way at once. When he left San Francisco in December 1866, bound for New York, he carried several letters of introduction to distinguished Eastern clergymen, politicians, and editors, but he also carried a reputation that tended to cancel out the letters. A ship's officer playfully listed him as "Mark Twain, barkeeper, San Francisco," and a "damned old meddling, moralizing" female prude on board scolded him for drinking too much and for playing cards. The elite group of passengers scorned him. When he tried to join the ship's choir in singing "Marching through Georgia" and "When Johnny Comes Marching Home," they would have none of him. His drawl was unmistakably that of a Southerner.[3]

Having arrived in New York, Clemens settled into the same hand-to-mouth, on-the-move, deep-in-debt tramp journalism he had known for fifteen years—making the rounds of the theaters, morgues, saloons, and police precincts, spending a night in jail for brawling on the street. A brief visit to his mother and sister in St. Louis brought back unwanted memories of a war whose wounds were still wide open in a border city where families and friendships remained estranged. Even in his mother's house ill feeling was in the air: the Prodigal Son, the family's last hope,[4] had not yet made good. Beyond an unwholesome reputation as a talented but eccentric scribbler of crude jokes, Mark Twain was still largely unknown in the East. It did not take him long to learn it was the jumping frog who was famous, not its author. Following his Eastern debut as lecturer on the savages of the Sandwich Islands in New York's largest hall in April 1867 (filled at the last moment by doling out free tickets to schoolteachers), Mark Twain signed up for the country's first modern luxury cruise to the Holy Land, which led to the publication of his second book[5] and first commercial success, *The Innocents Abroad,* two years later.

Still at loose ends after the Holy Land excursion, Clemens took a job in Washington as private secretary to Senator William M. Stewart of Nevada. The arrangement lasted barely two months. According to Stewart, Clemens was disreputable, seedy, sinister, and lazy, and helped himself too freely to Stewart's whiskey and cigars. When the senator threatened a thrashing, the secretary "resigned." Throwing himself into a bewildering tangle of newspaper and patronage projects,[6] Clemens rushed pell-mell through the winter of 1867, driven by ambition, the need for money, and an inability to decide who he was or what he wanted to do. Shortly after meeting the lovely, sheltered, and sickly[7] Olivia Langdon, daughter of a rich New York coal dealer, Clemens moved himself to New York, where he began to select his company on the basis of character and credit and to push his candidacy for membership in the Eastern establishment. With an ear finely tuned to the Northern mood for waving the bloody shirt at the defeated South, Mark Twain dropped his outdated strategy of self-defense and began to castigate the South herself. If any taints of treason remained from the Nevada years, his loud literary war against the South soon cleared him of all suspicion.

On March 4, 1869, in an article entitled "The White House Funeral," Mark Twain prepared for battle against the South by nudging himself into the front ranks of the Republican party. Using the art of political invective mastered after a few months of watching Congress—the only "native American criminal class"[8]—in action, he declared that the Democratic party was so corrupt that the only way to clean it up was to get rid of it. The party of Jefferson, Jackson, and Andrew Johnson was responsible for the most monstrous war in American history, for getting rid of President Lincoln "in an abrupt and peculiarly Democratic way," and for the stacks of dead bodies and barely-living skeletons that rolled and staggered out of Georgia's Andersonville prison after the war. Closing with his own version of Johnson's farewell address, Mark Twain depicted the Tennessean leaving the White House wet with tears and loaded down with public property: "I have . . . vetoed the Reconstruction Acts . . . the Freedman's Bureau . . . removed Stanton, everybody that the malignant Northern hordes approved. . . . I smiled upon the Ku-Klux-Klan . . . I pardoned Jeff Davis . . . I rescued the bones of the patriot martyr, Booth. . . . I die content."[9]

Turning from the Democratic party, which was, after all, a national as well as a Southern aberration, Mark Twain fired his opening shots at the South herself in 1869 and 1870. The refinements of civilization were finally beginning to appear in his native state, because Missourians were drowning horse thieves now rather than hanging them. Tennesseans were at last learning how to read and write, but Mark Twain doubted that this new hobby would outlast the velocipede as a permanent Southern institution. A news item stating that a pig with a human head was scaring the inhabitants of South Carolina led Mark Twain to ask whether such an animal was really rare down there. And when he learned that Brooklyn was planning to hold an annual tournament to commemorate the Middle Ages, Mark Twain switched the setting from Brooklyn to the South: he could understand the need for such "chivalrous absurdities" in prostrate Virginia, but Brooklyn scarcely had romance enough to recharge any Southern knight who came galloping North to Brooklyn to join in the medieval festivities. The idea of the "knight of Shenandoah" or the "knight of the Blue Ridge" coming up to joust in Yankeeland was preposterous. Better to let the "noble-natured, maiden-rescuing, wrong-redressing" Galahads of the Gilded Age retire permanently to the South, where they belonged.[10]

Taking the offensive into enemy territory in 1871 in "Journalism in Tennessee," Mark Twain, now a Yankee reporter, journeys south to improve his health. The two Tennessee towns which he visits are named Buzzardville and Blathersville. The five local newspapers are called the "Morning Glory and Johnson County War-Whoop," the "Semi-Weekly Earthquake," the "Moral Volcano," the "Higginsville Thunderbolt and Battle Cry of Freedom," and the "Mud Springs Morning Howl." The chief character in the story is a small-town newspaper editor who dresses like a gentleman (like Clemens's father, in fact[11]) and composes uplifting essays about the "encouraging Progress of Moral and Intellectual Development in America," while exchanging pistol shots, hand grenades, bricks, bombs, and insults with a varied assortment of local "asses." Indeed the Tennessee editor's overblown rhetoric rivals Mark Twain's own sorties against James Laird in Virginia City five years before. And, looking to the future, the Tennessean's concurrent praise of peace and practice of violence anticipates the fatal moral duplicity of the Grangerfords in the *Adventures of Huckleberry Finn.*

Two years later, in *The Gilded Age* (written in collaboration with Charles Dudley Warner), Mark Twain added squalor and laziness to his growing list of Southern traits. The drowsing and filthy village of Obedstown, Tennessee, is an unattractive replica of the real-life village of Jamestown, Tennessee, where John Marshall and Jane Clemens lived with four children and a slave shortly before Sam Clemens was born. Squire Silas Hawkins is an unsympathetic reproduction of Judge John Marshall Clemens himself.[13] The rest of the village is classic poor white. When the monthly mail rush of three or four letters arrives, the human cattle of Obedstown assemble to digest the contents communally. Like their Arkansas counterparts in *Huckleberry Finn* and *Life on the Mississippi*, the strain of standing erect for more than a few minutes is too much. In unison they climb aboard a fence, "humpshouldered and grave, like a company of buzzards," whittling, spitting, yawning, and scratching. One fence bird bunches "his thick lips together like the stem end of a tomato" and shoots a bumblebee. The others spit after him, burying the bumblebee. Eventually the squatters slide off the fence "like so many turtles" to view a dogfight.[14]

If the North liked Mark Twain's shirt-sleeve satire of the backwoods South, he had to learn the hard way that it preferred its nigger humor slightly toned down. In the fifteen years since Harriet Beecher Stowe published *Uncle Tom's Cabin,* Northerners had acquired a few notions of racial justice. Not that Negroes were equal; it simply was not good manners to belabor the fact that they were not.

It took the "Wild Humorist of the Pacific Slope" a while to figure this out. Stopping over in Key West, Florida, on his way East in 1867, Mark Twain cursed a conductor for unwittingly placing him in the back of a bus with some niggers and went on to talk about a topic that had been a favorite for at least fifteen years: black body odor. As a teenage reporter in Hannibal in 1853 Sam Clemens had assured his readers that they could tell when summer was approaching, because the town's "fat, lazy 'niggers' " would begin to "sweat and look greasy." In San Francisco in 1866 Mark Twain had compared the stench in a police courtroom with a polecat, a slaughter house, a soap factory, a graveyard after an earthquake, and a perspiring black man, and had concluded that to "stand to leeward of a sweltering negro" was perhaps the roughest experience of them all. In the Sandwich Islands Clemens jotted a ditty about white men who "smell berry strong but black man stronger." Now, en route East, Mark Twain told the California readers who were following him across the country through the *San Francisco Alta California* that blacks in Key West were actually a valuable addition to the community, because sailors lost on the high seas could point their ship in the direction of what they believed to be the "nigger quarter" and sniff their way safely into port.[15]

Once settled in New York, Mark Twain fell back several times on a subject he had first tested with unsatisfactory results in Nevada in 1864—miscegenation. It was a mistake, he wrote in 1869, to ask the Irish to accept Negro suffrage, because it would only lead them to think the country was asking them to "marry a nagur." In a similar mood Mark Twain found high humor in the fact that a petition circulated by black citizens in Buffalo, urging whites to support the renovation of an all-black schoolhouse, was signed primarily by whites, who thus became surrogate "parents of the colored children." Testing the limits of public tolerance on the subject, he bore down harder on miscegenation in an article about the escapades of one Jefferson Davis Othello. After a stormy courtship J. D. Othello manages to marry Desdemona only because this lovely young lady of alabaster complexion is unaccountably attracted to a black man. When he learns that his wife may not be satisfied with a nigger after all and that she may be seeing a white lover on the sly, Othello works himself into an emotional frenzy, tears his "raven kinks" to pieces, murders Desdemona, and, after stabbing himself, dies "all over the room."[16]

This sort of humor was tame compared to another kind of nigger joke which had to do with turning black bodies into cooked meat. In one of his notebook entries made shortly before he left the West, Clemens sprang the punch line:

"Where did you get that excellent venison at this time of year?"
"It isn't venison—it is a steak off that dead nigger."[17]

Possibly taking his cue from this notebook source, Mark Twain included part of the idea and discarded the rest in an essay about the vagabond career of his Bohemian newspaper friend, James Riley. Shying away from cannibalism but keeping the analogy between black flesh and well-cooked meat, he told a story about a black woman in Washington, D.C., who apparently fell asleep over a stove and was burned to death. The landlady of a boarding house next door, grieving sanctimoniously over the dead woman, insinuated that one of her beefsteaks bore some resemblance to the portion of the black woman's anatomy that came into contact with the stove. Asking one of her boarders, who happened to be Riley, to come up with a proper epitaph for the black woman's tombstone, Riley responded with: "Well Done, Good and Faithful Servant."[18]

For a man who repeatedly sought the approval of the Eastern literati and repeatedly asked to be confirmed, scolded, and corrected, Mark Twain had some trouble giving up certain forms of humor and certain colloquial expressions. While issuing blanket invitations to his troop of moral guardians—William Dean Howells, "Mother" Mary Fairbanks,[19] and, after 1868, Olivia Langdon—to supervise his moral and verbal regeneration, he rarely followed their advice in the late 1860s. It must have been distressing for Olivia Langdon—and especially for her father, who had aided fugitive slaves before the war and entertained abolitionists of the stature of William Lloyd Garrison, Wendell Phillips, and Gerritt Smith and was now supporting the education of freedmen and hosting Frederick Douglass—to read some of Mark Twain's newspaper quips and travel letters about niggers. With such sentries looking over his shoulder, however, it did not take him long to catch on that Easterners would not put up with the same sort of nigger humor that was still popular in the West; indeed would not put up with the word nigger itself. Ever sensitive to charges that he lacked cultivation and refinement, gilding and filigree, Mark Twain began to discard certain vulgarisms that were "not of a character to recommend me to the respectful regard of a high eastern civilization."[20] In 1867 he used nigger without quotation marks for the last time in print, except of course in *Huckleberry Finn*, where

Mark Twain is replaced by Huck. Although Clemens continued to use nigger this and nigger that in his notebooks and letters, he did so through force of habit, not malice, and after 1867 he took pains to keep this private habit under careful public surveillance. In 1867 he dropped "nigger" in favor of "contraband," then "freedman," then "colored," then "darkey." By 1869—the year he became engaged to Olivia Langdon—he had settled on "negro."[21]

By 1869, too, Mark Twain began to come out strongly against atrocities committed against blacks. In an article entitled "Only a Nigger" he satirized the lynching of a black man in Memphis, Tennessee, who was thought to have raped a white woman but was later declared innocent after being hanged. This unfortunate mistake was only a small blunder in the South's smoothly operating system of lynch law and was not to be regretted unless hanging, roasting, and beating black men to death began to keep Southerners awake at night. Otherwise the best way to preserve law and order and to nourish the "knightly hearts" of Southern gentlemen was to keep "the brand and the faggots in waiting" for other suspicious niggers.[22]

The following year Mark Twain lashed out again against racial violence, this time outside the United States. In Panama a "light-fingered gentleman of color" was sentenced to a chain gang for fourteen years for petty theft and was given "as a badge of honor a beautiful iron chain and a huge piece of iron rail to help him walk." When the prisoner tried to escape he was rewarded with a hundred-and-fifty-pound anchor. "The anchor is an emblem of hope, you know," Mark Twain wrote, "and the authorities bestowed it on him to cheer him up . . . and save him from dark(ey) despair." In the same article he denounced a Buffalo policeman for arresting a "slightly inebriated and noisy" black man. When "Mr. Negro" did not move along briskly enough to suit him the policeman "wasn't at all put out—he only persuaded him to go by jabbing his bayonet into the poor wretch's head with all his force, and then as the blood streamed over his face, striking him on the skull with the barrel of his musket." "I believe," Mark Twain added, "there was a darkey buried . . . the next day."[23]

Three years later, in *The Gilded Age,* he switched the emphasis from physical injustices to social indignities. The burden of his satire falls on "Colonel" Beriah Sellers, who is rightly remembered as half dreamer and half bunkum artist, but who is also a Southerner—a diehard Confederate struggling to adjust to changing times. Closely modeled after Clemens's Kentucky uncle, James Lampton, who prided himself on both his Southern pedigree and his ability to do business with the Yankee, Sellers too seeks to cash in on postbellum economic opportunities in the North, while retaining his hard-core Southernism. Like Lampton he insists that he is, and will always remain, "a Southern gentleman," the "finest type of gentleman in the Universe." But like Lampton (and Clemens) Sellers is apprehensive about his Confederate war record and eager to come to business terms with the North. "Bless you," he assures his cousin Washington Hawkins (alias Orion Clemens), "I'm reconstructed, and I go for the old flag, and an appropriation."[24]

The one facet of Northern life that Sellers, as a Southerner, cannot abide is the social position of the emancipated black man. Having known blacks as slaves, Sellers is not prepared to know them as freedmen. To be sure, "niggros" are still good for laughs: Sellers tells one of his servants in Hawkeye, Missouri, "the blackest niggro in the state," to clear out because his complexion "has brought on the twilight half an hour ahead of time."[25] But joking aside, niggros are lazy, immoral, and undependable and no amount of educational programs or emancipation proclamations can change their basic nature. In fact any attempt to educate former slaves will only give them more latitude to hang themselves. Though Sellers concedes that part of the white man's burden is to uplift the black man *spiritually* ("You can't make his soul too immortal"), he begs to be excused from touching "*him,* himself" and longs for the days when a man with a good business head could exploit niggros for honest profit. Early in the action of *The Gilded Age* Silas Hawkins (alias John Marshall Clemens) praises the financial soundness of one of Sellers's antebellum schemes to get rich: "When he got up that idea there in Virginia of buying up whole loads of negroes in Delaware and Virginia and Tennessee, very quiet, having papers drawn to have them delivered at a place in Alabama and take them and pay for them, away yonder at a certain time, and then in the mean time get a law made stopping everybody from selling negroes to the South after a certain day . . . mercy how the man would have made money! Negroes would have gone up to four prices."[26]

After the war Sellers switches from slavery to education as the way to make money from the emancipated black man. Not that book learning will do niggros any good: the schoolhouse simply replaces the auction block as the means to new fortune for the whites. In partnership with a sleazy senator from Cattleville, Kansas, who is named Dilworthy and patterned after Samuel Pomeroy (the Kansas Republican whom Mark Twain turned into one of the consummate villains of the Gilded Age), Sellers forms a shady enterprise to drive up real estate values in Tennessee by building a Negro university on land the two partners happen to own. Dilworthy, Sellers explains to Washington Hawkins, is "the father of the poor down-trodden negro . . . their Moses—their Aaron—their benefactor":

> "This glorious union has set the niggro free. What is the next step?"
> [Hawkins] "Support him, I suppose."
> "Well—a—not exactly, not exactly. Prepare him to support himself. Educate him—Make him a skilled workman—How shall we do this? Establish a University. . . . Where shall that University be located? In the Knobs of East Tennessee."[27]

While Sellers insists that the Eastern Knobs University for the Education of Negro Freedmen, otherwise known as the Negro University Swindle, is founded on his and Dilworthy's "great love for the niggro," Mark Twain makes it clear that profit, not uplifting the black man, is the controlling motive behind postbellum white schemes to educate the freedman. Indeed it is not too much to say that the Southern part of Colonel Beriah Sellers is a sort of flesh-and-blood Doppelgänger of the unreconstructed Sam Clemens of the 1860s. And, by 1873, the epitome of everything that Mark Twain found reprehensible.

So long as he stuck to white abuse of blacks, Mark Twain usually mixed humor and satire effectively. But when he shifted to blacks themselves he usually reverted to the minstrel stereotypes he had first tried out in the West. By whatever criteria—burlesque, satire, or character credibility—blacks *as* blacks fare poorly in *The Gilded Age*. "Uncle Dan'l," patterned after the middle-aged slave of the same name whom Clemens knew as a boy on his uncle's farm in Florida, Missouri, is a half-witted harlequin. In the stage production of *The Gilded Age* Mark Twain issued strict instructions that the actor who played Daniel must stammer constantly, an affliction from which the original Daniel did not suffer. He is also made the butt of a distasteful joke in which Sellers, when drunk, convinces Daniel that he can cure his stammering simply by whistling incessantly instead. The climax of Daniel's denigration, in the novel and the play, occurs when he mistakes a steamboat for the deity and vows first to defend the white children under his care: "O Lawd we's ben mighty wicked, an' we know dat we 'gwine to go to de bad place, but good Lawd, deah Lawd, we ain't ready yit, we ain't ready. . . . Take de ole niggah if you's got to hab somebody . . . take it outen de ole niggah—De ole niggah's ready. . . . Heah I is, Lawd, heah I is." Then the panic-stricken black man abandons all pretence at bluffing and runs into the woods, leaving it up to one of his white charges, who also has never seen a steamboat, to point out that the boat is not the devil. When the white boy accuses the black man of being a coward, Daniel becomes pettishly defiant: "I isn't 'fraid o' nothin."[28]

The important point about the steamboat episode is not that Daniel is ignorant or superstitious—Nigger Jim in *Huckleberry Finn* is both—but that here Mark Twain permitted whatever pittance of responsibility and dignity he originally gave a black man to be eclipsed by a white boy's superior capacity for reason and ridicule. Much the same thing happens to Daniel all over again in *The American Claimant,* published in 1892 but largely written in the 1870s as a sequel to *The Gilded Age.*[29] Daniel is now "Old Uncle Dan'l," an aged and decrepit postbellum servant but otherwise unchanged. Sometime between *The Gilded Age* and *The American Claimant* his master, Colonel Sellers, sold Daniel into the deep South. After the war Daniel and his wife Jinny[30] come wandering back north to Washington, D.C., pining for the happy days of slavery and too much in love with old Marster to hold a grudge against him for selling them into what border Southerners considered living hell. With not another lick of work left in their "old hides," Daniel and Jinny are waited upon by two younger black women provided for that purpose—"a situation," as Louis Budd remarks, "worthy of Thomas Nelson Page." When not pecking at each other, they play the role of pampered and fawning servants to the hilt: scurrying to the door to receive visitors, fleeing to the cellar to escape the minor duties assigned them, arguing over which one should carry out "dish-yer order de lord" (Sellers) has handed down to them, bowing, scraping, and simpering before white folks, and saying, "I's heah, suh," and "Well dat do beat all."[31]

The most striking feature about the behavior of these black characters is that the ballyhoo they carry on in the Sellers house is supposed to have gone on in the Clemens home as well, shortly after Clemens married Olivia Langdon in 1870. According to Paine, Clemens habitually exaggerated the loyalty and fondness of his servants, while complaining that they did little work and cavorted around too much. In *The American Claimant* Sellers insists that Daniel thinks the world of him, but that he is a heavy burden and does pretty much as he pleases. Also according to Paine, Clemens sometimes hid himself away in the shrubbery outside the kitchen at Quarry Farm[32] to listen to the two black servants, a "Dunkard" named Lewis and a Methodist named Aunty Cord, argue and insult each other. In *The American Claimant* Sellers orders Daniel, a "Dunker Baptist," and Jinny, a "shouting Methodist," to settle their theological differences in the kitchen and complains that the two jibbering ex-slaves "ought to be killed." At least once his paternalism approaches sadism. As part of a scientific experiment Sellers considers killing both Daniel and Jinny to see if their dead bodies can be converted into mechanical dolls—"modifiable, at will . . . sometimes turn on more talk, more action, more emotion" and all "adjustable—with a screw or something."[33]

Carried away with the ludicrous follies and schemes of one of his more likable and memorable white characters, Mark Twain did not seem to realize that his black characters had plummeted to the level of slaphappy darkies whose sole function is to amuse their white tormentor. Or perhaps it would be more charitable to say that he had not yet decided just where blacks belonged on his incompletely revised spectrum of moral and social values. After all, why should he? Since blacks were not equal, jokes about them were not out of character and, when handled with some concession to Eastern delicacy, were not out of taste. To charge Mark Twain with what a later generation called racism would be to burden him with the value judgments of another time, and to attach more significance to a single kind of humor than he himself attached to it. Indeed, given the enormous popularity of nigger humor, it would have been odd had he not tapped this lucrative professional source. To repudiate nigger humor would have demanded unusually strong convictions about black people—to have been essentially a neo-abolitionist crusader for racial justice. In the early 1870s Mark Twain was no more out to champion blacks than he was out to get niggers. He was neither negrophile nor negrophobe; like most Americans he stood somewhere in between.

Yet to raise the question of nigger humor is to raise another, even more fundamental question: To what extent can humor be used *at all* as an accurate index of the attitudes of the humorist? The question is as crucial as it is complex, for the discernment of authorial attitudes behind a mask or persona and behind the humor itself is an extremely hazardous business.[34] The very complexity of the comic mode suggests that the public pose of a professional humorist can rarely be equated with his innermost feelings. When expressing his views about blacks privately—that is, outside of his persona and with little or no pressure to be funny— Clemens still reflected certain regional and family traits. But as Mark Twain his seriocomic treatment of blacks was essentially the same as his seriocomic treatment of any other subject. Humor is by nature notoriously irreverent but not necessarily malicious or malignant. It *can* reveal racial attitudes but it does not automatically, or even customarily, do so.

One example should clarify the unreliability of humor as an index of the true attitudes of the humorist. At the time that Mark Twain was commissioned to contribute regular columns of humor to New York journals and newspapers, Samuel Clemens was undergoing the darkest period of his life before the 1890s. In the winter of 1870 and 1871 Olivia's father died, followed by the serious illness and near-death of Livy herself and of their newborn son Langdon, who relapsed and died the following year.[35] These family misfortunes caused Clemens to wonder seriously whether he was losing his creative powers as well as his sanity—a nagging fear not completely put to rest until the successful publication of *Roughing It* more than a year later. Out of these personal and professional worries came an extraordinary outpouring of "humorous" rage in 1870 and 1871, in a series of morbidly funny sketches that Mark Twain was compelled by contract to write for the Buffalo *Express* and the *Galaxy*. Some of these pieces have to do with injustices committed against blacks, but they also have to do with the plight of Chinese immigrants, the corruption of the Vanderbilt and Tweed crowd, the licentiousness of the press, the evils of universal suffrage, the hypocrisy of platitude-spouting clergymen, the venality of Congress, and so forth. The one thing these furiously comical writings have in common is a deep sympathy for sufferers of all sorts—underdogs, misfits, outcasts, victims of society—including, in a detached sort of way, Mark Twain himself.

The dark winter of 1870-1871 shows that while Clemens's misfortunes certainly colored Mark Twain's writing, they also opened the way whereby Clemens might rise above personal tribulations by suspending his identity through his persona. At the same time that Clemens was fretting over problems of self-interest and survival (money, family, fame, the compulsion to conform to Eastern standards), Mark Twain was perfecting the seriocomic pose which would largely free him from such problems. Pricked by what he regarded as Northern snobbery and extremely touchy about his own overlong probationary period in the East, Clemens took revenge on his critics by conforming to the cast-iron New England code as S. L. Clemens, while breaking it as Mark Twain. By submitting willingly enough to the strictures of membership by marriage in the Northern plutocracy, Clemens created the very atmosphere in which Mark Twain could best flourish as a writer, thus becoming at once the spokesman and the satirist of the age that made him famous and (as he would have it) finally betrayed him.

No one recognized this duality better than Clemens himself. Though he later complained that the price of such prostitution was too high, in the 1870s he was certain that the attractions far outweighed the disadvantages; and he was right. For all his masquerading as recalcitrant but reconstructible sinner, Mark Twain usually conformed only so far as his own evolving standards as a humorist *told* him to conform. In the process he placed the American public in the uneasy position of never quite knowing whether he was amusing them or making fun of them, baring his soul or simply taking them in—altogether a cunning mixture of preaching and mocking that opened the way for as much confrontation or retreat as he saw fit.

This goes far toward explaining Mark Twain's curious combination of comedy and seriousness, burlesque and satire, hoax and hyperbole that he used in his treatment of blacks as well as his treatment of everything else. When outraged by physical atrocities committed by whites against blacks, he met the whites with devastating satire. When seized by what he called "spasms of humorous possession"—some of them in his darkest periods of despair—he reverted to the long list of crotchety mammies, foolish aunts, hapless uncles, and wretched freedmen longing for the good old days of slavery that were available to him. Going into the seventies he still told a few off-color nigger jokes—such as telling a friend bound for South Africa to "give my love to the niggers"[36]—

49

and he still tended to treat black people largely as shadow figures: tin cutouts, grown-up children, spastic puppets whose walk-on parts are wooden and unconvincing. By the end of Clemens's successful initiation into Eastern respectability, the artistic image of blacks held by his persona, Mark Twain, was still one of gullible darkies capable of a primitive and unreliable loyalty to white folks. And, for that reason, more to be pitied and protected than admired or respected.

4

White Feuds
& Black Sambos

Yah-yah-yah. . . . Dat cake mighty *good;*
somebody *drap* dat, I reckon. (*Making ghastly
efforts to swallow it.*) But 'pears to *me* like dey'd
sumf'n *in* dat cake. I reck'n it's a *noos*paper.
Feel like a noospaper—*tas'* like a noospaper—an'
I bet she *is* a noospaper, too. . . . (*Gets it down
with a final frightful struggle, and caresses his
stomach, not altogether gratefully.*) By jing, she's
down at *las'*.
"*Tom Sawyer: A Play*" (1870s)

How to kill your man in a duel.—Take a rusty
old gun which you think is not loaded—let it go off
accidentally in the direction of the other man
with the distinct in[ten]tion & desire to miss him.
This will fetch him, sure.
Notebook (1878)[1]

WHAT GRADUALLY changed Mark Twain's artistic image of black people was his discovery of how he might make use of them as part of the slow process by which he began to reconstruct the idyll of Hannibal. The central drama of Mark Twain's life as a man of letters was his discovery of a usable past. Always his own biographer, his most astounding autobiographical discovery was how he might convert the antebellum South, from which he had consciously fled, into what Henry Nash Smith has called the Matter of Hannibal and the Matter of the River.[2] In the decade between 1874 and 1884, in a burst of creative energy and a wave of nostalgia, Mark Twain came as close as he ever would to embracing the antebellum South as Eden. One by one "A True Story," *The Adventures of Tom Sawyer,* and *Simon Wheeler, Detective,* followed closely by the first part of *Life on the Mississippi* and the *Adventures of Huckleberry Finn,* mark his pilgrimage back to the prewar South.

The pilgrimage began modestly enough in 1874 when he sent "A True Story" to William Dean Howells for publication in the *Atlantic.* As usual Clemens did not realize the full value of his creation. Though he told Howells he had taken great pains with the dialect ("a negro sometimes says 'goin' & sometimes 'gwyne,' & they make just such discrepancies in other words"), he thought a good deal more of another manuscript, "A Fable for Good Old Boys and Girls," which he sent along with "A True Story." Howells tactfully returned the "Fable" and announced that the "colored one" was one of the best short pieces he had ever read.[3]

Critics agree with Howells. Despite a heavy dose of Victorian sentiment "A True Story" ranks with Mark Twain's finest work. The central character, Aunt Rachel, is modeled after Aunty Cord, a former Maryland slave employed as a cook at Quarry Farm. In the privacy of a "Family Sketch" written twenty years later, Clemens left a memorable portrait of Aunty Cord:

Aunty Cord was six feet high, & nearly twice as black . . . & had strong notions about things, & a vigorous eloquence in expressing them if the opposing force were 'niggers'; for she had no great opinion of 'niggers.' . . . She petted the [white] children, of course, & also of course she filled their heads with 'nigger' superstitions. . . . According to her gospel, a spider in the heart of an apple must be killed, otherwise bad luck will follow. . . . Snakes must be killed on sight, even the harmless ones;

53

& the discoverer of a sloughed snake-skin lying in the road was in for all kinds of calamities.[4]

Ten years after this private note Mark Twain used Aunty Cord for the second time in fiction, this time as "Aunty Phyllis" in a story called "Refuge of the Derelicts":

Aunty Phyllis was born and brought up in Maryland—Eastern Shore. She was a slave, before the War. She is toward seventy, stands six feet one in her stockings, is as straight as a grenadier, and has the grit and the stride and the warlike bearing of one. But, being black, she is good-natured, to the bone. It is the born privilege and prerogative of her adorable race. She is cheerful, indestructibly cheerful and lively; and what a refreshment she is! Her laugh—her breezy laugh, her inspiring and uplifting laugh—is always ready, always on tap, and comes pealing out, peal upon peal, right from her heart, let the occasion for it be big or little; and it is so cordial and so catching that derelict after derelict [of Aunty Phyllis's "boarding house"] has to forget his troubles and join in.[5]

The overwhelming similarities between the real Aunty Cord and her two fictional counterparts, Aunt Rachel and Aunty Phyllis, suggest that Mark Twain's black women came from a single source and that he also relied heavily on this woman for Nigger Jim's vast store of superstitions. The real Aunty Cord had a low opinion of niggers; Aunt Rachel in "A True Story" constantly refers to her superior ancestry ("I's one o' de ole Blue Hen's Chickens, *I* is!") and looks down on all low-born niggers. Aunty Cord "petted" the Clemens children and "filled their heads with 'nigger' superstitions"; Nigger Jim pets Huck and "does magic" for him. Aunty Cord thought spiders brought misfortune; Huck will tremble with fear when he flips a spider into a candle. Aunty Cord believed a snakeskin caused "all kinds of calamities," while Huck's handling of a snake brings near-disaster to the two fugitives on Jackson's Island, when Jim is bitten by the snake's mate. Indeed it is not too much to say that Aunty Cord's chief contribution to American literature is not as Aunt Rachel, but as the source for most of the superstitious information that Mark Twain poured into the middle section of *Huckleberry Finn*. It seems most likely that this woman served as a more bountiful reservoir of darky superstitions than Clemens's hazy memories of Uncle Daniel a quarter-century earlier.

Aunt Rachel tells her story to "Misto' Clemens" at Quarry Farm "in her own words." Seated with the white folks on the farmhouse porch in the summer twilight, "respectfully below our level, on the steps—for she was our servant, and colored," Aunt Rachel is at first the model slaphappy darky, while her employer, Mr. Clemens, is the model naive Northerner who knows nothing whatever about darkies or about slavery. Carefully avoiding any mention that he was raised in a slaveholding society which had among its commonest institutions the physical punishment of blacks and the separation of slave families, "Misto' Clemens" plays the role of Yankee tenderfoot, asking Aunt Rachel how it is that she has managed to live for sixty years without any trouble or stress:

> She paused, and there was a moment of silence. She turned her face over her shoulder toward me, and said, without even a smile in her voice: "Misto C——————, is you in 'arnest?"

Taken aback by the darky woman's sudden loss of bubbling blackness, Misto C—————— stammers, "Why, I thought—that is, I meant—why, you *can't* have had any trouble. I've never heard you sigh, and never seen your eye when there wasn't a laugh in it"—a remark that upholds Clemens's conviction that the "adorable" black race was born "good-natured" and introduces the story's main theme of black survival through humor. Having set the stage for Rachel's recital, Mark Twain hands the story over to her, in the longest uninterrupted black monologue in his writing, climaxed by Rachel's account of the selling of her seven children at a Richmond slave auction:

> "Dey put chains on us an' put us on a stan'. . . . An' dey'd come up dah an' look at us all roun', an' squeeze our arm, an' make us git up an' walk, an' den say, 'Dis one too ole,' or 'Dis one lame,' or 'Dis one don't 'mount to much.' An' dey sole my ole man, an' took him away, an' dey begin to sell my chil'en an' take *dem* away, an' I begin to cry; an' de man say, 'Shet up yo' damn blubberin',' an' hit me on de mouf. . . . But I took and tear de clo'es mos' off of 'em an' beat 'em over de head wid my chain; an' *dey* give it to *me*, too. . . . Oh no, Misto C——————, I hain't had no trouble. An' no *joy!"*

Rachel's pride, passion, and power make her the first black character in Mark Twain's writing who is not a fawning and servile mammy or sambo. When she remarks to Clemens that she loves her children "jist de same as you loves yo' chil'en" and recounts the thirteen-year search for the only member of her family she ever sees again, she anticipates Huck's awed realization that Nigger

Jim cared "just as much for his people as white folks does for their'n" and actually missed his wife and children.[6] Yet for all her heartrending recollections of slavery, Aunt Rachel is not representative of Mark Twain's later black characters. Her sufferings are far in the past and there is a decidedly detached tone to the story: it could have happened anywhere in the antebellum South and it is told in retrospect by a postbellum Northern servant. As a work of literature about black people and slavery it stands midway between Mark Twain's offhand, detached treatment of darkies up to this point and his full artistic commitment to Nigger Jim in *Huckleberry Finn.* As in *The Gilded Age,* published one year before "A True Story," Mark Twain had not yet tied either blacks *or* himself very closely to his own Southern past—to Hannibal, Missouri. But he was on the verge of doing both.

In the 1870s two polar emotions nearly overwhelmed Samuel Clemens, and each led him to make his first extended explorations of his own Southern past. One was his marriage to Olivia Langdon. The other was his towering rage over the corruption and venality of the Gilded Age. Each in its own way helped to draw him back into the past.

Clemens's distress with the Gilded Age was proportionate to his complicity in it. As lavish host, entrepreneur, and inventor, busily pouring thousands of dollars into schemes and squabbles of all sorts, he was his own Colonel Sellers. For all his ranting over the era's multi-millionaires, he tried for thirty years to become one himself. And for all his championing of the common man in the eighties and nineties, Clemens in the seventies felt direly threatened by "this wicked ungodly suffrage," by the rise of organized labor, by the wave of Eastern European immigrants pouring into the country at the rate of five million each decade, and by the rumors of thousands of "communists" who were overrunning the country. Not that this "leather-headed Republic" didn't deserve to be overthrown by these radicals and troublemakers. It was just that too much of Clemens's own money and property (and Livy's inheritance) would go down with it.

In other ways too Clemens straddled his times. He was appalled when it was rumored that Henry Ward Beecher had committed adultery.[7] But he saw nothing wrong with Beecher accepting fifteen thousand dollars worth of stock from Jay Cooke for puffing the Northern Pacific Railroad; and when Cooke and Company collapsed in the Panic of 1873 some of Clemens's stock, and Livy's coal income, went down with it. While decrying special favors in business, Clemens expected—and received—numerous professional favors, including free advertising for his books and highly selective reviews by close friends or by men who owed him a favor.[8] While denouncing lobbying in Congress, he did a fair amount of congressional lobbying himself. But the most revealing glimpse into Clemens's bifocal view of his time is the gaudy polychrome-gingerbread mansion he built outside Hartford, Connecticut, in 1874. For all his grumbling about the garishness of the Gilded Age, Clemens's castle at Nook Farm was a classic of the era, complete with nineteen rooms, six servants, indoor garden and fountain, outdoor towers and turrets, a forest of chimneys, acres of artificially banked lawns, and a hole cut in the fireplace so Clemens could watch flames rising and snowflakes falling at the same time.[9]

Nonetheless personal involvement did not keep Clemens from raging over Cooke's corrupt railroads, or the shenanigans of Tweed and Tammany Hall,[10] or the Crédit Mobilier scandal, or the crude jobbery and cynical abuse of office under President Grant. (Grant himself, Clemens insisted, was honest: only his vice-president, his private secretary, his brother-in-law, his secretary of war, and his secretary of the treasury were corrupt.) Later, in the 1890s, he would refuse to give his blessing to Henry Demarest Lloyd's *Wealth Against Commonwealth* because one of Lloyd's Standard Oil scoundrels, Henry Rogers, was pulling him out of bankruptcy. But in the 1870s Mark Twain held two curious bedfellows responsible for most of the ills of the Gilded Age: "tainted money" (earned "dishonestly if we can; honestly if we must") and rampant Democracy. In an unsigned article in October 1875 called "The Curious Republic of Gondour" he proposed a sweeping if cumbersome solution to the danger of mob rule. Instead of restricting the suffrage, which would be unconstitutional, why not expand it by giving men of education and property five or even ten votes apiece—thus blending meritocracy and oligarchy?

Failing some such accommodation by America to his terms, Clemens would prefer to leave it. In less than two years he visited England three times; between 1872 and 1907 he spent more than eleven years abroad. First England and then Germany stood for the hallowed virtues of thrift and stability that his own country had lost in the rush and clatter of the Gilded Age. The United States was going mad; and if he did not wish to expatriate himself permanently the least he could do was to withdraw as much as possible by retreating aesthetically into the prewar past. Convinced that his anger was too great to be unleashed into imaginative literature about the American present, Mark Twain increasingly turned to the European and the American past for his literary material. All of his major books were to be tales of yesterday: the frontier West, the South before the war, the England of the Plantagenets, the France of Joan of Arc, the Germany of the Middle Ages, and finally the late fantasy stories in which distinctions between the past and present are blurred in nightmare. More than any other factor, it was the moral and mercenary decadence of the Gilded Age—by whose standards Clemens lived and whose values he alternately embraced and loathed—which drove Mark Twain to seek refuge in the dream world of the past.

If the corruption of the Gilded Age encouraged Mark Twain to consider retreat into an earlier era, Clemens's marriage to Olivia Langdon got him started and gave the retreat a special flavor and direction. The peace and prosperity that came with marriage into New England respectability became a talisman for recapturing a certain part of his past that Clemens had spent twenty years trying to forget. As early as 1870, fortified with domestic comforts and professional success, he began to view that past in a very different light. Four days after his marriage, while his bride napped upstairs in the forty-three-thousand-dollar brick mansion in Buffalo given the newlyweds by his father-in-law, Clemens sat down in his scarlet-upholstered study and wrote a long letter to "My First, and Oldest and Dearest Friend," Will Bowen, a Hannibal playmate. By a train of connections that took him back farther in imagination than in years—he was thirty-four, but he used the word old seven times—Clemens made some crucial associations between his recent marriage and his Missouri past:

The old life has swept before me like a panorama; the old days have trooped by in their old glory again; the old faces have looked out of the mists of the past; old footsteps have sounded in my listening ears; old hands have clasped mine, and the songs I loved ages and ages ago have come wailing down the centuries. . . . Laura Hawkins was my sweetheart—Hold: *That* rouses me out of my dream, and brings me violently back into this day and this generation. For behold I have at this moment the only sweetheart I ever *loved*, and bless her old heart [Livy was twenty-four] . . . for four whole days she has been *Mrs. Samuel L. Clemens!*[11]

Within a few years Clemens would grow bitter over the degree to which domestic harassments and lavish living devoured his energies and money. But in the early 1870s it was still possible to move from opulent present to the transfigured past and back again, from New England to Missouri, in and out of the dream. First Livy and the comfortable life in Buffalo, then Livy and the plush life at Nook Farm, caressed and quickened Southern memories and Southern habits: it was in New England that Clemens saw his first huckleberries, but he gave them as a name to a Southern character. In Hartford too he sang and danced once again the black spirituals and crippled-uncle hoedowns he had learned as a boy in Missouri—flinging himself on one winter's evening out of the New England snowscape and into the summertime South in an ecstasy of darky pantomime that left Howells and the other guests in a trance. By turning Hannibal from distasteful memory into detached nostalgia, Mark Twain had finally found the most attractive way to return in spirit to the antebellum South.

The initial result was *The Adventures of Tom Sawyer.* Off and on between 1874 and 1876, in the midst of lecturing, traveling, speculating, and entertaining, Mark Twain managed to sandwich in his earliest novel about the South. For the first time the fountains of his great deep were broken up—his favored metaphor for the unlocking of memory—and he rained reminiscences for three hundred pages. Of all Mark Twain's Southern writing *Tom Sawyer* is the most unashamedly sentimental, a Currier and Ives fantasy land in which the Gilded Age is transformed into a Golden Age of prelapsarian innocence and charm.

But Mark Twain's slumbering Eden is more than a hymn to the long ago and far away. It is also an ode to the sweet garden of the South, before its halcyon quiet was broken by the Yankee machine. St. Petersburg's Southernness lends an extra dimension to *Tom Sawyer*, for it means that from the beginning Mark Twain's Missouri idyll will have a tinge of terror to it. Behind the facade of the delectable[12] white village, drowsing in the sunshine of a summer's morning, lurks the horror of black slavery and the fear of physical vengeance at the hands of a terrifying villain who is

59

also a "man of color." Indeed one could say that Mark Twain had it both ways with Injun Joe. As a halfbreed this wicked specimen of interracial pollution calls up the deepest fears of a recent frontier people, while at the same time striking terror in the hearts of Southerners raised on the fear of another, even more formidable source of colored revenge—yet without making a direct appeal to prejudice against blacks. When Injun Joe vows to slit the Widow Douglas's nostrils and notch her ears,[13] he bares the threat of racial violence that lies beneath St. Petersburg's camouflage of summer-green hillsides and whitewashed cottages. Although racial revenge is barely suggested in *Tom Sawyer,* it announces, however mildly, that from the beginning Mark Twain's South is not to be purified of racial friction but shaped to embrace it.

Nevertheless in this first retreat into the past, the fear and guilt soon to be uncovered in *Huckleberry Finn* and *Pudd'nhead Wilson* are largely buried under a deluge of melodrama, romance, and burlesque. Lost in a fog of nostalgia and catering to a juvenile as well as an adult audience, Mark Twain stayed away from the black population of St. Petersburg almost entirely. When he did introduce a black character, he chose a happy-go-lucky nigger boy named Little Jim (no relation to Nigger Jim), who is tricked into whitewashing the fence. In a tedious and unsuccessful dramatization of the novel, however,[14] Little Jim plays a larger role which is disastrous. Loosely modeled after Clemens's memories of Jane and Marshall Clemens's slave boy Lewis, Little Jim is a happy lad but not very bright. He prances around the stage a good deal and ends most of his monologues with a foolish "Yah-Yah-Yah" expression which could have been twisted into a jeering taunt, such as Ned McCaslin's mocking "hee hee hee" in *The Reivers.* But Little Jim is no Ned McCaslin. His remarks are inane and his life is focused on the fear of being whipped by "ole missis" (probably Jane Clemens) for petty misconduct. His big moment in the play comes when he tries to swallow a cake wrapped in newspaper and finally gets it down, newspaper and all. As a last touch Mark Twain left unusually liberal instructions for anyone who might play this nigger boy on the stage. Little Jim could be played by anyone—boy or girl, man or woman, "6 feet high or 6 feet through"—it made no difference. "Only Huck & Tom," Mark Twain cautioned, "must not be burlesqued."[15]

In the book version of *Tom Sawyer,* Mark Twain wisely relegated Little Jim to a minor role in the whitewashing episode and turned to a more promising subject: the different manner in which Tom and Huck respond to blacks. Tom, being mischievous but respectable, will lower himself to the level of black boys while skylarking at the town pump. But this middle-class son of the South draws a rigid line between casual play and intimate association with niggers. When Huck, who is Tom's tie with the underworld, explains that he learned how to cure warts from a nigger, Tom makes it clear that Huck's knowledge of warts is therefore useless to him on two counts. For one thing, Tom has never seen "a nigger that wouldn't lie." For another, even if niggers were not liars, Tom does not know one well enough to verify Huck's information on warts. Since he does not care to see even Huck in public places, Tom can hardly be expected to really "know" a nigger.[16]

Huck on the other hand is compelled by his hogshead way of life to associate more intimately with blacks. He does so reluctantly of course, disclosing confidentially to Tom that he hauls water for the Rogers's nigger man Jake only because Jake occasionally feeds him: "That's a mighty good nigger, Tom. He likes me, becuz I don't ever act as if I was above him. Sometimes I've set right down and eat *with* him. But you needn't tell that. A body's got to do things when he's awful hungry he wouldn't want to do as a steady thing."[17]

The latter part of Huck's confession strikes precisely the tone the boy will adopt throughout his career. As a member, in however poor standing, of an antebellum Southern community Huck is all too aware of the hazards facing whites who consort with blacks. Though he does not know it yet, he eventually will have to go through a major mental struggle to choose between the Southern code of race and his own sound heart.[18] But that crisis happens in another book.

For two years after the publication of *The Adventures of Tom Sawyer*—between 1877 and 1879—Mark Twain frittered away his talent on a play and story of detective derring-do that he finally admitted was so "dreadfully witless and flat" that he gave it up.[19] *Simon Wheeler, Detective* is little known for good reason, but two minor incidents in the story deserve our attention. One involves a stereotyped darky and is a complete failure. The other offers an occasionally humorous caricature of Southern chivalry.

After his sympathetic portrayal of Aunt Rachel in "A True Story" just three years before, Mark Twain reversed himself completely in *Simon Wheeler.* The young black man in the story, Toby, is also an antebellum slave separated from his family, but there his resemblance to Aunt Rachel ends. There is absolutely no pathos about him. When chastised for childish behavior he is temporarily crushed but recovers rapidly with the good nature that is the birthright of his race—bowing with "embarrassed diffidence," smiling "widely and mollifyingly," moving humbly. In one scene of potential drama, when Toby expresses the same desire to see his slave mother that Aunt Rachel did to see her son in "A True Story," Mark Twain opted for a crippling burlesque. Since Toby cannot read or write, "being mighty ignorant fo' my size," he asks a white man to copy a letter for his mother from "The People's Ready Letter-Writer," a collection of nineteenth-century rhetorical nonsense that threw Clemens into convulsions of laughter: "Dey ain't nuffin in de worl' but what dat book know 'bout it . . . dah's *beautiful* words in dat book . . . dat dey ain't *no* man kin understan'. . . . Don't dem words taste good in yo' mouf! . . . don't dey . . . blobber-blobber-blobber along like buttermilk googlin' out'n a jug!"[20]

The problem with Toby is not that his lines are not funny: the business about buttermilk prose is mildly amusing. The problem is that there is nothing else *to* this black man. The white characters in *Simon Wheeler* are both good and bad, redeeming and ridiculous. Toby is incredibly lopsided. To be believable he would have to possess roughly the same balance of human traits held by his white counterparts: sadness and seriousness, stupidity and wit, strength and weakness—at least enough to persuade us that he is on hand for reasons other than as a walk-on comedian. Such is not the case. For all the attempt at humor in *Simon Wheeler*, Mark Twain was right: the story *is* "dreadfully witless and flat." More than any character in the story, indeed more than any other black character in his writing, Toby reinforces the suspicion that for Mark Twain by the mid-seventies the only workable alternative to Aunt Rachel's pathos was Toby's simple-minded foolishness.

In his burlesque of the chivalrous South, on the other hand, Mark Twain scored two points. One was his first severe indictment of his own father as a harmless but scarcely admirable Southern aristocrat; the other was his first extensive parody of Southern feuding. In the play version of *Simon Wheeler* Mark Twain dubbed Judge Horace Griswold an old ass and let it go at that. But in the novel Griswold is another man entirely. Whether as major, colonel, squire, or judge—and he is all four from time to time in this tired story—Griswold is also John Marshall Clemens. Like all of Mark Twain's self-styled aristocrats marooned in the backwater of the Mississippi valley, the judge is tall, spare, smooth-shaven, eagle-beaked, provincial, ignorant, and arrogant. His ancestors were Virginians and he is a Whig in politics, a free-thinker in religion, and a social snob: "In his eyes, a man who came of gentle blood and fell to the ranks of scavengers and blacklegs was still a gentleman . . . since the word did not describe character but only birth. . . . In his younger days, nobody had lightly used the word in the south. . . . The Judge was punctiliously honorable, austerely upright. . . . He was grave even to sternness; he seldom smiled . . . religion was a subject he never mentioned."[21]

Griswold's resemblance to Marshall Clemens is more than likeness of personality: it is character reproduction.[22] Clemens's father *is* Mark Twain's fallen aristocrat. The fact that Judge Clemens fell farther than either Judge Griswold or Colonel Grangerford in *Huckleberry Finn* is not very important. For, as Griswold reminds us so carefully, once a gentleman always a gentleman.

Nevertheless Griswold is so much the ass that he is not very effective. Far more damaging to the chivalric ideal is Mark Twain's first attempt to transplant the code duello of the Old South to the Mississippi Southwest in the Dexter-Burnside "feud." Later the same germ of an idea will appear as the celebrated Grangerford-Shepherdson blood feud in *Huckleberry Finn*, but with changes so profound as to be unrecognizable. Social embarrassment, not bullets, is the only wound suffered in *Simon Wheeler*. Southerners are always threatening each other but their threats seldom materialize. We recall that in *Huckleberry Finn* Colonel Grangerford will remind his son Buck, shortly before both of them are dead, that there is still plenty of time in Buck's young life for him to bag his quota of Shepherdsons. In *Simon Wheeler* Judge Griswold has difficulty instilling *enough* zeal in young Hale Dexter to go hunting for a Burnside. When Dexter does finally scare up Hugh Burnside in a stooped position, he assures him that he has no intention of taking advantage of him in such a posture. Thus does Mark Twain save the honor of the chivalrous South.[23]

The moral distance between the two feuds reaches its widest point in the last day of life for the Grangerfords in *Huckleberry Finn* and the final moment of glory for the Dexters and Burnsides in *Simon Wheeler*. Both last days are called dismal but that is certainly the only thing they have in common. While it is Huck's duty to report to the reader the sight of full-grown men shooting at wounded boys in the river, Judge Griswold's duty is to inform the elder Dexter that the sole surviving Burnside, after showing encouraging signs of recovery from a long illness, has relapsed and died. Cursing his bad luck that no Burnside offspring are old enough to kill (in *Simon Wheeler* gentlemen do not war on children), Dexter dies in bitter disappointment, leaving one son to shoulder the burden of the lost glory of the South.

The difference between feuding in *Simon Wheeler, Detective* and in *Huckleberry Finn* is the difference between burlesque and murder. It is the difference between Hale Dexter's willingness to give Hugh Burnside an equal chance in a more favorable position and the refusal of the Shepherdsons to give Buck Grangerford, floundering wounded and helpless in the Mississippi River, a second chance of any kind. Clearly something happened between 1879, when Mark Twain finally pigeonholed *Simon Wheeler,* and 1882, when he wrote the Grangerford chapters of *Huckleberry Finn.* What happened is that Clemens returned to the Mississippi valley in the spring of 1882. The journey back to his native land confirmed his suspicion that the South of *Tom Sawyer* and *Simon Wheeler* was a myth, and led directly to his savage attacks on both the antebellum and the postbellum South in *Life on the Mississippi.*

5

Paradise Lost: The Mississippi South Revisited

[I returned] like some banished Adam who is
revisiting his half-forgotten Paradise and wondering
how the arid outside world could ever have
seemed green and fair to him.

S. L. Clemens to Mrs. Boardman (1887)

[I found] a solemn, depressing, pathetic
spectacle. . . . There is hardly a celebrated
Southern name in any of the departments of
human industry except those of war, murder, the
duel, repudiation, & massacre.

Notebook (1881)[1]

In the autumn of 1874 Joseph Twichell, a Congregational pastor in Hartford and a close friend of the Clemens family, convinced Clemens that his years as a Mississippi River pilot held unusual literary appeal. Clemens "hadn't thought of that before."[2] Once reminded that he was uniquely equipped to translate an important part of the country's past into literature, he was eager to do so. The result was a series of articles published in the *Atlantic* in 1876 under the title "Old Times on the Mississippi." These articles contain some of Mark Twain's finest writing and constitute the best account of Mississippi steamboating ever written.

Halfway through his effort to enlarge the magazine articles into a book entitled *Life on the Mississippi*, Mark Twain's literary well ran dry. To recapture the flavor of those bygone days, Clemens decided to make his first trip back to the river since becoming one of the immovable fixtures of New England. He should have known better. As soon as he made the decision to return, he was in for trouble. In the twenty years since he left the South in 1861, Clemens's imagination had transformed the Mississippi Valley into a pristine paradise bounded by a river far finer than the one he had known as a pilot. In a letter to a schoolboy admirer in 1880 he had described this pastoral dreamland with intense nostalgia. He would be willing, Clemens had told the youngster, to go through his early life again only if he could emerge from childhood as a pilot on the Mississippi and remain one forever—gliding through an eternal Southern summer of magnolias and oleanders, "so that the dreamy twilight should have the added charm of their perfume."[3]

When he returned to the river in 1882 Clemens discovered that the one problem with his floating dream was that the Mississippi River no longer ran through virgin land. It ran through the postbellum South. And either the South, or Clemens, or both had changed a good deal in twenty years. Indeed the gap between his expectations and the reality so depressed Clemens that most of his notebook impressions never appeared in *Life on the Mississippi*— a book intended as a report about, not a funeral ode to, the river as a way of life. The northern stretches of the river were still lovely, but the southern half was in flood. Buzzards fished for drowned men. Trees were stripped bare by flood-starved cattle and mules. Even the river's surging brown current, once beautiful, now seemed oppressive. Cabins along the shore, once whitewashed (at least in Clemens's memory), loomed gray and spectral. Plantation mansions, "once so shining white," had "a decayed, neglected look."[4]

That spring Clemens found that the calm, peaceful river that flowed by St. Petersburg in *Tom Sawyer* had become a raging, swollen flood—and *that* was the river Mark Twain soon wrote into *Huckleberry Finn*.[5] Even steamboating was dead. The St. Louis levee, once lined with boats "with their *noses* against the wharf, wedged in, stern out in the river, side by side like sardines in a box," now housed a half-dozen "lingering ghosts and remembrances of great fleets that plied the big river," tied end to end, their fires out. Clemens did find a single steamboatman who still talked the colorful vernacular of the river's flush times, telling him about an old bitch who kept "the biggest whore house in St. Louis." But it was painfully clear to the returning pilgrim that the "old-fashioned, God-damn-your-soul," Brobdingnagian pilot of princely fame and salary—the kind of pilot Clemens imagined he had been—was a thing of the past, run over by the railroad.[6]

Clemens had discovered it was best not to try to go home again. From his position as adopted Yankee, the thing that bothered him even more than the polluted river was Southerners themselves. On the first leg of his journey he noted that the South did for a fact begin in his home state, where boots replaced shoes for a practical reason: Southern streets were paved with mud. Mustaches, which were in fashion in the civilized North (Clemens himself wore one), gave way to "obsolete and uncomely" goatees. Tobacco chewing, once a national disgrace, now started in Missouri, going south. And while Eastern loafers still managed to carry one hand "out-of-doors," Southwestern loafers kept both hands in their pockets—an important lesson in cultural geography. Along the flooded areas of the river malaria-racked Southerners could be seen slouching, squatting, leaning, and roosting on fences, stumps, and woodpiles, jaws cradled in their hands, gazing at nothing and discharging tobacco through crevices left by lost teeth. Malaria, still a pitiful part of Southern life, was now a tempting subject for Mark Twain's burlesque: the disease actually served a useful purpose by giving Southerners the shakes, thus enabling them to get some exercise without exerting themselves.[7]

By 1882 a large number of Mark Twain's Southerners were shabby, sick, lazy, ignorant, and profane. Even for Clemens

Southern profanity was "almost wicked" and their grammar was hopeless. In *Life on the Mississippi* Mark Twain complained that Southerners said "reckon" (one of Clemens's favorite words) and "don't" instead of "guess" and "doesn't" and that they tacked far too many "at's" onto the end of their sentences. Privately Clemens went further: Southern speech was gushy, flowery, fulsome, and sophomoric. But what bothered him more than the way Southerners talked was what they talked *about*. These people were forever yapping about the Civil War. Events were dated as "du'in' the waw," "befo' the waw," or "right aftah the waw"; and this kind of sport was growing so tiresome that Mark Twain offered a treasonous solution. To deflate Southern war leaders and to infuse them with a much-needed air of human fallibility, he proposed that the famous painting commemorating the last meeting between Stonewall Jackson and Robert E. Lee should be re-titled "Jackson Declining Lee's Invitation to Dinner—with Thanks" or "Jackson Asking Lee for a Match." Indeed of all the Southerners Mark Twain met only former slaves seemed capable of stripping away the utter nonsense about the war by adding a layer of humor to it:

> "What a splendid moon!"
> "Laws bless you, honey you ought to seen dat moon
> befo' de waw."[8]

Mark Twain had a ready explanation for Southern obsession with the war: Southerners still talked about the war because they still craved violence of any kind, in or out of war. Emerson had once remarked that "the Southerner asks concerning any man, 'How does he fight?,' while the Northerner asks, 'What can he do?' "—a comment that could serve as an epigram for *Life on the Mississippi*.[9] In chapter 26 Mark Twain tells the tragic story of two feuding families, the Darnells and the Watsons, who faced each other from opposite sides of the Mississippi and indulged in a bloodbath that inspired the Grangerford-Shepherdson vendetta in *Huckleberry Finn*. Privately, on his way down the river, Clemens added that the sole survivor of the Darnell-Watson feud, Old Darnell, did not learn very much from the violent deaths of his kinsmen. Apparently Darnell later attempted to seduce another man's wife and was shot by the woman's husband. Recovering sufficiently to kill a ferryboatman who had nothing to do with the feud, Darnell was in turn shot "through & through" and finally killed by the ferryboatman's friends. This sort of thing happened altogether too often in the South, and was usually accompanied by foul play: one Southerner, who discovered that his antagonist was unarmed, chivalrously threw down his revolver and slit the man's throat "all around" with a knife instead. Another Southerner, who thought his opponent was reaching for a weapon when he put his hand in his back pocket, began firing and, several shots later, managed to kill the man. A jury acquitted him.[10]

When Southerners weren't shooting at each other they seemed determined to do nothing at all. The result was that most things in the South were in disarray or disrepair. In Mark Twain's eyes the South was rapidly becoming one vast pigsty—a region of dirt, grime, and mud that he soon transferred from the postbellum South to the antebellum villages in *Huckleberry Finn*. Grand Tower, Illinois, was wearing the same coat of whitewash it wore the last time he saw it, twenty-one years earlier, and there was not much of it left. By contrast Point Pleasant was showing some progress: Clemens saw only one hog wallowing in the main street. Board walks had a habit of flying up and striking a passerby in the nose and Arkansas City was "a Hell of a place," with "19 different stenches at the same time" and enough mud "to insure the town against a famine in that article for a hundred years."[11]

Obviously Mark Twain forgot too easily that the river South was in flood that spring, but that did not keep him from trying to sum up this "new" South toward the close of *Life on the Mississippi*. The main difference between Northerners and Southerners was that Northerners worked and Southerners dreamed. Northerners also built schools, read books, and made money; so all that was needed was for Northerners to come south and bring their enterprise with them. As an apostle of progress busily investing in an engraving company, a publishing company, an insurance house, a watch company, a health food called Plasmon, a spiral hatpin, and the typesetter that ruined him, Mark Twain was delighted that the South was about to enter the nineteenth century as the rest of the country was preparing to leave it. Encouraged by signs of some Southern economic progress, he devoted long and dreary pages to new steamboat gadgets, cotton spindles, railroads, sewage systems, telephones, ice plants, and oleomargarine factories. Yet Mark Twain remained convinced that Southerners—because they *were* Southerners—would somehow find ways to cripple and retard even this much progress. And, most upsetting of all, in the process of updating themselves Southerners would lose the pristine beauty of the old preindustrial South Mark Twain longed for and mourned. By 1882 precious few magnolias were left on the "gray and grassless banks" of his muddy, mulatto Mississippi.[12]

Yet if Southern geography and economic conditions had changed— one for the better, one for the worse—Southern character had not. In *Life on the Mississippi* Mark Twain made the famous charge that Southerners were as bewitched as ever by Sir Walter Scott, the lunatic Englishman who had driven Southerners mad for two generations and may have caused the Civil War—presumably because Scott's novels were shipped to the South in carload lots before 1861. Though he admitted that other Americans were also bedeviled by Scott's romanticism, Mark Twain insisted that South-erners were ruined by it. Because of Scott, Southerners had little or no architecture worthy of the name; all they had was the silly Mardi Gras—which the young river pilot Sam Clemens had praised extravagantly in the 1850s.[13] Because of Scott's pernicious influence Southern writing was still juvenile, sentimental, and sloppy: instead of reporting matter-of-factly that a group of ladies boarded a pleasure boat and "shoved out up the creek," a Southern newspaper had to spread itself out and say that "the gallant little boat . . . proud of her fair freight . . . glided up the bayou." So long as Southerners continued to write such flowery and idiotic trash and to pine for the "maudlin Middle-Age romanticism" of "an absurd past that is dead and out of charity ought to be buried," they would never become wholly modern, or moral, men.[14]

It is not necessary to belabor the shortcomings of the Scott thesis. We are concerned here with Mark Twain's opinions, not with his accuracy as a historian of the South. As a matter of fact his charge against Scott was, for him, unusually tentative. When he wrote that "something of a plausible argument might, perhaps, be made in support of that wild proposition" that Scott was "in great measure responsible for the war," Mark Twain did not (quite) say that Scott caused the war. Actually he thought it "a little harsh" to blame one man. What he did say was that Scott's influence was "rather more" decisive than anyone else's—a different emphasis, if not a different charge, than the one customarily ascribed to him by critics.[15]

It should not even have to be said that Mark Twain's attack on Scott reached far beyond the man himself. When Huck and Jim encounter the wrecked and sinking steamboat named the *Walter Scott* on the river, they encounter (depending on one's taste) either a symbol of the extent to which Scott had wrecked the South, or a symbol of the extent to which Walter Scottism itself may finally be foundering. At any rate Scott himself was clearly a convenient whipping boy for the South's sins. Mark Twain's indictment of Scott is more than an eccentric, hyperbolic flight of fancy, though it is that too. For all its absurdity it stands as a bold, imaginative, and sweeping criticism of Southerners and of Southern institutions.

For this reason alone the diatribe against Scott is vastly more interesting than the celebrated but tepid chapter that Mark Twain left out of *Life on the Mississippi,* supposedly on the grounds that he did not wish to offend the South *that* much. He needn't have worried. The "suppressed" chapter is mild stuff indeed. In one section Mark Twain paid tribute to Frances Trollope, the English visitor who was "holily hated" in the South for exposing Southerners as "tissue-cuticled" barbarians masquerading as Greek philosophers; but he passed on quickly from Trollope's antebellum observations to his own evaluation of the postbellum South. The one thing he found missing after an absence of twenty years was slavery. That horror was finally gone and, with a casual stroke of the pen, Mark Twain declared that all black Southerners were now free and happy. But white Southerners were as far from moral emancipation as ever:

In one thing the average Northerner seems to be a step in advance of the average Southerner, in that he bands himself with his timid fellows to support the law (at least in the matter of murder), protect judges, juries, and witnesses, and also to secure all citizens from personal danger and from obloquy or social ostracism on account of opinion, political or religious; whereas the average Southerners do not band themselves together in these high interests, but leave them to look out for themselves unsupported; the results being unpunished murder, against the popular approval, and the decay and destruction of independent thought and action in politics.[16]

Mark Twain was not at his best when he dropped satire for calm commentary. Yet the latter part of the passage contains the rough rationale for Colonel Sherburn's unpunished murder of Boggs and his harangue of the Bricksville lynch mob in *Huckleberry Finn.*[17] Mark Twain had struck a vein of violence that could be mined either for its terror or for its humor, and he began to work both heavily—first the humor in *Life on the Mississippi,* then the prospects for terror in *Huckleberry Finn.* In his river notebook Clemens reported that a certain Southern major had been "shot in the backside" and could not sit down. "Let us have a law," Clemens scrawled with obvious delight, "that *all* duels shall aim at that part." Or, better yet, why not do away with dueling pistols altogether, replacing them with small and dainty French swords, which carried with them the assurance of "French immunity from danger"? Reworking the idea a bit in the chapter omitted from *Life on the Mississippi,* Mark Twain noted that bowie knives, sabres, rifles, bullets, and other outmoded tools of the dueling trade were now being replaced in the South by safety revolvers with blank cartridges, guaranteed not to go off and not to harm anyone if they did. If the mere threat of a duel was replacing the duel itself, perhaps eventually the threat, too, could be eliminated.[18]

The man who had tossed off some dueling threats of his own in Virginia City in 1864 had come a long way.[19] Eventually the distance which Mark Twain placed between himself and the South would pose some disturbing literary problems; but for the time being his anti-Southern outlook opened up a new and rich area of exploration. For if he was distressed by the white South, he was charmed and delighted by the black South. Clemens's river notebooks contain several stories, sketches, and anecdotes about black people, most of them bearing little resemblance to the tedious monologues reeled off by Little Jim and Toby in *Tom Sawyer* and *Simon Wheeler, Detective.* He was still amused by blacks, but his amusement took a new direction: blacks were now just the same as everyone else—nothing more, nothing less.

As a novelist Mark Twain had little to say about the social and economic conditions of blacks in the postbellum South. He was a man of letters, not a sociologist; his interest focused on individuals, not on classes. It was not that he lacked compassion. It was just that each time he saw a black face his mind veered off in another direction—away from the 1880s and back toward the 1850s. Each time he heard a nigger joke or watched a nigger being called down by a white, the sights and sounds of another time came flooding into his conscience. Each joke and each beating, once viewed as a natural part of life on the Mississippi, now struck Clemens as shocking and tragic. As a young pilot in the 1850s he had filled his river notebooks with statistical data about shifting sandbars, submerged snags, clogged channels, and drifting islands. Now, twenty years later, Clemens still recorded some data about drifting islands, but he seemed especially interested in one island called Jim Bayou, where a band of pirates had holed out before the war and killed white men for a fee of ten dollars, niggers for five. A nigger, Clemens wrote in 1882, "had rather go overboard than be landed at Jim Bayou."[20]

Each time Clemens started to take notes about the miserable lot of blacks in the South of the 1880s, his vision was almost instantly blurred by a succession of nightmare images of a South of another time. Only once did these two black Souths come together, in a conversation Clemens overheard between two black laundresses on board the steamer *Gold Dust* going downriver. The year was 1882, but it might as well be 1858 or 1860. One of the laundresses goes into ecstasy over the beauty and charm of a passing plantation on the riverbank, only to have the other laundress cut her short by reminding her that "many a poor nigger" was killed on that plantation before the war and fed to the catfish. When the first laundress insists that it would be nice to "have the old times back again, just for a minute, just to see how it would seem," the other replies that she does not need a historical resurrection to remember that slavery was "mighty rough times on the niggers" and that if she had been sold "furder down" the river before the war she would not be alive now. Clemens reminded himself to use the conversation in an article ridiculing "the Wretched Freedman who longed for Slavery" school of postbellum literature.[21]

He never got around to it. But he did eventually make a story out of another memory stirred by his return to the river. In his notebook while going downstream Clemens jotted a few lines about a man he had known as a pilot who "used to bet on niggers," and reminded himself to write about the time the "nigger better" on board Clemens's own boat used a slave as collateral in a card game. Though he admonished himself to "make it realistic," especially the part where the slave "appeals dumbly to the passengers" for help,[22] twenty years later when he finally got around to writing about it Mark Twain did not take his own advice. In a rough sketch called "Mr. Randall's Jew Story" a young border Southerner filled with "variegated southern prides and self-complacencies and aristocratic notions" (probably Clemens) tells a tale about a card game on board a steamboat in the 1850s. The three players are a professional gambler and slave trader named Hackett, a Jew,

74

and a Southern planter. The planter has a pretty teenage daughter and an attractive slave girl named Judith at his side.[23] In a last desperate bet he offers Judith as collateral, and on the next draw of cards loses her to Hackett. Judith, "crying and sobbing," looks "timidly from face to face, as if she might . . . find a friend and saviour there." Hackett shouts "You will come with me, wench" and implies he may make a prostitute out of her.[24] Unlike the incident Clemens remembered, however, all turns out well in the melodrama: the Jew kills Hackett and Judith is saved. In a later version of the same tale Mark Twain narrowed the gap between fact and fiction by placing the card game on the same boat he piloted in 1860, the *Alonzo Child*. Hackett becomes Jackson; Judith is changed from a black wench into a more fetching, "almost white" mulatto straight out of dime-novel fiction; the Jew interferes again; and Jackson is once again killed.[25]

For all the dramatic potential inherent in these stories, Clemens's most convincing river notes deal neither with the past brutalities of slavery nor with the present economic conditions in the South, but with the two aspects of race which always brought forth his best work: white bigotry and black humor. Already well into both subjects in *Huckleberry Finn* before he returned to the river, Clemens filled his notebooks with current samples of white nigger jokes and black dialect. Going downriver on the *Gold Dust,* he scribbled a conversation with a bartender who informed him that niggers had faulty tastes: they would "go to Hell for a watermelon," then turn around and drink anything he offered them so long as it looked pretty. The bartender was making a fortune selling "a pint of all kinds of worthless rubbish" to black steamboat hands simply by adding a liberal dose of red dye to it. Another white employee on the boat, a bullying roustabout named Dad Dunham, told Clemens that he had once been hauled into court in New Orleans for striking a "nigger with a *left* handed axe handle." Now "who in hell," Dunham asked Clemens, "ever heard of a left handed axe handle?"[26]

Southerners had not changed much. But Mark Twain had, and the change is reflected in the kind of jokes he told about blacks— jokes which have little in common with those he heard from the Dad Dunhams of the South. The main difference between Mark Twain's nigger jokes of the sixties and those of the eighties is that blacks no longer occupy a special humorous category—no longer seem funny just because they are black. They are still stupid, of

75

course, but so are whites: one darky watches the same steamer pass a given point on the river thirteen times and concludes that he has seen thirteen different boats; elsewhere Mark Twain assigns a similar misjudgment to a white man. Moreover blacks can be depended upon to lie or to distort the facts the same as whites in order not to *appear* to be stupid: one old black uncle swears that a certain steamboat going downriver was just loafin' along, then changes his estimate of the boat's speed to *"a-sparklin'"* when he learns it was the *Eclipse,* a boat noted for its swiftness. Elsewhere Mark Twain makes liars out of several white pilots. Blacks are also guilty of pulling social privileges: a black stoker informs rival niggers at a ball in St. Louis that he "fires de middle do' on de *Aleck Scott!"*—a distinction which earns him special privileges with the women. Immediately following this story Mark Twain switched the hypocrisy of using steamboating as a status symbol from black male to black female: a middle-aged matron tells her teenage daughter to "come in de house dis minute" and stop "stannin' out dah foolin' 'long wid dat low trash" on the street corner when "de barber off'n de *Gran' Turk"* is waiting inside to "conwerse wid you!"[27] Elsewhere Mark Twain ridicules whites for the same obsession with status and rank.

The point is obvious: both races are hypocrites and are therefore eligible for chastisement. We may recall that in his introduction to *Joseph Andrews* Fielding warned that misfortune is never a fit object of comedy, but hypocrisy is. One must not laugh at a man because he is poor, but if one sees a man in rags emerging from a coach and six, then one can make fun of him. If we apply Fielding's standard to Mark Twain's humor, we find that he was always at his best when he aimed his satire at people—black or white—who put on airs or pretended to be something they were not. Since blacks are members of the fallible human race, humor at their expense *can* be funny; being human, they qualify as fools. They also (occasionally) qualify as wise men adept at putting one over on the race long accustomed to putting jokes over on them. When Clemens visited Hannibal on his way back up the river he was kept waiting at his hotel by a distinguished-looking coachman who, when he finally arrived, took the stuffing out of Clemens's anger by explaining that "de time is mos' an hour en a half slower in de country en what it is in de town," and that Clemens should try to shuck his city ways and make allowance for the "diffunce in de time."[28]

What we have in these samples of black dialect and commentary is a preview of Nigger Jim's character and performance in *Huckleberry Finn*. The best piece of all is an unpublished (and almost certainly fictitious) dialogue between two deckhands on board the *Gold Dust,* who argue themselves to the conclusion that God Himself is a fool and " 'sponsible" for man's sins. The passage anticipates Nigger Jim's superb dialect and his resounding defeat of Huck in the celebrated dispute over "Sollermun" and the French language:

"O de hell you say!"
"Yes, de hell I say.—Do a dove ever want to hurt anybody?"
"Coase not."
"Do a rabbit?"
"No."
"Do a fishin'-worm?"
"Ke-he!—no."
"Do a cat fish ever want to soak whisky en git drunk?"
"No—coase he don't."
"Do a butterfly ever cuss & swääh?"
"O hell no, coase he don't."
"Do de bull-frog tell lies en steal?"
"No."
"*Well,* den! He don't make *no* dove dat's bloody-minded; He doan make *no* catfish dat loves whisky; He doan make *no* butterfly dat cusses & swäähs; He doan make no bullfrog dat lies & steals! What do all dat show? . . . He could a made de mankind so *dey* wouldn't ever want to rip & cuss & kill folks, & git drunk & so on, if he'd a wanted to. But he didn't *want* to. . . . He made most all of 'em so dey'd be a set of ornery blame' scoun'ls,—& now you reckon he gwine to roas' em to all everlast'n for what He done his own seff? No, *sir*—He's 'sponsible—shore's you's bawn he is; & dey jist ain't no way for Him to git aroun' it."[29]

For all the shortcomings of each race, the fact remains that most white Southerners who appear in *Life on the Mississippi* displeased Mark Twain, while most black Southerners delighted him. Nevertheless it would be a mistake to box Mark Twain's thinking about the South into two categories and label the one "black" and the other "white"; for by the spring of 1882 he was beginning to "see" several different Souths, each deriving from the deep disillusionment he felt over what he saw, or thought he saw, when he returned to the river. Although he certainly did not expect to find the same South he had known twenty years earlier, he was ill prepared for the profound sense of personal loss that he felt. Ironically, at the same time that he was making almost a subsidiary career out of lambasting the South in print and speech, Mark Twain found that he solely missed what he saw, in retrospect, as an antebellum Southern Eden that grew far more attractive the more it receded into the past. It did not take him long to discover that the best way to remember the Southern ideal was to stay away from the actuality. The best place to view the American South was, after all, from Hartford, Connecticut.

By 1882 Mark Twain's vision of an antebellum Arcadia clashed so harshly with the mechanized and polluted postbellum South that he began to make a sharp distinction between the two, a distinction that grew sharper as the years passed. Aside from marking off the black from the white South, he began to envision no fewer than three distinctive white Souths: an innocent pastoral South before the war; an evil manmade South also before the war; and an economically progressive but morally bankrupt postbellum South. The last of the three takes up most of *Life on the Mississippi,* but the other two can be found in scenes where Mark Twain simultaneously denounces antebellum Southern romanticism and mourns the passing of the "romance of the river" itself.

Without question the river is the key to Mark Twain's changing image of the South. More than for any other Southern writer, the Mississippi River *was* Mark Twain's South—and that South changes markedly halfway through *Life on the Mississippi.* In the first twenty chapters of the book, written in 1876 while he was perched high in his octagonal, steamboat-shaped study overlooking the misty blue hills and shimmering Chemung River in New York, Mark Twain presents the Mississippi River as nature's noblest creation. In the last half of the book, written after his return to the South, the river is a mass of notebook statistics. Barges, buoys, bridges, and the railroad have made the steamboat obsolete. The government has mechanized even nature itself, tearing out snags, uprooting islands, enlarging channels, dredging out sand-bars. Far from dictating economic terms for the South as it had before the coming of the railroad, the river is now a subsidiary part of the real South, increasingly at odds with the society on its banks. No longer the heart of the South, the Mississippi River has become an escape hatch—the best way to *avoid,* not to return to, the machine culture that corrupts the shore. The result is not only a natural and cultural transformation but, for Mark Twain, something close to literary chaos: a hymn to nature almost constantly broken by the chant of the dynamo.

A profound ambivalence underlies Mark Twain's thinking about the South, antebellum and postbellum alike. Just what *was* the South really like? Or, more important for the artist, which South—the real one or the ideal one—would finally gain the upper hand in Mark Twain's imaginative reconstruction of his own Southern experience? By 1882 the artistic choice, if not the final moral decision, had been made: the shore is the real South, the river a bewitching illusion, and the distance between the two is becoming too great to be bridged. While continuing to be entranced with the South as a majestic natural setting, Mark Twain was becoming increasingly distressed by the fact that the region was, regrettably, inhabited by Southerners.

The idea is barely suggested in *Life on the Mississippi*, where the values of both the garden and the machine are unpersuasively reaffirmed. Nevertheless the gap between the river as ideality and the shore as actuality was very much in Mark Twain's mind when he returned to New England to take up the unfinished novel which gave these two Souths their highest artistic expression.[30] In a strictly logical sense his feelings about the past contradicted one another; yet each was strong and deep, and each was embedded in *Huckleberry Finn*. The journey back to his native ground had proved a shattering experience. Yet the tension between the two rivers—and the discordant Souths—that came out of that journey provided the vital roughness, as well as the controlled nostalgia, that Mark Twain soon poured into the vibrant middle section of his finest work. Though he did not know it at the time, he had gained far more than he had lost.

6

A Lot of Prejudiced Chuckleheads: The White Southerner in Huckleberry Finn

Human nature cannot be studied in cities
except at a disadvantage—a village is the place.
There you can know your man inside & out.
Notebook (1882)

Mildmay, if we would happily live in the
South, we must not look so deeply and darkly
upon the things around us.
Thomas Bangs Thorpe,
The Master's House[1]

THE *Adventures of Huckleberry Finn* is Mark Twain's masterpiece, the product of a brief period in his career when he brought his talent and his view of the damned human race into a constructive relationship.[2] It is also his most ambitious examination of the society which nurtured him and his most intense denunciation of the five Southern institutions he had long singled out for special condemnation: slavery, violence, bigotry, ignorance, and Sir Walter Scott's jejune romanticism. Slavery was gone when Mark Twain wrote his novel, but the other four Southern "afflictions" were, as he observed in *Life on the Mississippi,* alive and flourishing in the 1880s. Inevitably *Huckleberry Finn* damns the postwar as well as the prewar South.

Two types of white Southerners largely populate the novel: good ones who have been partly warped by their environment and bad ones who have been totally twisted by it. It is almost as clear-cut as that. There are degrees of difference, but Mark Twain organized most of his characters around distinct cultural types as he saw them, tailoring his episodes to fit those types. Pap Finn represents the lowest mudsill type of Southerner. This archetypal figure appears in fewer than two dozen pages, yet he is permanently etched on the reader's consciousness. Old Man Finn is the offal of Southern civilization, a nightmarish man with a revolting, unbuttoned frankness that fascinates while it repels. His beady eyes, half-hidden behind a tangle of greasy hair, shine through "like he was behind vines." The color of his face is "a white to make a body sick, a white to make a body's flesh crawl— a tree-toad white, a fish-belly white"—enough indeed to make one prefer the color of the niggers he despises.[3]

But Finn is more than a physical horror. His incomparably obtuse reflections on the "gov'ment" show him to be, in his ignorance and prejudice, not outside of Missouri society but merely the most vicious form of it. In deriding the government Finn distills three feelings that Mark Twain thought were shared by too many white Southerners: fear of books, fear of blacks, and hatred of government. It is bad enough to have a son going to school and learning to read, but when he meets a free "nigger p'fessor" from Ohio[4] and has to shove him into the ditch before the arrogant black man will concede the right of way, Finn approaches apoplexy. Learning that blacks in Ohio can vote, he views that state as a freak and wonders why the federal government does not prove itself useful for once and force Ohio to reenslave its blacks. Ranting about the free nigger vote, Finn lets slip that he was too drunk on the last election day to make his own way to the polls. He affects contempt for the black professor's gold watch and silver-headed cane because he wants that watch and cane. He derides the man's intelligence because it is more satisfying to be contemptuous than to be jealous. That this "prowling, thieving, infernal, white-shirted free nigger" is "most as white as a white man" merely adds insult to injury, and cements Pap Finn's position at the bottom of the white South's social trash heap.[5]

There are, however, a host of other Southerners who are not too far above him, especially when it comes to the one trait that unites a good many Southerners in *Huckleberry Finn:* violence. In the course of his journey down the river with Jim, Huck literally moves from one scene of Southern bloodshed to another. The list of violent deeds or threats begins in St. Petersburg, Missouri, and ends eleven hundred miles and thirteen corpses later in Pikesville, Louisiana. In chapter 6 Pap, reeling with delirium tremens, tries to kill his son with a knife and Huck sits out the night with a gun, ready to kill his father if he tries again. The following day the boy stages his own mock murder by spilling a pig's blood and flees to Jackson's Island. Shortly thereafter the comparatively civilized citizens of St. Petersburg threaten to lynch Pap, whom they blame for Huck's "murder," just as they threatened to lynch Muff Potter and Injun Joe in *Tom Sawyer.* Later, in the house of death floating on the flooded Mississippi, Jim finds Pap shot in the back; and Huck himself is responsible for leaving the three thieves and would-be murderers stranded on board the sinking *Walter Scott,* thus condemning them to death by drowning. All the male members of the Grangerford family are wiped out in a single battle, with Huck again acting as the innocent agent of death by delivering Sophia Grangerford's elopement note to Harney Shepherdson. Even those immortal frauds, the King and the Duke of Bilgewater,[6] are first seen running from two separate mobs who mean business. The King has just been warned by one of the niggers whom he despises to flee from a village where respectable, middle-class citizens are "getherin' on the quiet" to give him a headstart, hunt him down, tar and feather him, and ride him out of town on a rail—a foreshadowing of the subsequent fate of these two con men. In Bricksville, Arkansas, Huck watches the farmer Boggs die on the main street ("they tore open his shirt. . . and I seen where one of the bullets went in"). And the town's leading citizen, Colonel Sherburn, is almost lynched by the same citizens who enjoyed watching Boggs die.

When Southerners are not violent in this novel they are likely to be promiscuous or perverted. The house of death floating down the river with Pap's naked corpse is a former brothel, and its walls are scrawled with obscenities. Some of the notes Mark Twain made for the novel but did not use, such as "Southern Courting—Making a gelding," imply that the Southerners who moan, groan, and gyrate to a relay of frenzied preachers at the Pokeville camp meeting may be using the occasion to whip up their own sexuality.[7] And the Arkansas audience that roars over the King's obscene stage antics in the nude[8] suggests that the Duke was not idly boasting when he said he knew the type of theatrical performance that would draw large Arkansas crowds. As Mark Twain saw it, far too many Southerners were bigoted, crude, ignorant, superstitious, or immoral.

Too many, but not all. Actually most Southerners were kind-hearted and decent; fools surely, but not knaves. Aunt Polly, the Widow Douglas, Uncle Silas and Aunt Sally Phelps—even Sister Hotchkiss, who prattles on about runaway niggers on the night of the evasion at the Phelps's farm—all have a redeeming side. They read the Bible regularly, feed boys homemade jam, set supper tables in summer breezeways, and preach Sunday sermons down on corner lots of their one-horse plantations.

These Southerners are not grotesques. By and large they know right from wrong; but this is precisely what locks them into a moral dilemma over slavery. Repeatedly Mark Twain drives home the irony that to be a Southerner in good standing one must preach good and practice evil. The novel is replete with Southerners who contradict themselves over slavery. The Widow Douglas is a gentle and well-meaning woman. But when she fetches her slaves in for bedtime prayers early in the novel, St. Petersburg's facade of starched propriety suffers irreparable damage. Setting black souls free merely facilitates keeping black bodies in bondage; and, since most Christian Southerners are in on the act, only innocent heathens like Huck, who take the gospel literally, are capable of revealing the hypocrisy of Southern notions about salvation. The Widow tries her best to teach Huck right from wrong and tells the boy that he "must help other people, and do everything I could for other people, and look out for them all the time"[9]—and then the ungrateful Huck turns around and tries to help and to do everything he can for a black slave.

Throughout the novel decent white Southerners unwittingly trap themselves over slavery. Mrs. Judith Loftus of St. Petersburg is a kind and hospitable if prying woman, eager to help Huck and to do what is right. Doing right includes telling Huck that she is the only one in the village with sense enough to send some men, including her husband, over to Jackson's Island to hunt for the runaway Jim with bloodhounds and guns. Later, on the river, the two men in the skiff who ask Huck if his companion on the raft is white or black are so sincerely distressed to learn that Huck's father, mother, and sister Mary Ann are afflicted with the smallpox that they float forty dollars' worth of conscience money across the water to help the family survive the plague. They are also professional slave hunters. Even Huck retains his credibility as a Southerner by continuing to echo Southern sentiments about niggers long after he has changed his mind about Jim. Repelled by the King's and the Duke's behavior in the Wilks episode, he vows that "if ever I struck anything like it, I'm a nigger." And when he learns he is supposed to be Tom Sawyer and must tell Aunt Sally Phelps a convincing lie about his tardy arrival by steamboat, Huck says what comes naturally and Aunt Sally responds with what also comes naturally:

"We blowed out a cylinder-head."
"Good gracious! anybody hurt?"
"No'm. Killed a nigger."
"Well, it's lucky; because sometimes people do get hurt."[10]

Slavery, ignorance, and violence give many Southerners in *Huckleberry Finn* a fragmentary quality, an angularity and rigidity of moral posture that make them less than whole persons. The most depraved examples are the villagers of Bricksville, Arkansas, who seem to be intimately related to the Southerners Clemens saw (or thought he saw) on his return to the river in 1882. In the notebook he kept on that journey he wrote: "Human nature cannot be studied in cities except at a disadvantage—a village is the place. There you can know your man inside & out."[11] By the time the raft carrying Huck and Jim reaches Bricksville, the "little one-horse town . . . pretty well down the state of Arkansaw," Mark Twain has found his village. But there are precious few Southerners in it worth knowing. Unlike the St. Petersburg of *Tom Sawyer* Bricksville has no visible Sunday School superintendents or Aunt Pollys. With the single exception of Colonel Sherburn, this Southern village is solidly poor white.

It is also filthy and decadent—a drab replica of the dilapidated villages Clemens saw on his return to the flooded Mississippi in 1882. We recall that in *Tom Sawyer* (1876) Aunt Polly's garden in St. Petersburg, Missouri, still grew a few tomatoes amidst the jumble of jimpson weeds. Eight years later and several hundred miles farther south in Bricksville, gardens run to ashes, boots, bottles, rags, and "played-out tinware." Hogs wallow in the main street and loafers yawn, stretch, scratch, slouch, and chaw their way through nine long paragraphs, flavoring their "lazy and drawly" speech with "considerable many cuss-words" and setting fire to a turpentine-splattered dog. Conversations are devoted to speculations about who stole the last piece of tobacco from whom. These ragtag whites are quarrelsome ("*You* give him a chaw, did you? So did your sister's cat's grandmother"), stingy ("You pay me back the chaws you've awready borry'd off'n me, Lafe Buckner, then I'll loan you one or two ton of it"), and cunning—a certain loafer "borry'd store tobacker and paid back nigger-head."

When they learn of the approaching showdown between Colonel Sherburn and the farmer Boggs, a large crowd of loafers, drunks, and normally law-abiding citizens pack the town's main street, "listening and laughing" and egging Boggs on, eagerly awaiting the murder. Except for two of Boggs's friends no one tries to stop the killing and no one goes for the sheriff. After Sherburn shoots Boggs, the crowd rams its way to a ringside position near the dead man, "squirming and scrouging and pushing and shoving" to have a look, while those on the fringe complain that it is not fair for the same viewers "to stay thar all the time, and never give nobody" else a chance to view the corpse. To speed Boggs's arrival in heaven the rednecks put a heavy Bible on his chest, then pull out hip bottles to toast the lanky man in the stovepipe hat who reenacts the murder for them. Rather than arrest Sherburn, they try to lynch him.[12]

Colonel Sherburn, the one person visible who is not a redneck, comes off only slightly better as a murderer. Although not of the planter crust, he is the best Bricksville has to offer and must therefore abide by the cavalier code—up to a point. When Boggs insults him, Sherburn responds with impeccable manners. His ultimatum to Boggs is courteous, courtly, and overdone. He is punctilious ("I'll endure it till one o'clock") and he carefully repeats the warning: if Boggs opens his mouth once after one o'clock Sherburn will kill him. The Southern gentleman draws the line, the redneck is foolish enough to step over it, and what begins with formal lip service to the code of the Old South ends in murder. Once Boggs fails to live up to his side of the arrangement, Sherburn drops the genteel facade and shoots an unarmed man.[13]

Up to this point Boggs, "the best-naturedest old fool in Arkansaw," is surely the more sympathetic of the two. The villagers assure Huck no fewer than four times that the drunken farmer is harmless, and Sherburn knows that as well as anyone else. Here, however, a problem arises: if Boggs is a sympathetic and harmless victim, and Sherburn an insensitive egomaniac, how can we possibly reconcile the brutal murder of Boggs with Sherburn's later heroic repulse of the lynch mob? How can the same man perform the same acts—one that elicits our disgust, the other our applause?

The answer may be that Mark Twain had two Sherburns in mind. There is the bad Sherburn, patterned after the "damned son of a bitch" William Owsley, an arrogant Hannibal storeowner, formerly from Kentucky, who "smoked fragrant cigars—regalias" and shot the "kind and good" farmer Sam Smarr on the streets of Hannibal when Clemens was nine years old.[14] And there is the good Sherburn, who courageously faces the mob and is not so much Sherburn the murderer as Mark Twain the moralist, who used the fictional protection of a Southern gentleman to insert the antimob material he had lacked the courage to leave under his own name in *Life on the Mississippi*.[15] The conceited Sherburn who kills Boggs is a counterfeit aristocrat. The courageous Sherburn who repels the mob is still Sherburn, but he is also the man Clemens quite candidly confessed he would like to be: the fearless loner who puts down mobs in *The Prince and the Pauper*, *Life on the Mississippi*, *Huckleberry Finn*, *A Connecticut Yankee in King Arthur's Court*, *Joan of Arc*, and *The Mysterious Stranger*.[16]

If Sherburn is both attractive and repulsive, what about the Grangerfords? Where do they belong in Mark Twain's cross-section of Southerners? For all their sham they belong close to the top. The Grangerfords are in fact the only Southern aristocrats in Mark Twain's writing for whom we feel some pity. We feel pity not because they are aristocrats, but because they die for *being* aristocrats. Like Colonel Sherburn the Grangerfords are practitioners of a vicious and perverted code. Unlike Sherburn they pay dearly for their loyalty to that code.

As Mark Twain's one composite example of country gentry gone to seed on the Mississippi frontier, the Grangerfords must bear a heavy burden of virtues and vices. They are hospitable, kind, proud, provincial, arrogant, and foolish. Generous to a fault, they own slaves and hunt men. Owners of "a lot of farms and over a hundred niggers," they are lazy and ineffectual farmers: Huck has to walk over a good deal of rough ground to reach their house. Pointedly named after the hard-working farmers who formed the Granger movement in the 1870s and 1880s, the Grangerfords spend little time farming and more time trying to kill a family just as pointedly named the Shepherdsons. Capable of intense love, they are consumed—and finally killed—by hate. For all their honorary titles and niggers-in-waiting, this fiefdom is set down among backwoods barbarians.

The family's duality is maintained in the domestic trappings. The house is the finest Huck has ever seen, but Huck would be the first to admit that is not saying much: for each feature of gentility there are several counterfeatures implying that the Grangerfords have not been successful in transplanting the tidewater South to the Mississippi Southwest.[17] The house is large, plastered, carpeted, and whitewashed; but it is built of rough-hewn logs, not brick or marble. There is a library in the parlor, but it consists of the Bible, a hymnbook, the speeches of the Kentucky peacemaker Henry Clay, and—in a family at war—*Friendship's Offering*. The books are "piled up perfectly exact," implying they are to be seen but not read; during the two weeks he stays with the family Huck is the only one who does any reading. The fancy parlor clock rarely runs unless a peddler has recently "scoured her up"; then it outpaces all rivals for a few hours and breaks down again.[18] Huck himself is certain the piano must have "tin pans in it," and the colorful, rakish mantel ornaments are mere chalk crockery that, when Huck presses them to hear them squeak, fail to "open their mouths nor look different nor interested." Even the artificial fruit in the cracked crockery basket could stand as a solitary symbol of the corroded society Mark Twain is mocking: both the chipped fruit and the thin veneer of Grangerford gentility are in such poor repair that the hypocrisy, "or whatever it was, underneath," shows through with embarrassing clarity. If parlor decor accurately reflects the character of those who furnish it, the Grangerfords are trying to look finer than they are.[19]

Physically they look fine indeed. The shabby and cracked household furnishings suggest the disorderly state of the Grangerfords, but their physiques do not. They look like quality. The womenfolk are beautiful, the men are handsome. Colonel Grangerford, like Mark Twain's other self-appointed aristocrats, has a certain sartorial splendor: he is tall, thin, high-browed, beak-nosed, and fierce-eyed, with the "thinnest kind of lips," the "thinnest kind of nostrils," and a "darkish-paly complexion" that sets him apart from rednecks.[20] Though vaguely reminiscent of the julep-sipping lords of manor in tidewater fiction, the colonel is no scholar-planter. In his spare time he does not read Virgil or anything else. His virtues, as he sees them, are courage, pride, and loyalty. His vices, as we see them, are clannishness, impetuosity, ignorance, and simplemindedness. For all his outward dignity Colonel Grangerford has the mentality of a child.

From the moment when Huck arrives wet from the river after the steamboat has rammed into the raft, and someone tells him not to move while the Grangerfords find out if he knows any Shepherdsons, the feud dominates the two Grangerford chapters. Unlike Huck the reader is aware almost at once that the family's blueblood facade is a bloody one.

Mark Twain took pains to make the Grangerford-Shepherdson feud realistic. In the notebook he kept on the river in 1882 Clemens reminded himself about a skirmish he was certain he had come "very near being an eye-witness to" while piloting on the river before the war: "At a landing we made on the Kentucky side [in 1860] there was a row. Don't remember as there was anybody hurt then; but shortly afterwards there was another row at that place and a youth of 19 belonging to the Mo. tribe had wandered over there. Half a dozen of that Ky. tribe got after him. He dodged along the wood piles & answered their shots. Presently he jumped into the river & they followed on after & peppered him & he had to make for the shore. By that time he was about dead—did shortly die." Elsewhere in the same notebook Clemens added: "Once a boy 12 years old connected with the Kentucky side was riding thro the woods on the Mo. side. He was overtaken by a full grown man and he shot that boy dead." And again: "Refugee from a wornout feud in Kentucky or Tenn. Told his story. Afraid he might be hunted down. Fictitious name. Saw his boy of 12 riddled but he and his ambushed an open wagon of the enemy driving home from church."[21]

All these incidents appear in the Grangerford-Shepherdson feud. The boy in the second quotation becomes Buck Grangerford's fourteen-year-old cousin Bud; the full-grown man is Baldy Shepherdson. All versions, fictional and historical, share the final death scene, in which teen-aged boys are besieged behind a woodpile that crops up in no fewer than four feuds in Clemens's notebooks or in Mark Twain's writing. Clemens also set down an unlikely but colorful incident in which the Darnell and Watson families (the actual contestants in *Life on the Mississippi*) were forced to attend the same church services. "Part of the church," Clemens wrote in his river notebook, was "in Tenn. part in Ky.," with the aisle serving as neutral territory between the two armed camps. Although Mark Twain did not keep the state boundary bisecting the church when he placed the scene in the novel, he did transfer intact the irony of each side's praying for "brotherly love, and such-like tiresomeness," with shotguns propped between their knees.

Of all the Grangerfords the boy Buck is the central figure of tragedy. Introduced in his nightshirt, sleepily dragging a gun larger than himself with which he would "a' got one" of the Shepherdsons if he were not "always kept down" and denied his right to kill, this fourteen-year-old boy is a true son of Mark Twain's South. When Huck confesses that his mudcat ancestry has left him ignorant of the ways of feuds, Buck wants to know "where was you raised." He casually mentions that there is no school in the region now, presumably because of the feud, and stresses the emotional detachment of the whole business: Buck tries to kill Harney Shepherdson, his sister's lover, only "on account of the feud." He feels no personal animosity. When Huck wonders what Harney has done to Buck, he is astounded to learn that Harney Shepherdson has "never done nothing" to Buck.[22]

The most shocking part of this boy's moral makeup is his callous attitude toward members of his own clan foolish enough to get themselves killed. Buck shows no compassion for his dead cousin Bud, because the boy should have known better than to go around unarmed. He even respects old Baldy Shepherdson for murdering the boy, "which he would naturally do of course." Buck reports the casualty list for the current year ("we got one and they got one") with a chilling matter-of-factness. In fact murder is such a natural way of life for this boy that he will not learn the inevitable outcome of prolonged feuding until he is trapped behind Mark Twain's well-used woodpile on the riverbank, the sole surviving male Grangerford with only a few minutes to live. Surely there can be no more traumatic farewell to Southern feuding than the sight of full-grown Southerners running along the riverbank, shooting at wounded boys in the water and shouting, "Kill them, kill them!"[23]

By the time all the male Grangerfords are dead, Huck Finn is sick of Southern feuding. The one time Huck cries in the novel is when he drags Buck Grangerford's body from the river and covers his face. The breakup of this Southern family is all the more sorrowful for this poor white boy because he is honest enough to admit that he was quite taken in by the deceptively lazy and hedonistic way of life at the Grangerford house: toasting each other's health in the morning, taking picnics in the woods, being waited on by niggers, loafing on the grass at midday with the dogs. Somehow it was too bad that the same code that gave the Grangerfords grace, dignity, and charm also demanded that they kill people, that their life should be made attractive by the very qualities of decorum, pride, and clannishness that destroyed them.

In the end, however, the pretentious parlor decor, the dazzling clothes so white that they "hurt your eyes," and the Sunday sermons about brotherhood stand no chance against Grangerford violence. In their failure to see the gap between what they preach and what they practice the Grangerfords are actually no different from most Southerners in *Huckleberry Finn,* except that almost alone among Mark Twain's Southerners they finally reap the consequences. Even Huck halfway understands this. The orphan boy who finally found a home among a family of whites whom he could admire and love learns too late that the destiny of each member of that family, male and female alike, is determined by violence. Forced to flee the dark and bloody ground of the river South for the freedom of the river itself, Huck will find his true home, and his fullest measure of peace and freedom, only when he is compelled to switch his allegiance from the dead Grangerfords back to a black slave.

7

Heroes or Puppets?
Clemens, John Lewis, &
George Griffin

Unconsciously we all have a standard by
which we measure other men . . . we admire them,
we envy them, for great qualities which we
ourselves lack. Hero worship consists in just that.
Our heroes are the men who do things which we
recognize, with . . . a secret shame, that we
cannot do.

Autobiography (1909)

Out of love, they [the Clemens family] did
not twit [George Griffin] . . . but out of love, I
did—and rubbed it in, sometimes.

"Wapping Alice" (1907)[1]

NIGGER JIM is a composite portrait of three black men Clemens knew intimately or casually during his lifetime. One was Uncle Daniel, the Missouri slave whom Clemens vaguely remembered as a boy.[2] Another was John Lewis, a handyman on the farm where the Clemenses spent their summers. By far the most important source of inspiration for Nigger Jim was George Griffin, the Hartford butler who served the Clemenses during the eighteen years in which Nigger Jim appeared in three books.

Uncle Daniel's importance as a source of literary inspiration after *The Gilded Age* has been greatly exaggerated.[3] John Lewis, on the other hand, contributed three traits to Nigger Jim's makeup: physical strength, a bucolic air which was not a part of George Griffin's character, and perhaps a complacent simplemindedness which crops up in Nigger Jim's behavior in the last part of *Huckleberry Finn*, in *Tom Sawyer Abroad*, and in "Tom Sawyer's Conspiracy." Aside from these three traits of Lewis's, which were transplanted to Nigger Jim, the most intriguing part of the story of John Lewis is not Lewis himself, but Clemens's reaction to Lewis.

On August 25, 1877, while the Clemenses were summering at Quarry Farm, John Lewis looked up from the manure he was shoveling and saw a runaway horse careening down the road carrying a cartload of Livy Clemens's relatives to what Clemens, panting desperately after them, considered certain disaster. Lewis planted himself squarely in the path of death and jerked the horse to a stop.[4]

Clemens at once added Lewis to his list of demigods. Although probably the most popular figure of his era, he seemed to feel the need to compare and to pit himself against a number of men less great than himself.[5] The Lewis incident is important not because Clemens found yet another hero, but because this time he gave the wreath to a black man. Before the runaway episode Lewis's greatness had completely escaped Clemens: indeed he had regarded this black man as a mere buffoon, a rustic boor who watched a magnificent sunset with Clemens at Quarry Farm and then remarked that the sight was "dam [*sic*] funny." But after he fetched that horse "up standing," this bowed and bent black scarecrow in "fluttering work-day rags" suddenly became Lewis the Prodigious, a man of superhuman strength and sterling character.

95

Still slouching on the same manure wagon he had always slouched on, Lewis, once crude and boorish, was now beautiful. Overnight he became Clemens's first black Adam.[6]

Chagrined that Lewis's greatness had eluded him before, Clemens set about making up for lost time. When Livy's relatives asked him if a gold watch would be an appropriate medal of honor for Lewis, Clemens at once set himself up as authority-at-large on how to reward deserving members of the colored race.[7] Warning that any scoffer who dared to question the propriety of giving a black man a watch would have to answer to Clemens personally, he declared that Lewis would actually appreciate this fine toy far more than the more valuable rewards, totalling nineteen hundred dollars, that the Langdons and Cranes showered on him. Bright shiny playthings appealed to black people more than expensive gifts. Four years later Clemens congratulated Joel Chandler Harris for shedding light on the black man's faulty "estimate of values by his willingness to risk his soul and his mighty peace forever for the sake of a silver sev'm-punce."[8]

The most astounding part of Lewis's behavior was that he remained modest in the midst of his new fame, humbly giving all the credit to "divine providence" for saving those "presshious" Langdon lives. The man seemed blissfully unaware of his greatness, thereby standing even taller in Clemens's eye. Like Ulysses S. Grant, another of Clemens's heroes, Lewis was noble in spite of himself—an unassuming fellow whose simplicity added to his dignity and to his power over Clemens. Surely here was a natural man with great literary possibilities.

Yet when Lewis finally made his fictional debut more than a quarter-century later, he was a disaster. In a sterile tale about Admiral Stormfield's efforts to erect a monument to Adam as founder of the human race (rightly labelled by Paine as "one of M. T.'s mistakes"), he appears as Uncle Rastus Timson. Although Lewis was actually shorter than Clemens, Uncle Rastus Timson is a ragtag giant: "[He] has a pronounced Atlas stoop, from carrying mighty burdens upon his shoulders; wears what is left of a once hat—a soft ruin which slumps to a shapeless rumple like a collapsed toy balloon when he drops it on the floor; the remains of his once clothes hang in fringed rags and rotting shreds from his booms and yard-arms, and give him the sorrowfully picturesque look of a ship that has been through a Cape Horn hurricane—not recently, but in Columbus's time."[9]

For all his titanic strength, Uncle Rastus Timson is a mental pygmy, a feeble black barometer set up to measure superior white intelligence and to respond to white jokes with such expressions as "Bless yo' soul, honey," "Well, dat do beat me!" and "Sure as you bawn." The problem with Uncle Rastus is that he was modeled after an ordinary handyman who turned out to be even less than ordinary: a timid and foolish darky who "hain't ever struck" anyone so intelligent as Admiral Stormfield, who is even more insane than Colonel Sellers in *The American Claimant*. Only late in the story, when Mark Twain trots him out into the dusty summer road to pull down the horse and rescue the white folks, does Rastus regain part of his dignity. Growing melodramatic, Mark Twain declared that after that episode white people eagerly took Rastus "by his horny black hand and gave it a good grip, and many said, 'I'm proud to do it!'"[10]

But it was too late and too forced. Despite his tardy heroism, Uncle Rastus Timson is not credible because neither Lewis himself nor his heroism was as striking as Clemens made them out to be. The most unusual event that occurred that summer day at Quarry Farm in 1877 was not Lewis's act of courage but Clemens's emotional response. Though he unquestionably admired Lewis's courage, Clemens seemed to admire even more his own capacity to admire Lewis. He could get away with such theatrics in his private relationship with Lewis. But when Mark Twain tried to stitch together a gullible darky and a courageous black hero into a single composite character, the two traits cancelled each other out. We may prefer to remember Lewis's influence on Nigger Jim as the natural shaman of woods and river in the middle portion of *Huckleberry Finn*. But the fact of the matter is that Lewis's more lasting contribution to the character of Nigger Jim was as the powerful but timid giant with the mentality of a child who appears in the last quarter of *Huckleberry Finn*, in most of *Tom Sawyer Abroad*, and in all of "Tom Sawyer's Conspiracy." Fortunately in most of *Huckleberry Finn* Lewis is eclipsed by another very different black man.[11]

Sometime in 1875 a large man with a "clear black and very handsome" complexion came to the Clemens home in Hartford to wash windows for one day and, as Clemens put it, accidentally stayed for eighteen years.[12] His name was George Griffin.

In a family sketch that he wrote in the 1890s Clemens noted

that Griffin had been a slave in Maryland and a Union general's bodyservant during the war. He described Griffin as "handsome," "faultlessly dressed," "well built, shrewd, wise, polite, always good-natured, cheerful to gaiety, honest, religious, a cautious truth-speaker, devoted friend to the family, champion of its interests," and the children's idol. Griffin was also a confidant for Clemens, a successful gambler, an astute debater, a money-lender in the Hartford black community, and a "strenuously religious" deacon of the African Methodist Episcopal Church.

When Clemens wrote that there was nothing commonplace about Griffin he might have added that there was nothing commonplace about what Clemens expected of him, either. Griffin answered the door ("it takes George all of two minutes to answer the door-bell when he is in a hurry, and I have never seen him in a hurry"), and sorted the mail while the Clemenses were summering at Quarry Farm. He acted in family theatricals, served as court jester at the dinner table, and played horse, camel, or elephant for the Clemens children on African safaris. Aside from these regular duties Clemens called on Griffin to use his mollifying tongue in breaking up insurrections in the kitchen, to roar election returns and news reports through a speaking tube up to the billiard room during Clemens's stag parties, and to fire a revolver at three ruffians lurking on the lawn and yelling obscenities at Clemens. Apparently Griffin also served as a scapegoat. When Clemens began swearing on the telephone to a person he presumed was the operator, only to learn that the woman was actually a family friend, he persuaded her that she had just been talking with George and that Clemens would have to upbraid his butler for his indecent language.[13]

To put it mildly, Griffin was a butler in the loosest sense of the word. When he wasn't scapegoat he was, as Howells put it, Clemens's interpreter—that is, Clemens's liar. When Clemens told Griffin he would not come down from the billiard room to see the twelve apostles or the Holy Ghost, much less an unsolicited visitor who was banging on the door, he expected Griffin to modify the curse to the point that the intruder would leave thinking that Clemens was on his deathbed. Clemens himself expressed satisfaction that he had trained Griffin to be a well-behaved, loyal, and lying sentinel, stationed at the front door to guard his master's privacy.

Yet Clemens also placed an uncommon amount of trust in Griffin, writing that he felt perfectly safe in discharging the police officer he had hired to prowl the premises for imaginary burglars, because he trusted Griffin to perform that task. Clemens also gave his butler, who did not drink, a key to the liquor cabinet and placed him in charge of seeing that the other servants did not raid it—for Clemens a remarkable sign of trust. Griffin, for his part, sometimes showed embarrassment over his employer's crudities of behavior. When Clemens gleefully treated several distinguished dinner guests to some cheap cigars that brought the evening to an abrupt close, Griffin reported with shame that the driveway was strewn with half-smoked "long-nines."[14]

If Clemens expected and received unusual service and loyalty from Griffin, he also credited him with unusual intelligence, especially in matters of finance where Clemens, with good reason, was uncertain of his own prowess. In the election of 1884, when Clemens bolted the party (much to Griffin's disgust) and voted for Grover Cleveland, Griffin laid his usual heavy bets on the Republican candidate, James G. Blaine. When Blaine committed political suicide with his "Rum, Romanism, and Rebellion" speech, Griffin seemed headed for financial ruin. Instead he won handsomely by covering his bets three-to-one a few hours before the news of Blaine's disastrous speech reached the rest of Hartford. In addition to taking care of his own pocket, Griffin apparently "settled" several criminal cases involving blacks out of court; Clemens did not say how. He also conducted a thriving banking business in the black community at what Paine (who usually played back what Clemens told him) called ruinous interest. And when several of Hartford's elite citizens gathered at the Clemens home on Friday evenings to play billiards, Griffin detained them in deep and mysterious financial discussions in the front hall, which amused Clemens because as a Southerner he recognized that high-class Northerners enjoyed being milked by a black butler.[15]

Of all Griffin's endowments, the most aggravating for Clemens was his "disposition to gallantry" with black cooks in the kitchen. Griffin's unwillingness to adopt a hands-off policy led Clemens to screen his prospective cooks carefully. The principal requirement in a black cook (other than that she be "*tidy*—because when a colored cook *is* untidy she is likely to be intemperate in it") was that she be "old enough, or grave enough,—or above all, strong enough & wise enough, to resist George's fascinations." When Griffin threatened to live with his wife for a change if Clemens did not provide a cook to his taste, Clemens urged him to do just that. Finally things got to the point where Clemens had to issue a household ultimatum: there would be no more black cooks until Griffin experienced what Clemens tactfully called a change of heart.[16]

If Griffin occasionally taxed Clemens's patience, surely it was Griffin whose patience was usually more heavily taxed—and not only by the master of the house. Clemens's daughter Clara recruited Griffin to rattle and bang his "huge black paws" over the piano keys, because "he was the only person in the whole wide world I could hound into the misery of becoming my pupil." Susy Clemens, the oldest daughter, scolded Griffin for his gambling, and Livy sometimes did not "approve of George." According to Clara, the only time Griffin ever looked after anyone's needs was in the presence of guests, when he "could rise to great heights of professional service and throb with feverish excitement." Otherwise Griffin "explained that the intellectual inspiration he received in the dining–room saved him from the bad effects of life in the inferior atmosphere of the kitchen." Closing her commentary on Griffin's dinnertime behavior, Clara added: "Often did we hear a prompt laugh filling the room from a dark figure at ease against the wall, before the rest of us at table had expressed our amusement at one of Father's remarks. George was a great addition to the family and afforded Father almost as much amusement as Father did George."[17]

Clemens amused Griffin in a variety of ways, but primarily by acting out the role of father-protector to an erring child. (He once told Howells that he kept a black butler because he could not bear to give orders to a white man.) When Griffin charged into Clemens's billiard study one day in a "high state of excitement" and demanded his employer's revolver to kill a black man with whom he was at odds, Clemens perceived at once that what Griffin needed was not a gun but a man of wisdom, stability, and high authority to talk him out of such a move. Accordingly Clemens slipped into the role of august adviser, first feigning support for Griffin's violent plan to throw him offguard, then countering with "wise & righteous counsel" for a black man who had shown a "bad streak in him." Griffin went away convinced and converted.

Shortly after this episode Clemens was forced to discharge Griffin for financial reasons. By 1891 his household expenses had gotten so out of hand that he decided to cancel his subscription to *Harper's Magazine* and find a cheaper brand of toilet paper. When these two reductions proved insufficient, he decided to take his family into voluntary exile in Europe to cut down on domestic expenditures. Before he left he secured a position for Griffin as a waiter at the Union League Club in New York. On one of his numerous business trips back to the states during the family's nine-year stay abroad, Clemens sought Griffin out in New York, took him by the arm, and led him into the *Century* publishing house. Describing the episode later, he poked fun at the clerks who looked aghast at this unprecedented breach of etiquette. Glorying in the fact that everyone "took a sight of George & me," Clemens sought out the top editors and introduced them to Mr. Griffin; everyone but Clemens was embarrassed, and everyone but Clemens stopped talking. When the chief editor finally recovered, he asked Clemens to pass judgment on the quality of a certain manuscript they had just received ("You are just the man!"). Instead Clemens collared Griffin, who was decamping toward the door, and read a paragraph of the manuscript to him, asking him how the "literary quality of it struck him." Griffin gave his opinion and Clemens handed the manuscript back unread, stating that that was his opinion too.

Pleased with his performance, Clemens next led Griffin into the *St. Nicholas Magazine*'s editorial room down the street for an encore, this time asking Griffin for his opinion on a new cover design. Griffin complied and Clemens again endorsed his view. Again the ensuing conversation with the editors was not fluent, but Clemens left happy. Still later, on what proved to be a long day for Griffin, Clemens took him on a stroll through the streets for refreshments with a Mr. Carey of *St. Nicholas Magazine*. When Griffin dropped behind the two white men on the sidewalk, Clemens brought him forward and placed him between Carey and himself. When Griffin admitted that he had won six hundred dollars on a prize fight between a white man and a black by betting on the white man, and was challenged by Carey whether it was patriotic to bet against his color, Clemens credited Griffin with the proper reply for a New York businessman in 1893: "Betting is business, sir, patriotism is sentiment. They don't belong together. In politics I'm colored; in a bet I put up on *the best man,* I ain't particular about his paint. That white man had a record; so had the coon, but 'twas watered." At the end of the day's entertainment, Carey and Clemens agreed that Griffin was, indeed, "no commonplace coon."

The publishing house episode takes up most of the nonfiction sketch Clemens wrote about Griffin. But this black man also appears in two highly dissimilar pieces of fiction. The last and most revealing is a nightmare tale called "The Great Dark" written in 1898. The other is a story called "Wapping Alice," supposedly about a female servant who turns out to be a man ("why he unsexed himself was his own affair") but actually starring Griffin in the lead role as a black servant named George, who is employed by an author named Mark.

In "Wapping Alice" Mark Twain played upon two contradictory qualities in George's character—one commendable, the other deplorable. The commendable quality was George's lively interest in family affairs, which Mark Twain took pains to explain: Griffin was "an institution—he was a *part* of us, not an excrescence—we had a great affection for him, and he for us; when he said to people 'my family' . . . he meant *my* family, not his."[18] Yet in striking contrast to everything Clemens ever said about the nonfictional Griffin, the most conspicuous trait of the fictional George is not his loyalty but his vanity and selfishness. In "Wapping Alice" George is a master of deceit. When the family leaves town, relying on George to take care of the house and grounds, he leads the entire brigade of servants off on a week-long excursion to the Northampton horse races and manages to keep the news about his negligence as a caretaker from leaking out. But when "Mark" returns and puts George on the spot, the black man tries to lie his way out, first insisting that he always sets the burglar alarm before departing on excursions, then gradually crumbling under Mark's relentless interrogation until he admits that he rarely, if ever, sets the alarm. The longer Mark plays the role of cunning detective the more George resorts to desperate rationalization: the mere *presence* of a burglar alarm, he assures his employer, is enough to discourage burglars. There is no need to turn it on.[19]

In "Wapping Alice" George is not only irresponsible; he is greedy. When Mark reminds him that the house could have been burglarized while George was off on an excursion, the black man pales "to the hue of old amber" (in the "Family Sketch" he bleaches "to the tint of new leather")[20] and bounds upstairs to make sure his private cache of fifteen hundred dollars is still hidden between his "mattrasses." Mark, a bit put out over his butler's lack of concern for the safety of his master's property, accuses George of betting fifteen hundred dollars on the sweeping effects of a "religious epidemic" in the African Methodist Episcopal Church and pocketing the results. The charge pricks the black man's conscience badly, and leads Mark to pour it on: "I could see that that wounded him—poor old George . . . it was a sore spot with [him] . . . but as he never went quite far enough to say it was a lie, and as he was something of a purist in language, this subtle discrimination was noticed by the family, to his damage. Out of love, they did not twit him with it; but out of love, I did—and rubbed it in, sometimes."[21]

Out of love Clemens rubbed a bewildering variety of experiences into Griffin; still there can be no question that butler and boss exchanged a good deal of affection and respect. Griffin's feelings for the family are brought out clearly in a letter he wrote to Clara from New York in 1893, two years after he left Clemens's employ:

Miss Clara I have almost lost sight of Hartford it seems so long since we were there and like yourself I am having such a good time here. . . . Now Miss Clara don't think that I have lost sight of the old family, for that cannot be, for life is too short. . . . One year ago I did miss you all so mutch but today I feel at home in New York and I am glad to say that I am happy. . . . Now Miss Clara I am going to ask one favor of you and this is this, please write me a letter so I can have it to read Christmas morning. I will enjoy it so much and it will be so home like and all I want it to caust you, is the time that it will take to write and a five cent stamp.

You don't know how I enjoy looking at your Pictures Sundays when I am off and it seems as tho I was in Hartford and not in New York. . . . In spring I think I shall go to work on the rail road if I can get a parlor car that runs out west. I want to see the west very much. . . .

From your old Servant

"George."[22]

On his global lecture tour in 1895 Clemens jotted in his notebook that Australia, "with its specialties of piety & horse-racing, would be heaven for George" and added a reminder to tell all about his butler in a future article. He never got around to it. On June 2, 1897, he scribbled tersely in his London notebook that Griffin was dead.[23]

The most striking part of the story of George Griffin is not Griffin himself, but the similarities between Griffin and Nigger Jim. Both are large, intelligent, argumentative, grand "distorters of the truth," sentimental, polite, usually "cheerful to gaiety," deeply religious, and profoundly loyal to white folks. In the nineteenth-century spectrum of black characters depicted by whites, they stand together somewhere between Harriet Beecher Stowe's complacent Uncle Tom and George Washington Cable's savage Bras Coupé. Both Griffin and Nigger Jim are buffoons when locked into a civilized environment; both are noble when released into a state of nature: Jim on the river, Griffin at sea in his last fictional appearance in "The Great Dark."

Even more striking are the similarities between Huck and Jim on the one hand, and Clemens and Griffin on the other. Early in *Huckleberry Finn* Huck's relationship with Jim is marred by the boy's lack of compassion and sensitivity, which eventually brings him to remorse and apology. Clemens's association with Griffin was sometimes marred by callousness which led to regret and, occasionally, to defending Griffin against criticism by other members of the family.[24] We also recall that Huck tries to explain Jim's goodness by the fact that he must be white inside; Clemens reversed the color scheme by calling Griffin "as good as he was black." Both Huck and Clemens were fond of commenting on the unswerving loyalty of their black companions: Huck is flabbergasted and embarrassed by Jim's declarations of affection; Clemens was flattered and awed by Griffin's affirmations of devotion. Above all both Huck and Clemens were careful to point out that their black charges were unusual people and not necessarily to be confused with the rest of their race. Huck repeatedly calls Jim an uncommon nigger; Clemens insisted that his relationship with Griffin was wholly proper, because Griffin was by no means a "commonplace coon."

It is this precarious up-and-down relationship, alternating between compassion and callousness, companionship and rivalry, that makes George Griffin's last fictional appearance memorable. Mark Twain's late and shattering story entitled "The Great Dark" is at once a fitting end to Griffin's career and the best possible point of departure for a discussion of Nigger Jim and Huck in *Huckleberry Finn*.

Toward the close of the century Mark Twain took himself on one of the dream voyages that litter his last manuscripts. While looking through a microscope one evening at a drop of rainwater (to which he has added some whiskey to stir up the microbes) a man named Edwards, alias Clemens, gets bored and falls asleep. During his nap a dark-clothed Satanic figure disguised as the Superintendent of Dreams appears from nowhere, awakens Edwards, and offers to take his entire family on a long pleasure excursion inside the drop of rainwater. Edwards agrees and sails off with his wife Alice (Livy) and their two daughters, one named Susy and born on the same day as Susy Clemens, who died six years before the story. What begins as fantasy turns into nightmare as the family is cast adrift on a haunted ship strewn with dead or dying passengers. For ten years the derelict ship plows through a pitch-dark Antarctic wasteland, dodging icebergs and chasing another phantom ship that has kidnapped Susy and remains just beyond reach. To compound the difficulties, whales with "hairy spidery legs" feed on each other and threaten to overturn the ship and devour the passengers. Before they die, most of the passengers go mad.

At the outset of the story the Edwardses' servant George[25] (an ex-slave like Griffin) is little more than a chuckling stage darky who bares white fangs in huge grins, says "Bless yo' soul, honey" to Alice, and hardly seems aware that a nightmare is going on. When he reminds Edwards that it is time for their daily boxing exercise on board ship, Edwards responds with the kind of "solid good cussing" that Clara Clemens remembered as the way her father "explained things to George." Edwards finally agrees to box, however. In the sixth round of a lively fight he knocks the big, brawny black man out cold.

It is not likely that Clemens, who once compared his biceps with an oyster wrapped in a rag,[26] ever tested his strength against George Griffin's. But the incident momentarily throws *us* off balance by suggesting that Clemens may have fantasized about such a vicarious physical victory over Griffin. Actually the final message of this story is not hostility but friendship. In striking contrast to his role in "Wapping Alice" George plays the role of hero in "The Great Dark." When an octopus threatens to swallow the ship, he rescues the Edwards children by hiding them in the hold; and we are reminded that John Lewis saved the Langdon children by stopping a runaway horse and that Nigger Jim saves Tom Sawyer from blood poisoning in *Huckleberry Finn* by insisting that Huck go for a doctor after Tom is shot in the "evasion."

After a decade of aimless wandering, the phantom ship comes to a dead stop as the sea begins to boil and to turn into molten brass—dried up by the merciless white light from the microscope lamp. The compasses spin crazily, the surviving crew mutinies, spider-quids attack and consume the surviving passengers, and it becomes George's duty to inform Edwards that his wife and children are dead.[27] In the last scene of this grim story two human beings are left on the planet—Edwards (an adult Huck) and George (a late Jim), sitting and consoling each other in the middle of nothing. The fetching image of Huck and Nigger Jim squatting together in peace and contentment on a sandbar, watching the dawn spread over the river and listening to the sounds of a waking world, has been replaced by two old men imprisoned in a wasteland called the Great White Glare. In the last decade of his life, fifteen years after finishing *Huckleberry Finn*, Mark Twain left one black and one white to share one another's company, briefly, before the snuffing out of the human race.

8

Everything All Busted Up &
Ruined: The Fate of Brotherhood
in Huckleberry Finn

Brotherhood . . . is our most precious possession,
what there is of it.
Pudd'nhead Wilson's New Calendar (1897)

After all this long journey . . . here it
was all come to nothing, everything all busted up
and ruined.

It's too good for true, honey, it's too good for true.
Huckleberry Finn (1884)[1]

Nigger Jim is the conscience of *Huckleberry Finn.* More than
Huck he is the moral standard by which other characters in the
novel are measured and found wanting.[2] This black man is a new
kind of character in American fiction, a highly complex and original
creation.[3]

Huck learns compassion from Jim. Without this black man the
boy's rebelliousness would be confined to petty stealing, lying,
putting his feet up on the widow's furniture, and running away. Jim
makes Huck's revolt more than a personal reaction to etiquette
and niceties; when Jim is taken from the raft and put in prison,
Huck loses the stature he gained from being with a black man.
It is this feeling of heart and expression of conscience, exhibited
by a black and emulated by a white, that makes the relationship
between Nigger Jim and Huck memorable.[4] It is the central theme
of *Huckleberry Finn* and the most appealing dream of interracial
brotherhood in our literature.

Huck and Jim first meet in the novel on the level they will assume
whenever superstition is at issue; Jim as teacher, Huck as learner.
When the boy sees his father's tracks in the snow, he sets out at
once to discover how it is that Pap, whom he has not seen for a
year and had hoped was dead, is after all alive and about. To
find out what Pap is up to,[5] Huck goes to the highest possible
authority—Nigger Jim's hairball oracle.

At this point the two future companions are casual acquaint-
ances, brought together because they are both in the power of
white women. Jim is owned by the Widow Douglas's sister Miss
Watson; Huck, driven into respectability as the price for joining
Tom Sawyer's gang, is being housed and tutored by the widow
herself. The striking feature about this first encounter is that Jim
dominates the situation. Anxious to find out what Pap has in mind,
Huck wants Jim's hairball to speak out at once; but it won't say
a thing until the white boy forks over twenty-five cents! Although
the quarter is a fake, the hairball accepts it and Jim in effect gives
Huck a counterfeit prophecy in exchange for a counterfeit quarter
which he converts into passable currency by removing the brass
stain. In doing so the slave scores a triumph over the white boy,
who not only has faith in a ball of mucus taken from the fourth

stomach of an ox, but accepts without question the black man's prognosis.

Jim's prophecy to be sure is a bright one—and filled with ironies of color. Pap has two angels hovering over him, one white and good, the other black and evil. Huck too is being watched over by two girls, one dark and poor, the other—the one he will marry—light and rich.[6] Through compassion for Huck Jim tells the white boy what he wants to hear; but in doing so the black man remains in complete control of the relationship.

Despite Jim's good intentions Huck is not able to evade Pap as easily as the hairball predicted. The next spring he is captured by his father and taken across the river to a cabin deep in the Illinois woods. When Pap gets drunk and almost kills him, Huck simulates his own murder and flees to Jackson's Island. There he meets Jim. Both are fugitives fleeing from their respective forms of bondage—Jim from Miss Watson whose Christian principles could not withstand a slave trader's offer of eight hundred dollars, Huck from the disagreeable alternatives of Miss Watson's peckings and Pap's beatings.

Huck pretends to be Jim's protector, but Jim is the one who actually lays the groundwork for a satisfactory relationship. His readings of the signs of nature are accurate and his folk cures usually work. It is Jim who suggests that they seek higher ground in the cave before the arrival of the storm which would have drowned them, Jim who builds the wigwam on the raft captured in the June flood, Jim who finds Pap's body in the floating house of death and shields Huck from the knowledge by covering Pap's face. Throughout the middle part of the novel this natural man of woods and river is the final authority on storms, stars, snakes, and birds. He corrects, admonishes, and instructs. He explains how to ward off bad luck and helps Huck strike a reasonable compromise between his conscience and his taste for food by suggesting that they steal only corn, melons, and chickens and stay away from rotten crabapples and out-of-season persimmons. Since both are convinced that witchcraft and woodcraft control their lives, Jim is Huck's natural superior.[7]

He is also Huck's superior in affection and loyalty. Knowing that Pap is dead, and denied the opportunity to lavish affection on his own family, Jim takes on the role of foster father to an orphan boy. He calls Huck "honey," "boss," and other pet names and vows, to Huck, that he will never "forgit you . . . honey." Huck on the other hand is in no shape at the outset to enter into a relationship that requires equal respect or affection. Even though he despises tricks and jokes of all kinds, he tricks Jim several times. On Jackson's Island Huck kills a rattlesnake and curls it up at the foot of Jim's bed, expecting the darky to react with wall-eyed minstrel horror. When Jim is bitten by another snake wrapped around the dead one and shows every ability to take care of himself by swallowing a jugful of Pap's whiskey to kill the poison, Huck refuses to accept the consequences of his joke. To avoid having to confess, he throws both snakes away.[8]

Part of Huck's reluctance to change his feelings about Jim is based on the fact that he has no intention of leaving his home ground. Jackson's Island appeals strongly to the boy because it serves as a convenient halfway point between the discomforts at the widow's and a full commitment to the monstrous big river. The serene village of St. Petersburg lies just across the water, and Huck hesitates to abandon this ideal way station between civilization and savagery. He does so only when he thinks he has to: learning from Mrs. Loftus that slave hunters are approaching the island looking for Jim, Huck forgets that no one is after *him* (he is, after all, officially dead), and shouts the three words—"They're after us!"—that constitute his first real commitment to Jim.[9] When the two fugitives push the raft out into the dark and flooded river, Huck, though he is not yet willing to admit it, has finally become a "low-down Abolitionist."

Once on the river the boy begins to show some real affection for Jim, in part because he is bound to the black man by nighttime travel on the raft, in part because he is getting lonely. The words lonesome, loneliness, and lonely occur repeatedly on the river, rarely while Huck is on shore. Indeed the river provides an opportunity for a measure of compassion and commitment that Huck never would have tolerated on Jackson's Island. Before going ashore to try to save the thieves stranded on the sinking *Walter Scott*, he carefully hides Jim. Later, on one of the few occasions when the two find themselves on the river in daylight, Huck makes Jim lie down in the canoe "because if he set up people could tell he was a nigger a good ways off."[10]

The change in Huck is especially striking when he begins automatically to share with Jim. He divides the loot taken from the *Walter Scott* and splits the forty dollars that the two slave hunters float over the water to save his family from the smallpox.

He also becomes aware that Jim's eagerness to let things "blame' well alone" is founded not on cowardice but on a sharp sense of survival; when Huck returns from leading the two slave hunters away from the raft he finds Jim in the water "with just his nose out." After the steamboat smashes into the raft, Jim follows Huck to the Grangerfords at a distance because, as Huck explains, Jim "didn't want nobody to pick *him* up and take him into slavery again." When Huck finally realizes that rescue from a natural disaster on the river would be well for him but a catastrophe for Jim, he has reached a new understanding not only of Jim's predicament but of Jim himself.[11]

While the two are on the river Jim's principal role is to teach Huck some manners, especially manners pertaining to friendship. Huck is not a model student. He tries repeatedly to offset Jim's natural superiority by claiming his superiority as a white (his bed on the raft is made of straw, Jim's of cornshucks), or by pitting himself intellectually against a nigger who he already knows has an "uncommon level head." When he does so Huck usually winds up on the bottom. In the famous battle of wits over "Sollermun" and the French language Huck disastrously undertakes the role of Tom Sawyer, using books captured from the wrecked *Walter Scott* to teach Jim "about kings and dukes and earls and such." To a point Jim responds in the usual minstrel manner: his eyes bulge out, his lips quiver, and he is convinced that a harem must be some kind of "bo'd'n-house" where "mos' likely dey has rackety times in de nussery." If a Frenchman ever said "Polly-voo-franzy" to Jim, he would "take en bust" the Frenchman's head in—"dat is, if he warn't white. I wouldn't 'low no nigger to call me dat."

Jim's ignorance is not only funny; it is credible and compassionate, and carries no tones of inferiority or humiliation.[12] His failure to understand the moral behind the Solomon tale is counterbalanced by his genuine horror over Solomon's threat to slice the child in two. Huck's dismal efforts to convince Jim that the child is in no danger—and that the important part of the story is to get the moral *"point"*—is lost on Jim because his attention is riveted on the child, not on "de point." Jim's compassion—and Huck's limitations as an abstract thinker—reach an even greater impasse over their dispute about the French language. Jim's amazement that "french people" do not talk "de same way we does" not only goes farther than minstrel humor; it goes farther than Huck's mind is prepared to travel. When Huck argues that it is natural and right for Frenchmen to talk differently from Americans, on the grounds that cows "talk" differently from cats, Jim simply notes the difference between animals on the one hand and the common cultural brotherhood of all men on the other. Huck, the uncomfortable intellectual poseur who despairingly says that "you can't learn a nigger to argue," has himself been out-argued.[13]

And Mark Twain has used a black man to express his deep conviction that kindness and compassion are the highest moral values. Nine chapters later he repeats the point, this time replacing Jim's concern about the child Solomon " 'uz gwyne to chop in two" with his remorse over mistreating his own daughter. Although the incident takes up less than six hundred words, it strikingly demonstrates Jim's feelings for Huck and Huck's growing attachment to Jim. The raft is drifting down the river at night, Jim is standing watch, Huck is asleep: "Jim didn't call me when it was my turn. He often done that. When I waked up just at daybreak he was sitting there with his head down betwixt his knees, moaning. . . . He was thinking about his wife and children, away up yonder . . . and I do believe he cared just as much for his people as white folks does for their'n. It don't seem natural, but I reckon it's so. He was often moaning and mourning that way nights, when he judged I was asleep. . . . He was a mighty good nigger, Jim was."

When Huck questions him, Jim confesses that he once struck his four-year-old daughter for not obeying his command to shut a door: "I fetch' her a slap side de head dat sont her a-sprawlin' . . . jis' den, 'long come de wind en slam [the door] . . . behine de child, ker-*blam!*—en my lan', de chile never move'! . . . Oh, Huck, I bust out a-cryin' en grab her up in my arms, en say . . . De Lord God Amighty fogive po' ole Jim, kaze he never gwyne to fogive hisself as long's he live! Oh, she was plumb deef en dumb, Huck, plumb deef en dumb—en I'd ben a-treat'n her so!"[14]

The moral distance between Huck's disregard for Jim's feelings for the child in the Solomon episode and the boy's compassion for Jim's confession of his own abuse of his deaf and dumb daughter suggests how far the two have traveled together. The surest indication that this black man has finally been accepted as human is Huck's willingness to accept his fallibility. It is Jim's capacity for both cruelty and remorse that places him solidly within the wicked and contrite human race. The insensitivity, violence, and remorseful suffering attributed by the author to his character is also the best indication of Mark Twain's great if erratic capacity for accepting a black man as a man.

Two moral lessons, the Solomon story and Jim's confession about his daughter, prepare the way for Huck's three great moral crises in the novel. The first occurs when he springs still another joke on Jim, but this time accepts the consequences and humbles himself to a black man. The second occurs when Huck almost betrays Jim to the slave hunters on the river. The third, and the high point of the book, comes when Huck wrestles with his conscience, whips it, and decides to free Jim from reenslavement and to be damned. Each is a different kind of study in the boy's growing commitment to Jim.

On a night too foggy to run the river Huck sets out alone in the canoe with a towline to tie the raft up to an island in midstream. The raft tears loose from the island and goes booming down the flooded river, with Jim on board alone. It does not occur to the boy to paddle off in another direction and let both raft and slave drift out of his life forever, though he might have done just that if he had thought of it. Huck's decision to pursue Jim in the fog is not a decision but a spontaneous reaction. He chases after the raft without considering the consequences, though he is a little put out that the black fool does not think of beating on a tin pan to indicate his whereabouts. When Huck catches up with the raft toward dawn, it is littered with branches and dirt from smashing into towheads, snags, and eroding banks. One oar is broken: "So she'd had a rough time." Jim is asleep, exhausted. Huck lies down beside him and pokes him awake. Jim's joy on seeing the boy alive is completely lost on Huck, who busies himself with persuading Jim that the harrowing chase was only a dream. There has been no fog, no separation, no chase, and no reunion. When Jim asks Huck to look him in the eye and tell him the truth, the boy looks him in the eye and tells more lies, encouraging Jim to interpret his dream in the stereotyped manner of the superstitious darky. Jim does so, stretching the actual chase out of all proportion until he has, indeed, turned himself into a "tangle-headed old *fool*," a word Huck uses several times to describe him.

Finally, in the growing light of morning, Huck springs the nub of the joke: what part does all the debris on the raft play in the dream? Just where do leaves, dirt, and broken branches fit into the overall " 'terpretation"? Preparing himself for a laugh, Huck's joke is cut short by the black man's unexpected reaction. From a slapstick teller of tall tales, Jim suddenly assumes new dignity: "When I wake up en fine you back ag'in, all safe en soun', de tears come . . . I's so thankful. En all you wuz thinkin' 'bout wuz how you could make a fool uv ole Jim wid a lie. Dat truck dah is *trash;* en trash is what people is dat puts dirt on de head er dey fren's en makes 'em ashamed."[15]

This is Jim's finest moment in the novel, and it marks a turning point in the relationship between the two. From now on Huck must be humane if he wants to receive Jim's affection. Although this second trick does not harm Jim physically like the snake bite that nearly killed him, Huck thinks it far worse. It is the utter *righteousness* of Jim's rebuke that bothers the boy and prompts him to enter the wigwam and apologize to a nigger, and never feel "sorry for it afterward, neither." Nevertheless this first crisis is far from complete. Huck's apology is not voluntary but forced and selfish. The stigma of trash is not lost on the boy. If niggers are inferior—and yet a nigger feels free to quit his position of inferiority and call a white person trash—then surely the behavior that prompted such a remark must be deplorable and ought to be amended. By getting Jim to repudiate what he said about trash, Huck makes them both feel better. Jim's dignity is restored— and so is Huck's superiority as a white.[16]

The second crisis comes about when Huck's growing commitment to Jim collides with the feeling that he really ought to turn the slave in at the earliest safe opportunity. For Huck it is one thing to drift passively downriver with a runaway slave when turning the slave in would mean turning himself in as well. It is quite another to continue to harbor a runaway black if he can find some means of turning Jim in without endangering his own position as a runaway white. Huck prefers to stay away from shore and postpone the decision as long as possible. The problem of what to do with Jim becomes acute only when geography forces Huck to stop procrastinating. The raft, he realizes, must be approaching the mouth of the Ohio River at Cairo, Illinois, the one possible turning point north to freedom by water. Huck must finally come to grips with "what this thing was that I was doing."[17]

Jim's loving expressions of gratitude to the boy for bringing him to the brink of freedom do not help any. His joy on approach-

ing Cairo, and his bold words about what he is going to do as
soon as he is free, provoke Huck to thinking about the terrible
crime he has committed against the South: "He wouldn't ever
dared to talk such talk in his life before. Just see what a difference
it made in him the minute he judged he was about free. It was
according to the old saying, 'Give a nigger an inch and he'll take
an ell.' Thinks I, this is what comes of my not thinking. Here was
this nigger, which I had as good as helped to run away, coming
right out flat-footed and saying he would steal his children—children
that belonged to a man I didn't even know; a man that hadn't
ever done me no harm."

"All in a sweat to tell," Huck suggests that the town on the
riverbank may not be Cairo and that he should paddle ashore
alone to find out where they are. For once the boy's lie turns
out to be the truth: the raft has passed Cairo in a treacherous fog.
Jim, however, is convinced that the village is Cairo and Huck is
afraid it might be. Possibly suspecting that the boy's career as "a
low-down Abolitionist" is suffering its first severe test, Jim pours
it on, calling Huck "de bes' fren'" he's ever had and placing his
worn-out coat in the canoe for the abolitionist to sit on. Halfway
across the river, with Jim's farewell shout ("Dah you goes, de ole
true Huck") ringing in his ears, Huck runs into two slave hunters:

"There's five niggers run off to-night up yonder, above the head of the
bend. Is your man white or black?"
   I didn't answer up prompt. . . . I warn't man enough—hadn't the
spunk of a rabbit. I see I was weakening; so I just give up trying,
and up and says:
   "He's white."[18]

An accomplished liar, Huck thinks he has just responded in
character. Actually this particular lie is far more difficult than
most, for the enticing location of the slave hunters, smack in the
middle of the river halfway between the burden of distrustful
Southerners on the shore and the burden of Nigger Jim on the
raft, must have tempted the boy sorely. Since he dislikes the idea
of exposing himself by exposing Jim, what better way for Huck
to relieve himself of both Jim *and* the awkwardness of another
confrontation with Southerners than to hand the black man over,
quite literally, in midstream? Huck's lie is, after all, something
close to heroic. Anxious to avoid danger, he has just committed
himself to greater danger. Cairo is behind them, and the raft is

moving deeper into the Deep South. With the geographic dilemma settled once and for all by default, Huck has finally committed himself to Jim.

Huck's final crisis starts when the King sells Jim for "forty dirty dollars"[19] in a card game in Pikesville, Arkansas. It ends when Huck, after severe emotional anguish, decides to reject Christianity, to free Jim, and to "*go* to hell."

When he learns that Jim has been sold and is a prisoner on a nearby farm owned by one Silas Phelps, Huck first toys with the idea of risking the truth for a change and writing old Miss Watson in St. Petersburg to come pick Jim up, "as long as he'd *got* to be a slave." He abandons that idea only after realizing that Miss Watson would be so disgusted with Jim's "ungrateful-ness for leaving her" that she would fall back on her original plan and sell him down the river. But the thought of writing Miss Watson leads Huck to reexamine his own delicate position: "And then think of *me!* It would get all around that Huck Finn helped a nigger to get his freedom; and if I was ever to see anybody from that town again I'd be ready to get down and lick his boots for shame. . . . It hit me all of a sudden that here was the plain hand of Providence slapping me in the face and letting me know my wickedness was being watched all the time from up there in heaven, whilst I was stealing a poor old woman's nigger that hadn't ever done me no harm."[20]

Repeatedly in his final agony Huck must do battle with the theological jargon he has picked up from Southern sermons up-holding slavery. We recall that earlier in the novel Miss Watson prattled on about heaven and good works, while plotting to sell Jim down the river. Now Huck, her unregenerate pupil, thinks "awful thoughts" and says "awful things" that would have shocked Miss Watson, all the while plotting somehow to keep in God's graces *and* free Jim. Realizing finally that he can't have it both ways, Huck sits down at the edge of the river which gave him his largest measure of freedom and, to avoid damnation, beseeches God's help in turning Jim in, but "the words wouldn't come." Failing in prayer, he writes the letter to Miss Watson to save his soul:

I felt good and all washed clean of sin . . . and I knowed I could pray now. But I didn't do it straight off, but laid the paper down and set there thinking . . . how near I come to being lost and going to hell. And went on thinking. And got to thinking over our trip down the river; and I see Jim before me all the time: in the day and in the night-time, sometimes moonlight, sometimes storms, and we a-floating along, talking and singing and laughing. . . . I'd see him standing my watch on top of his'n, 'stead of calling me, so I could go on sleeping . . . and would always call me honey, and pet me, and do everything he could think of for me, and how good he always was . . . and then I happened to look around and see that paper.[21]

Huck tears up the letter and risks hell. Though he frets most over the crippled clichés of Southern Calvinism, we are likely to be more impressed with the careful manner in which he separates Jim from slavery. Huck's decision to free Jim is not prompted by moral insight or outrage, but by the memory of Jim on the river. Slavery hasn't been dislodged; it is only Jim who is no longer for sale. Huck will be damned for devotion to a single black man, not for repudiation of the peculiar institution *as* an institution. In the most ingenious irony in the novel an immoral, poor white boy behaves like a Christian by rejecting Christianity, does right by doing wrong, and, in doing so, widens the gap between himself and the respectable, religious, and righteous South.

But then there is the end of the novel, an ending that comprises one-quarter of the book. For many readers the notorious evasion episode on the Phelps's farm is a peculiarly well-named disaster—a device for quite literally evading the complex moral issues Mark Twain had raised on the river.

Critics agree that the problem lies in the reappearance of Tom Sawyer, who in defiance of the laws of fictional probability turns out to be related to the family holding Jim in bondage, Uncle Silas and Aunt Sally Phelps. When Tom comes down from St. Petersburg to Pikesville, Arkansas, for a visit, he already knows that Jim is a free man, freed by Miss Watson herself. But he tells no one and at once takes the lead in liberating Jim. For Tom Jim is not Jim at all but an ebonized replica of one of Scott's or Dumas's doomed prisoners, complete with an escutcheon that reads, "*Maggiore fretta, minore atto* . . . the more haste, the less speed"—a pointed reminder that Jim's liberation, by Tom's calculations, is going to take a long time.[22]

We expect this kind of behavior from Tom. Far more upsetting is the fact that Huck, after discovering on a thousand miles of river the folly of tormenting a black man, contributes some in-delicacies of his own.[23] He worries that Jim may not survive the number of years it will take to surround his prison with moats and to dig him out through solid rock with kitchen knives. Earlier in the novel Jim, when bitten by the snake on Jackson's Island, bled real blood. Now, in Huck's most insensitive remark in the novel, this inhuman creature bleeds red "ink" to write his prison journal with, yet feels no pain.

If Huck suffers a serious decline, Jim is reduced to the level of farce.[24] When Tom and Huck enter his prison on the Phelps's farm, he cries for the fourth time in the novel and makes it clear that he is eager to be gone. But the white boys prevail upon him ("Jim he said it was all right") to endure three weeks of vaudeville stunts that approach sadism and leave them all "pretty much fagged out . . . but mainly Jim." The list of indignities seems endless: though he could free himself by slipping the chain off the leg of his bed and walking out the door, Jim must saw the bed leg in two and eat the sawdust. He must allow rats to bite him several times a day to keep his ink fresh and must discover brass "pens" to write his prison memoirs with by biting into them when he eats his corn pone, which "mashed all his teeth out" and therefore worked "just . . . nobel."[25] He must also grow a flower in his "donjon" and water it daily with his tears, which flow generously when Tom puts onions in his coffee. He must permit rats, snakes, bugs, caterpillars, frogs, spiders, and a dozen other stage properties, borrowed from a thousand minstrel scenarios,[26] to crawl over him and give him a "noble good time" while he lulls them to sleep with a Jew's harp.

Most disturbing of all, Jim must put up with all these indignities passively. Occasionally he pleads with his rescuers to stop this nonsense (*"Please*, Mars Tom . . . I can't *stan'* it!"), and he even threatens to leave for good if Tom brings a rattlesnake into the prison. (He does leave once, to help the white boys roll a large grindstone into the donjon so he can scribble prison laments.) By and large, however, he is content to suffer and to forgive. When he misbehaves he takes his verbal whippings submissively and promises to try harder. In a final gesture of indignity Tom considers sawing Jim's leg off. When we recall that Jim later comes out of hiding to help the doctor treat Tom's wounded leg after the aborted evasion, the betrayal of the noble black man seems com-plete.[27]

For all the arguments showing that Tom's reappearance brings the novel full circle back to the beginning (which, after all, was hardly the high point), Hemingway's judgment that the evasion is cheating[28] remains as sound as ever. The nature and quality of Mark Twain's lengthy notes for this part of the novel—two-thirds of the entire outline he made for the book—suggest that he had entertainment in mind more than a burlesque of Tom Sawyer's efforts to revive dead chivalry in blighted Southern air. It would also have been high entertainment to have Tom get soundly trounced by Jim's and Huck's superior common sense, but this does not happen. In the process of playing charades with a black man, Tom desecrated Jim's dignity so cruelly and completely that the damage is unforgettable and irreparable.

The evasion episode leads to two disturbing conclusions about the relationship between Jim and Huck and the fate of interracial brotherhood in *Huckleberry Finn*. Mark Twain's constant shuffling between sympathy, pathos, disinterest, and even hostility toward Jim suggests that he could not make up his mind about where this black man stood in his scheme for the novel. In a state of nature Jim is noble. On shore he is a comic buffoon. In his finest moments he is a marvelously subtle character: superstitious and practical, somber and playful, illiterate and smart, loyal and stubborn, timid and bold. But there can be no doubt that Jim is primarily a measure of the moral growth (and the subsequent decline) of Huck. It is Huck's moral regeneration, not Jim's role as instructor, that the novel is about. In the climactic chapter, when Huck decides to go to hell for Jim, Jim is not even nearby. For long periods he simply disappears, hiding on island, raft, or swamp, leaving Huck to work his way out of other mishaps that have nothing to do with Jim.

In a nineteenth-century book about a slave society as seen through the eyes of a white boy, Jim can be the conscience of the novel but he cannot be the main character. By the end of chapter 31 Jim's function as moral instructor is over, with one-quarter of the action ahead. Indeed one could say that Jim assumed the role of Huck's moral instructor on the river only at the risk of becoming the boy's moral burden on the shore—and one that eventually became too great for Huck. After deciding to free Jim the boy willingly, even gratefully, turned the task over to Tom Sawyer. The implications of such a desertion are awesome and portentous:

blacks may for a time act as the white man's conscience, but sooner or later that conscience becomes too much to bear.[29] Such subtleties of course are lost on Jim as well as on Huck. At the end of the novel, clutching his forty-dollar gift "for being prisoner for us so patient," the liberated black man is "pleased most to death" with the way things have turned out. "*Dah*, now, Huck," he boasts, "what I tell you? . . . I *tole* you I got a hairy breas', en . . . gwineter to be rich . . . en heah she *is!*" The moments on the river have been forgotten.[30]

The second conclusion about Jim and Huck goes beyond the novel to take in Mark Twain's growing pessimism about the possibility for any sort of permanent interracial harmony or brotherhood—and here we are reminded of the fate of Edwards and George in "The Great Dark." While on the raft, Huck and Jim try to practice a code of compassion and decency. "What you want, above all things, on a raft," Huck explains, "is for everybody to be satisfied, and feel right and kind towards the others." But their intentions are constantly thwarted by nature and by men. The raft, a fetching symbol of freedom, is vulnerable to steamboats, slave hunters, and the King and the Duke. It lacks independent power and can only carry the fugitives downriver into what Mark Twain considered a descent into hell. When Huck and Jim are forced to land the raft to take on supplies, Huck runs into feuds, murder, and a spurious Christianity. Even the river, the highest symbol of freedom, drowns people, wrecks rafts, provides a one-way movement into the deep South, and generates a fog that makes Cairo invisible, thus concealing the way to freedom. Moreover even if the evasion had been successful, there are precious few miles of river left below Pikesville, Arkansas, before the journey must come to an end. Though both raft and river are enchanting symbols of freedom,[31] they are just that—symbols.

The most excruciating irony of all is that the flight down the river has nothing whatever to do with Jim's final attainment of freedom. Poor Miss Watson,[32] whose greed started the two down the Mississippi in the first place, provides that. Though this woman's deathbed manumission is plausible, when Jim gains his freedom through the last will and testament of one of the novel's most unlikable characters we, like Hemingway, feel cheated: Jim's liberation on land will probably bring him less freedom than he enjoyed as a slave on the river, and it certainly spells the end of a possible relationship of equality with Huck. Jim can be freed from bondage but not from the disability of being black. To acknowledge this is to admit that the final fate of brotherhood in *Huckleberry Finn* is as disappointing as it is realistic. If freedom and brotherhood are possible only outside of society—if blacks and whites can really know each other only in isolation from other men—then there is not going to be very much brotherhood. Love and nature are not enough. With this admission, one of the high hopes of *Huckleberry Finn* goes down to defeat, drowned at the river's edge. As Huck says after the King sells Jim, the journey really *has* come to nothing. Everything, indeed, is "all busted up and ruined."

However, to end here would be another form of cheating. There *is* another dimension to the novel that transcends defeat. If the end of *Huckleberry Finn* suggests the way things are, the river portion of the novel provokes our sense of the way things ought to be. The thousand-mile flight down the river is, after all, a symbolic quest for freedom, a quest so utterly charming that after the disappointment of Tom Sawyer's evasion we are likely to take Hemingway's advice and return to the middle of the novel: to Jackson's Island, or the raft, or perhaps to Huck's description of the sunrise at the beginning of chapter 19. "Here," the boy tells us, "is the way we put in the time." Squatting waist-deep in the shallow water of a sandbar in midstream, Jim and Huck watch the dawn spread over the river. The effect is, as Jim says once, "too good for true," an exhilarating feeling of freedom and escape, peace and contentment. Repeatedly in the course of the journey downstream Huck reminds us of the delights of dawn and darkness, of going without clothes most of the time, of not talking much, and of being with Jim.

What the raft and the river come to mean is a marvelous condition of unreality—a shucking of our bondage to men, time, and codes of morality in exchange for a kind of freedom and companionship that can never be reached on shore. Long after Tom Sawyer's evasion has blurred into the background of our memory, the image of a black man and a white boy on a raft remains—a fantasy of brotherhood as appealing as it was perishable.

9

We Ought to Be Ashamed of Ourselves: Mark Twain's Shifting Color Line, 1880-1910

The change is in *me*—in my vision of the evidences.
S. L. Clemens to W. D. Howells (1887)[1]

In THE LAST three decades of his life Mark Twain tried to practice some of the attitudes of brotherhood he had introduced into *Huckleberry Finn*. Interracial harmony may be doomed to failure, but that did not exempt him from doing what he could to prove himself a personal exception. He was not always successful and he did not always employ the same strategy or technique. When upset over racial atrocities, he saw the racial situation as a moral problem, which indeed it was. When concerned with collecting raw material for his art, he saw blacks as fallible individuals, which indeed they were. Shuffling constantly between burlesque and satire, humor and pathos, compassion and callousness, Mark Twain remained inconsistent to the end. In doing so he opened himself to the posthumous charge of racism, which is to miss completely what he was trying to say. Like the rest of the human race, blacks were cowardly and courageous, foolish and smart, pitiful and honorable. To deny them an equal share of human faults would be to deny them their rightful position within the brotherhood of man.[2] It would also be to deny Mark Twain the right to use his superb gifts of vernacular and mimicry to help him make what Nigger Jim might have called "de point."

From the 1880s onward Mark Twain began to make the point with increasing fervor. Sometimes he did it through his persona, sometimes through the actions of S. L. Clemens, influential private citizen. In 1881 Clemens tactfully reminded President-elect James A. Garfield of his help in getting Garfield into the White House and suggested that he would now appreciate in return a favor for a friend of his, Frederick Douglass, who was about to be dismissed from his post as marshall of the District of Columbia:

I offer this petition with peculiar pleasure and strong desire, because I so honor this man's high and blemishless character and so admire his brave, long crusade for the liberties and elevation of his race.

He is a personal friend of mine, but that is nothing to the point, his history would move me to say these things without that, and I feel them too.[3]

Perhaps because of Clemens's good offices Douglass was given another federal appointment. About this time Clemens also began donating money to various black causes. In 1882 he gave $2,500 to Lincoln University for black scholarships; six years later he supported at least one and possibly as many as five black scholars through Yale Law School.[4] When Karl Gerhardt, a young sculptor enjoying an apprenticeship in Paris on Clemens's money, suggested that Clemens finance a similar experience for a promising black artist, Charles Ethan Porter, Clemens agreed at once. He was amply rewarded by Porter's gratitude. In his first letter to the Clemenses from Paris Porter thanked them for their support and for their interest in his character development, which was "quite as dear" to him as his art. In a second letter, slightly more than a year later, Porter noted that he had not yet received a reply from Clemens and added that he was eager to prove through personal example that his race was quite as capable as the white.

No evidence survives that Clemens ever answered Porter. But when he received a letter from Karl Gerhardt's wife complaining about Porter's living habits and lack of morals, Clemens responded in a manner suggesting he was still much interested in Porter:

I want to know everything about him, good and bad; for if he is worthy of help I want to turn out and see what can be done for him; and if he is not, I want to at least act with caution. At the same time I must remember, and you must also remember, that on every sin which a colored man commits, the just white man must make a considerable discount, because of the colored man's antecedents. The heirs of slavery cannot with any sort of justice, be required to be as clear and straight and upright as the heirs of ancient freedom. And besides, whenever a colored man commits an unright action, upon his head is the guilt of only about one tenth of it, and upon your heads and mine and the rest of the white race lies fairly and justly the other nine tenths of the guilt.[5]

In striking contrast to his profane outbursts against rumors of treachery committed against him by white men,[6] Clemens's response to Porter's alleged misconduct was cautious, optimistic, and scrupulously fair. If Porter proved beyond redemption, Clemens would only say he was not sure what he would do. White guilt required bending over backward for blacks. By implication it also required the moral reconstruction of a good many whites.

The same thought appears again the following year, when Clemens admitted that he too often lost his temper "over a certain class of business [begging] letters except when they come from colored [& therefore ignorant] people." To avoid confusing such letters from blacks with those from whites, Livy proposed a rule of thumb for her husband that Clemens explained to Howells:

A drop letter came to me asking me to lecture here for a [Baptist] church debt. I began to rage over the exceedingly cool wording of the request, when Mrs. Clemens said "I think I know that church; & if so, this preacher is a colored man—he doesn't know how to write a polished letter—how should he?"

My manner changed so suddenly & so radically that Mrs. C. said: "I will give you a motto, & it will be useful to you if you will adopt it: 'Consider every man colored till he is proved white.' "

It is dern good, I think.[7]

Whatever paternalism we may detect in Clemens's remarks was utterly unconscious on his part. He meant well, and he usually lived up to his wife's motto. This is not to say that he stopped telling nigger jokes. He told them privately for the rest of his life; but he did so less often in the eighties and nineties than in the sixties and seventies and his alter ego, Mark Twain, gave that kind of humor up almost entirely. From the 1880s onward Mark Twain began to replace his old darky jokes with carefully selected readings about blacks, delivered before both black and white audiences. In 1881 he wrote Howells that he had just had "a most rattling high time" reading Joel Chandler Harris's "Tar Baby" in Joe Twichell's high-class Congregational church in Hartford, and that he was "going to read to the colored folk in the African church here, (no whites admitted except such as I bring with me,)" and he wanted Howells and Livy on hand for acclamation. In 1889 he read selections on lynching and dueling from *Huckleberry Finn* to a "dusky audience" in Hartford and "Tar Baby" once again at the Brooklyn Academy of Music.[8]

When Clemens did tell jokes about blacks, they tended to be of the sort that could just as well (or almost as well) have been about whites. In 1877 he chortled over a newspaper article about thirteen "innocent, marveling, chuckled-headed Bermuda niggers" who were drifting around the Atlantic Ocean in a "sailless, mastless, chartless, compassless, grubless old condemned tub," begging bread and water from passing steamers "like any other tramp" because they had lacked sense enough to provision the ship before leaving port. The incident is an excellent example of the difference between Clemens and his persona: Clemens telegraphed President Hayes to urge him to rescue the vagabond niggers, while Mark Twain wrote Howells that he was eager to have "one of those darkies" come up to Hartford and tell him all about it, so he could write a "delicious" article about their foolish behavior.[9]

Had he written such an article, Mark Twain probably would have based it less on the incident itself than on the opportunity it afforded to show off his remarkable powers with black dialect. Privately, in notebooks and letters and on loose bits and scraps of paper, Clemens was constantly practicing his skill with black vernacularisms—playing with alternative spellings and pronunciations, honing the sound and the nuance to the highest possible pitch of perfection. His notebooks of the eighties and nineties are filled with dialect scribblings, most of them in the form of folksy religious phrases such as "we lean on de railin's o' heben & look down & see'm a fryin' in hell," or "Good mawnin' Massa Jesus, how'd you leave yo' pa," or the "po' $22-nigger" who will "set in Heaven wid de $1500 niggers," or "Come yo' seff Lawd, doan sen' yo' son, dis ain' no time f' chillun." One notebook entry about a black woman Clemens met on his return to the river in 1882 offers insight into Roxana's theological cant and short-lived conversions in *Pudd'nhead Wilson:* "Locate Clara's black swearing chamber-maid (fat and black) in some Arkansas town & make her good natured & perfectly overflowing with variegated profanity. Then 'Did you think I said dat bad word? No, I said it's de con-demdest hotel, dat's all what I said—I ben converted las' week an' I doan use dem kine o' words no mo', now.' Then let her heave in Scripture & piety honestly & occasionally forget & hurl in a sounding oath."[10]

Clemens was only mildly interested in black theology. It was the manner more than the matter that really fascinated him. In a letter to his publisher, written in the white heat of struggling with Nigger Jim's dialect in *Huckleberry Finn,* he showed the pains he was taking with vernacular humor:

I's gwyne to sen' you de stuff jis' as she stan', now; an' you an' Misto Howls kin weed out enuff o' dem 93,000 words fer to crowd de book down to *one* book; or you kin shove in enuff er dat ole Contrib-Club truck fer to swell her up en bust her in two an' make *two* books outen her. . . . I don't want none er dat rot what is in de small onvolups to go in, 'cepp'n jis' what Misto Howls *say* shel go in.

I don' see how I come to git sich a goddam sight er truck on han', nohow.

Yourn truly
S L Clemens

P.S. I wrotened to Cholly Webster 'bout dem goddam plates en copy-rights.[11]

An unpublished letter of 1888 also shows his mimic gift. Apparently Clemens and several friends, seated around a breakfast table in the Arlington Hotel in New York, decided to send a round-robin birthday greeting to President Grover Cleveland. Reconsidering, they decided to convey the message through Cleveland's wife. Clemens observed that "the colored waiter had been showing signs of distress from the very beginning of the conversation" and that "he had now reached the limit of suffering: so he broke ground—to this effect":

Gentlemen . . . I's a ole han' in dese-yer gov'ment marters. Now, concernin' er dat letter, *dey's etiquette for dat.* (No K-sound in that 'etiquette.') Yassir, dey's etiquette for it, an' you want to go mighty slow an' don' make no mistake. Dish-yer's de rule—de rule of de etiquette: you can't write no letters *to* de President wife, an' you can't bust no compliments at her—*in de fust pusson,* you understan'. . . . De rule is, you got to jis jumble an' jumble it aroun' widout lettin-on which un um you's arter, in partickler; an' jis' tak'n mush-up de compliments all in 'mongst de words, so's *you* knows dey's *dar,* but nobody else don't know it an' dey don't *stick out* nowhers. Yassir, dat's de way, an' de onliest way for to write to de White House folks—*it relieve um fum embairsment.*

The message to Mrs. Cleveland was drafted in "light of these instructions."[12]

This sort of humor got out of hand only when Clemens switched from jokes *about* blacks, usually told in the first person with emphasis on the manner rather than the matter, to traditional nigger jokes told in the third person with little or no effort to intrude black vernacularisms. When Clemens did make the switch, the jokes were usually second-rate. In 1886, in a curious betrayal of his twenty-year policy of not using the word nigger in public, Mark Twain responded to a toast in his honor at the Whitefriar's Club in London by declaring that actually he, and not Henry Stanley, had ridden blacks and other beasts of burden all over Africa looking for Livingstone. It was fortunate that Mark Twain found him when he did, because Livingstone's unfaithful niggers had deserted him and he was about to be boiled and eaten. Four years later, in an outline for a similar after-dinner speech which he probably never gave, Mark Twain used the same African setting but took a different tack, declaring that when he finally caught up with Stanley, the Englishman "smiled a smile which I judged he had imported from Africa. . . . He hunts people, of course; but he travels there largely for his complexion. . . . I don't know— that is, I don't know any reason that would fit in between your intellectual horizons,—but I will say this much, in the strictest confidence: that if he goes there for his complexion he's making the biggest mistake he ever made in his life." Two years later, in 1892, Clemens brought the matter of color up again by defining pumpernickel, the dark Westphalian ryebread of speckled black and white color, as "niggers & white folks sleeping together—six in a bed."[13]

In these three instances there can be little doubt that Mark Twain (or Clemens) was getting maximum mileage out of the traditional nigger joke, in which the subject takes precedence over the manner of telling the story and no effort is made to impersonate black speech. The distinction is an important one, for it suggests that Mark Twain opened himself to the charge of racism only when he surrendered his superlative gift for telling black jokes from the black point of view and gave in entirely to the white side of the joke—that is, to nigger humor. The question was not whether jokes about blacks were going to be different from jokes about whites: blacks *are* black; they look and talk differently from whites and are susceptible to a different kind of humorous treatment. The question, as Mark Twain well knew, was whether he was going to deal primarily in nigger jokes, or in jokes about blacks. When he told first-person vernacular jokes stressing manner over matter, he told jokes about blacks. When he told third-person nonvernacular jokes stressing matter over manner, he told nigger jokes. This is precisely where the late Mark Twain parts company with the early Mark Twain. In the 1860s and early 1870s he almost invariably told nigger jokes from the white point of view, whether he used dialect or not. By the 1880s, with the exception of the three samples of humor just cited, Mark Twain was telling jokes on, or about, or in defense of, blacks. With only three specimens of nigger humor to go on over a period of thirty years, there does not seem to be much point to arguing that Mark Twain pursued a policy of racist humor. Indeed, compared to his lifelong jokes about decayed corpses, physical freaks, or animal and human copulation, delivered with what Howells tactfully called "Elizabethan parlance," Mark Twain's nigger jokes actually are rare slips through what was a very tight censorship he had imposed on himself by the 1880s.

↭

The person most responsible for setting a high example for Clemens, and for encouraging Mark Twain's self-censorship, was George Washington Cable, the postbellum South's leading man of letters after W. G. Simms's death. Scholars have long noted Cable's imprint on *A Connecticut Yankee in King Arthur's Court*,[14] but he probably exerted a more direct influence on *Huckleberry Finn* and *Pudd'n-head Wilson*. Cable visited Hartford several times shortly before Mark Twain wrote the Arkansas portion of *Huckleberry Finn*, and he spent a long convalescence in the Clemens home in January 1884, when Clemens was reading proof for *Huck Finn*.[15]

Much of Clemens's attraction to Cable was based on the deep respect of one master of dialect for another. Shortly after meeting him in New Orleans on his return to the river in 1882, Clemens wrote Cable that the "charm," the "pain," and the "deep music" of *Madame Delphine* was "still pulsing" through him after he read it in a single evening. In *Life on the Mississippi* Mark Twain stated categorically that the only Southern writers worth reading were Cable and Joel Chandler Harris.[16] Yet Clemens's respect for Cable went far beyond literary craftsmanship. Cable's deep Southern background fascinated Clemens, in part because it contradicted his own experience of the border South, in part because Cable's ideological disloyalty to the South paralleled Clemens's own. As an ex-Confederate raised in New Orleans but soon to go into Northern exile for his heretical beliefs, Cable was in an excellent position to give Clemens an up-to-date liberal view of conditions in the postbellum South.

Far more than Clemens, Cable was making those views known. When the U.S. Supreme Court upheld the emerging pattern of segregation in the South in the civil rights case of 1883, Cable answered with his celebrated "Freedman's Case in Equity," which raised an uproar throughout the South. Southern newspapers urged Cable to remove himself from the South on the grounds that he was a traitor to his homeland and that besides, he was not a true Southerner anyway. (Henry W. Grady pointed out that Cable's mother came from Indiana.) At the peak of Cable's friendship with Clemens, no man of letters was more hated in the South. Mark Twain by comparison had not yet received even the mild abuse that followed on the heels of the South's tardy awareness that *Huckleberry Finn* was a subversive book, and he declined to comment on either the civil rights case of 1883 or on Cable's "Freedman's Case in Equity." Indeed the immense popularity of

Cable's essay in the North remained a sore point with Clemens.[17]

It was typical of Clemens that jealousy of Cable was matched by respect.[18] Even before Cable wrote the "Equity" essay, Clemens had proposed that they join forces and tour the Northeast, Great Lakes, and border South for fifteen weeks in the spring of 1884, reading selections from their works. The tour was an immense success. Cable sang Creole songs and quoted passages from several works, including *The Grandissimes,* a novel about miscegenation and racial violence. Mark Twain's repertoire included the folk story about the darky who dug up his dead wife's "golden arm," the hardships of Aunt Rachel in "A True Story," and selections from the forthcoming *Huckleberry Finn,* carefully timed to coincide with the appearance of several chapters of the novel in *Century Magazine.* Though he was cautious not to sacrifice popularity or profits for viewpoint, Clemens deserves credit for recognizing the attraction of having two reconstructed Southerners appear together in probably the most widely publicized and widely attended "anti-Southern" lectures given on the nineteenth-century stage.[19]

Inevitably the tour ruined the friendship. Each lecture became an ego contest and after ten thousand miles of late trains and greasy food Cable became "the pitifulest human louse" Clemens had ever known—a "pious ass" who spent too much time on the rostrum (almost as much as Mark Twain), pilfered hotel stationery, charged his laundry to Clemens, drank nothing stronger than water, and went to church too much. For Cable, Clemens became unbearably rude, coarse, irreverent, and hot-tempered. But before Cable's piety and Clemens's profanity soured the friendship, the two had several conversations on what Clemens mysteriously called a deep subject. Based on an entry Clemens made in his notebook, the deep subject almost surely had to do with miscegenation and with the possible overthrow of white supremacy in the South[20]—the one soon to appear in Mark Twain's *Pudd'nhead Wilson,* the other in a manuscript he wrote in 1902. As the most hated as well as the greatest man of letters in the deep South, Cable was uniquely fitted to point Mark Twain on the road toward the flattering title of "desouthernized Southerner" that Howells finally gave him in 1910—a title appropriate for the later New England career of George Washington Cable himself.

By the 1890s the "desouthernization" of Mark Twain was veering away from humor about blacks and toward satire aimed at whites who mistreated blacks. On no subject was Mark Twain more quick to work himself into a rage—or more quick to lose his sense of humor. His campaign on behalf of justice for blacks did not result in much memorable prose; but it did provide some of the era's sharpest attacks on racism. At a time when many of his countrymen were self-righteously linking imperialism with the white man's burden, Mark Twain was linking imperialism with racism. On his global lecture tour in 1895 he struck hard at the involuntary recruiting of natives of the Sandwich Islands for chain gang labor on Queensland sugar plantations—a form of "black-birding" which he insisted was not very different from antebellum Southern slavery. In fact the more he saw of white people around the world, the more Mark Twain was reminded of the South: "In more than one country," he wrote in *Following the Equator*, "we have hunted the savage . . . with dogs and guns through the woods and swamps for an afternoon's sport, and filled the region with happy laughter over their sprawling and stumbling flight, and their wild supplications for mercy. . . . In many countries we have . . . made him our slave, and lashed him every day, and broken his pride, and made death his only friend, and overworked him till he dropped in his tracks."[21]

Traveling through Tasmania, Mark Twain pricked the British government's method of exterminating the natives:

How glad I am that all these native races are dead and gone, or nearly so. . . .

The government wanted to save the Blacks from ultimate extermination, if possible. One of its schemes was to capture them and coop them up. . . . Bodies of Whites volunteered for the hunt. . . . But it was suspected that in these surprises half a dozen natives were killed to one caught—and that was not what the government desired.[22]

After all the Tasmanians were killed, one white man in New South Wales concluded that the mass murders were actually acts of God wrought against the "ungodliness and unrighteousness" of black people. That, Mark Twain wrote, settled it.

Yet when he reached South Africa the man who was beginning to be called the Moralist of the Main oddly lapsed into his old views about both imperialism and race. Always either an ardent Anglophile or a raving Anglophobe, Mark Twain was in a temporary state of euphoric Anglomania; so he focused his attention on diamond mining and mentioned only in passing that black miners were not permitted to consume alcoholic beverages and that they had a habit of stealing other people's diamonds and wives. As for the wretched housing, curfew laws, barbed fences, billy clubbings, and working conditions in the mines, Mark Twain knew they were deplorable but made no effort to interview anyone, or to see the mines, or to write about them.[23] Indeed black Africans seemed to be a disappointment to him, perhaps in part because he actually saw them: in the Pacific Islands he had championed dark-skinned Hawaiians—from on board the ship, anchored well off-shore. He also defended the Australian and Tasmanian aborigines, who were extinct. By comparison real live black Africans came off rather badly. They were cheerful enough, but once you had seen one you had seen them all, and they did not seem to be worth much. In the privacy of his African notebook Clemens started to write that the mass slaughter of blacks in South Africa had been a great loss to the country, then scratched it out and scribbled: "No, not that."[24]

Nonetheless as the nineteenth century dragged on toward its mock-heroic finale on San Juan Hill and his own country began to do what he had condoned the British doing, Mark Twain began to make some embarrassingly specific connections between imperialism and racism. Thirty years before, in 1867, young Clemens had scrawled disdainfully in his notebook that niggers in Latin America were so fond of revolutions that United States intervention in these countries was justified at any time and under any circumstances.[25] Now, in the late nineties, disgusted by what he saw as an unholy alliance of Christianity, cash, and colonialism masquerading under the collective name of civilization, Mark Twain became one of the first prominent Americans to condemn U.S. involvement in Cuba and the Philippines, and on grounds of race as well as sordid self-interest. When "that slimy creature," Major-General Leonard Wood, "penned up six hundred helpless savages in a hole" in Cuba "and butchered every one of them, allowing not even a woman or a child to escape," he was guilty, Mark Twain charged, of race brutality. When President Theodore Roosevelt ("the Tom Sawyer of the political world of the twentieth century") congratulated Wood "for thus 'upholding the honor of the American flag,'" he put "the heart and soul" of a racist nation into the message.[26]

    Almost alone among white antiimperialists Mark Twain saw a connection between conquest abroad and suppression of blacks at home. The paltry rights and privileges granted black and brown citizens in the Caribbean and the Pacific Islands taken by the United States were about the same as those granted blacks in the South. In an outspoken (and characteristically unsigned and unpublished) review of the career of the Philippine rebel Aguinaldo, Mark Twain compared Aguinaldo's youth in the Spanish-owned Philippines to opportunities open to black youths in Alabama and concluded that there was not much difference. Indeed by the turn of the century the only area of the world that rivaled the United States in racial atrocities was the Belgian Congo. In a savage essay entitled "King Leopold's Soliloquy," published privately because no magazine in the country would touch it, Mark Twain raged over the masses of black Africans who were being starved, beaten, burned, and crucified under Leopold's orders. "It was wrong to crucify the women," Leopold admits ruefully; "it would have answered just as well to skin them." Belgian soldiers, held responsible for each cartridge fired, were making up for poor marksmanship by cutting off the hands of some blacks who were very much alive. Eighty-one hands were reported drying over a single fire preparatory to delivery in Brussels; bones were being stacked in piles; one man's head was being used for a bowl; and Mark Twain was certain that an "osseous fence" of 15,000,000 Congo skeletons could be stretched, single-file, from New York to San Francisco.[27]

It was a short step from foreign atrocities to the lynchings, burnings, and castrations of blacks in the postbellum South.[28] As his indignation grew in the 1880s and 1890s, Clemens began collecting samples for a book on lynching, with special emphasis on those that took place in his native state.[29] The incident that finally prompted Mark Twain to take up his pen occurred in 1901 in Pierce City, Missouri, where a band of whites lynched three black men, burned several homes in the black section of town, and drove thirty black families into the woods. Mark Twain's response was to write "The United States of Lyncherdom." Urging all American missionaries to stop trying to civilize the Chinese and to come home to deal with barbarisms in their own country, he cited as an "appetizing" example a recent incident in Texas, where a black man was burned slowly so he would not *die too quickly.*" Toward the close of the article Mark Twain asked his readers to imagine what it might have looked like if the 203 black men lynched in the United States in the past year had died in the same place and at the same time:

Place the 203 in a row, allowing 600 feet of space for each human torch, so that there may be viewing room around it for 5,000 Christian American [spectators]; . . . make it night, for grim effect; have the show in a gradually rising plain, and let the course of the [burning] stakes be uphill; the eye can then take in the whole line of twenty-four miles of blood-and-flesh bonfires unbroken. . . . There should be no sound but the soft moaning of the night wind and the muffled sobbing of the sacrifices—let all the far stretch of kerosened pyres be touched off simultaneously and the glare and the shrieks and the agonies burst heavenward to the Throne.[30]

Late the same year Mark Twain complained that Southerners were at it again and urged that a federal law be passed to keep them from lynching blacks on Christmas Day. Yet he eventually agreed with his publisher, Frank Bliss, that if he actually undertook the multivolume history of "*all*" lynching in the United States that he had in mind, he would not have "even half a friend left" in the South. Besides, such a book would probably not sell well "down there."[31] So he gave it up, and even added "The United States of Lyncherdom" itself to his growing pile of warehoused manuscripts. It was not published until after his death.

By discarding the lynching-book project and pigeonholing "The U.S. of Lyncherdom," Mark Twain seemed to confirm a remark that his biographer made about him in 1906. "He did not," Paine wrote, "undertake any special pleading for the negro cause; he only prepared the way with cheerfulness."[32] As an example Paine cited Mark Twain's performance in Carnegie Hall on the twenty-fifth anniversary of the founding of Booker T. Washington's Tuskegee Institute, where Mark Twain said not a word about the Institute but told a lot of jokes. In a dictation for his autobiography the following day he said this about Washington and his program:

It was at a Fourth of July reception . . . that I first met Booker Washington. I have met him a number of times since, and he always impresses me pleasantly. Last night he was a mulatto. . . . It was a great surprise to me to see that he was a mulatto and had blue eyes. How unobservant a dull person can be! Always, before, he was black, to me. . . . He has built up and firmly established his great school for the colored people of the two sexes in the South. In that school the students are not merely furnished a book education, but are taught thirty-seven useful trades. Booker Washington . . . has taught and sent forth into Southern fields among the colored people six thousand trained colored men and women. . . . A most remarkable man is Booker Washington.[33]

This is the only remark that Mark Twain ever made about the foremost black educator of his day. Washington's program was at once worthwhile and rather boring to talk about; the author of Tom Sawyer's whitewash swindle just couldn't get very excited about manual arts at Tuskegee. Indeed when circumstances involving race relations demanded something more than humor or satire, Mark Twain was notably less successful. While in London in 1907 to receive an honorary degree he became embroiled in a controversy over the election of a black student to the fraternity of American Rhodes scholars. When asked by the authorities to urge the embittered white students to accept the black scholar, Mark Twain agreed to "do my best to convince them that their position was not wise, and not just." First he tried to persuade the students that they were obliged, under the terms of the Rhodes contract, to accept any student elected to membership. When that did not work he appealed to their sense of humanity and justice. When that too failed, Mark Twain backed off. Learning that the black scholar had scored high on every criteria of candidacy except personal popularity, he declared that to grant the black youth a scholarship would be "to defeat one of Mr. Rhodes's dearest purposes" in setting the scholarship up in the first place, namely to reward popularity. Rather than puffing the black lad as he had promised to do, Mark Twain "refrained from any reference to the matter in dispute" when he addressed the Rhodes students "and confined my talk to other and cheerfuler things."[34]

His use of the word "cheerfuler," and Paine's use of "cheerfulness," are apt. Mark Twain was always at his best as a humorist. The role of artist sheltered him from accountability for his actions and allowed maximum freedom to use his vernacular and mimic gifts in a colorful and often socially useful fashion. Aside from writing and lecturing the most attractive outlet for his talent was what can be loosely called theatrics: he loved the stage, wanted to be an actor, and wrote bad plays. But the form of stage art that most appealed to him was "the real nigger show—the genuine nigger show, the extravagant nigger show." That he loved minstrel song and dance is as much a part of the Mark Twain Legend as the tales about entertaining guests by jigging his own nigger hoedowns or wailing his own mournful darky ditties.

Black minstrelsy came to mean far more to Clemens than the mere satisfaction of his craving for theatrics. Perhaps more than any form of artistic expression it fulfilled his sense of beauty and his longing for the past, a longing that he put into a letter to Joe Twichell, written shortly after entertaining the Jubilee Singers in his home in Lucerne in 1897: "Away back in the beginning—to my mind—their music made all other vocal music cheap; and that early notion is emphasized now. It is utterly beautiful, to me; and it moves me infinitely more than any other music can. I think that in the jubilees and their songs America has produced the perfectest flower of the ages."[35]

Even more than literature, minstrel music became for Clemens the most attractive combination of drama, poetry, and romance and, especially in his last years, the most appealing way to call up his lost youth. In the middle years of his career, when he was writing his best books about the South and filling his notebooks with black dialect and superstitions, he rarely bothered to record even the title of a minstrel song. Years of fortune, happiness, and seemingly unlimited opportunities simply did not inspire the recollection of this part of his past. Beginning in the 1890s, however, when he wrote less about the South but was driven through family misfortune farther into the past, Clemens's minstrel scribblings became frequent and detailed. Long lists of darky songs piled up in his notebooks, followed by a sentimental stanza or two.[36] Unlike his notebook entries of the previous two decades, these late jottings cannot possibly be ideas for future books. Clemens knew his writing days were over. Like his rudimentary but soul-felt piano playing these pitiful memory-shakers are the longings of an old man for bygone times. When Clemens sang and played the piano, he usually sang and played minstrel songs and spirituals. The night Livy died, this was the form of comfort he sought—riding on a wave of emotion that was captured perfectly by his daughter Clara when she wrote that her father's rendition of spirituals was "an emotional outcry, rather than a song."[37]

This simple statement says more about Mark Twain's affinity for blacks than any number of letters to presidents on behalf of Frederick Douglass, or telegrams on behalf of stranded Bermuda niggers, or speeches and articles puffing Booker T. Washington and denouncing Southern lynchings. Whether he was lashing out against mistreatment of blacks, telling jokes about them, yarning their stories, or singing their songs, Mark Twain's response to black people was volatile, dramatic, sentimental, and intensely personal. For a man of such special gifts, passion, not programs, was the greatest contribution he could make to the cause of black justice.

10

The Black & White Curse:
Pudd'nhead Wilson &
Miscegenation

You's a *nigger!—bawn* a nigger en a *slave!* . . .
Thirty-one parts o' you is white, en on'y
one part nigger, en dat po' little one part is yo' *soul.*
Pudd'nhead Wilson (1894)

I have no race prejudices, and . . . no color
prejudices. . . . [Black Africans] should have been
crossed with the Whites. It would have
improved the Whites and done the Natives no
harm. . . . Nearly all black and brown skins are
beautiful, but a beautiful white skin is rare. . . .
Where dark complexions are massed, they
make the whites look bleached out, unwholesome,
and sometimes frankly ghastly.
"In Defense of Harriet Shelley" (1893)
Following the Equator (1897)[1]

Notwithstanding his fondness for black culture and causes, by the 1890s Mark Twain had a serious, even shattering color problem. On the one hand he had persuaded himself that persons of dark skin were physically more attractive than those of white skin, and he said so. Moreover he was convinced that the greater tragedy of the South was not miscegenation, but the curse that white Southerners had placed upon it. *The Tragedy of Pudd'nhead Wilson* is Mark Twain's most eloquent declaration of conscience on these two subjects.

Yet Clemens also had a private, more or less conscious craving to find a credible sexual being in that most incongruous and puzzling of all places in the nineteenth century, namely a *white* woman. The result was an extraordinary amount of color confusion in his private thinking and in his art, culminating in Mark Twain's two-toned portrait of the mulatto slave woman Roxana in *Pudd'n-head Wilson*. At the same time that Roxana's small drop of black blood made the point about the tragedy of racial mixture in a slave society, Mark Twain's Victorian teachings demanded that her skin be white. By painting this woman in a baffling black-and-white collage he tried to have it both ways: to satisfy the requirements of the Victorian code, while calling down the curse of the South. The ultimate outcome was chaos; but in the process of making a shambles of Roxana, Mark Twain let slip some revealing opinions about color. The purpose of this chapter is to trace the curiously shaded patterns that ripple over this woman and to place them in the context of Mark Twain's changing notions of skin color and of miscegenation.

Roxana was not an entirely original creation. During the 1880s the earlier halfbreed villain of Fenimore Cooper's novels (and of the Injun Joe type) was being superseded in American fiction by a new stereotype, the Tragic Mulatto, who was tragic precisely because he or she was not visibly a mulatto. Far from being physically degenerate and morally perverted like the Malicious Mulatto,[2] this new literary figure was a sympathetic creature who boasted the finest qualities that could be given him by the master race, yet possessed none of its social advantages. Since the Tragic Mulatto appeared to be white he could, under favorable circumstances, "pass." More often than not, however, he was a marked man, sooner or later to be unmasked, humiliated, and brought back across the color line. The reason for the shock and pathos that white readers felt in the presence of the Tragic Mulatto was that he was (almost) like them. Indeed the Tragic Mulatto might better have been called the Incongruous Mulatto, for what made him so tragic was that he was doomed to the same outcast position as blacks, but he *looked* so much better.

Mark Twain was not the first to explore the plight of the Tragic Mulatto: Cable, Melville, Stowe, and Howells were there before him.[3] But sometime in the 1880s Mark Twain also began to sense the pathos in the subject. Possibly inspired by conversations with Cable before and during their lecture tour, he sketched a four-page outline for a story about the misfortunes of a mulatto man who has the same amount of Negro blood as Roxana in *Puddn'head Wilson.* Although the story is rough and incomplete, it is Mark Twain's most compact and explicit statement about miscegenation, and it merits full quotation:

> Before the War he is born—1850
> The Accident—Mrch or Apl—1860
> The Sale, April, 1860.
>
> The War.
>
> The Wanderings.
> (His father <u>his</u> master & mean.)

Does not deny but speaks of his n blood. His struggles—education—advertises & hunts for his mother & sister—at last gives them up. At last, seeing even the best educated negro is at a disadvantage, besides always being insulted, clips his wiry hair close, wears gloves always (to conceal his telltale nails,) & passes for a white man, in a Northern city.

Makes great success—becomes wealthy.

Falls in love with his cousin, 7 years younger than himself—he used to "miss" her, on the plantation.

She & her father are very poor; he blows & gasses & talks blood & keeps up the lost cause fires, & she supports him. She is a very fine & every way noble & lovely girl; but of course the moment the revelation comes that he is 1/16 negro, she abhors him. Her father & she wears [*sic*] fictitious names, to indulge his pride, & he makes a mystery of their former history—which enables him to aggrandize it & at the same time prevents either of them from saying anything which would lead XX to recognize them.

XX keeps his early history a secret, of course—& it is the only secret which he has from *her.* All the towns people try to dig out his secret, but fail.

At the climax when his mother & sister (who is waiting on the table) expose his origin & his girl throws him & her cousin (proud, poor, & not sweet), voices *her* horror, he is at least able to retort, "Well, rail on; but there is one fact which Atlantics of talk cannot wash away; & that is, that this loathsome negro is your *brother.*

At time of the climax he is telling the stirring tale of the heroic devotion of a poor negro mother to her son—of course not mentioning that he was the son & that *his* is the mother who bears the scar which he has described. Then she steps forward & shows the scar she got in saving him from his own father's brutality. So this gassy man is *his* [*sic,* whoever XX is] father, & it is his niece whom XX loves, & who with (perhaps) his daughter, supports him.[4]

Apparently the mulatto boy was sold by his master-father directly after the unknown "accident," which may have been the blow suffered by his mother in attempting to protect him. Freed by the war, he courts and perhaps marries the cousin he used to address as "Miss" on the antebellum plantation, but whom he does not now recognize. The girl soon learns that he is part Negro, but she is too ashamed to reveal her knowledge to him. This leaves the way open for the mulatto to be dramatically exposed by his long-lost, and now freed, mother and sister. From there the genealogical ramifications of the plot grow more confusing, but they include the revelation that other people who had been under the illusion that they were all-white are also tainted.

In this brief sketch Mark Twain uncovered the fear, doubt, hypocrisy, and guilt of white feelings about mixing with blacks. The implications of this unfinished story become fully explicit only in the light of *The Tragedy of Pudd'nhead Wilson,* Mark Twain's last American novel and his last published outcry against the American South. That the story turned out to be so anti-Southern was more accidental than planned.[5] Having begun with the notion of chronicling the absurd adventures of an extraordinary pair of Siamese twins—one virtuous and fair, the other vicious and swarthy— Mark Twain was chagrined to find that a stranger named Pudd'nhead Wilson, a mulatto woman named Roxana, and another mulatto named Tom Driscoll were taking over the story. Dimly aware that the plot was veering from comedy toward tragedy, he attempted to solve the problem of his hybrid creation by performing what he called a "literary Caesarian operation," yanking out the Siamese twins altogether. The extraction, though physically complete, was artistically incomplete and the novel remains a semiserious, semi-comic grotesque—a hodgepodge of characters and events which somehow still reveal the traumatic divisions and cruelties that Mark Twain had come to associate with the antebellum South.

The white characters and the setting are people and places we have seen earlier, under other names. Dawson's Landing, hugging the banks of the Mississippi in 1830, is a confusing combination of the St. Petersburg of *Tom Sawyer* and the Bricksville of *Huckleberry Finn*. The cozy flower-decked homes belie the somberness of the story, and the pretentious rollcall of ex-first families of Virginia tells us that the people who lord it over this shabby village are the same crowd of counterfeit aristocrats we have met in *Simon Wheeler* and *Huckleberry Finn*. Colonel Cecil Burleigh Essex has fathered an illegitimate child with the mulatto slave Roxana, but has died before the narrative opens. Judge York Leicester Driscoll, patterned after Mark Twain's father, is murdered late in the story by the mulatto Tom Driscoll, whom he has adopted as his presumably all-white son. Pembroke Howard, a friend of the judge, is a minor character who acts as second in a burlesque duel in which a bullet ricochets off the nose of Roxana standing nearby. Percy Northumberland Driscoll, brother to the judge, is Roxana's master who threatens to sell his slaves down the river for petty theft, but repents and sells them locally instead, setting the charitable act down in his diary "so that his son might read it in after years, and be thereby moved to deeds of gentleness and humanity himself."[6]

Only the mulatto characters are wholly new creations. At the outset of the story the young slave woman Roxana, ex-mistress of the shadowy and deceased Colonel Essex, gives birth to his son, who is one-thirty-second black and whom she names Valet de Chambre (shortened to Chambers) because it sounds aristocratic. On the day Chambers is born, the wife of Percy Northumberland Driscoll bears *him* a legitimate, all-white son named Thomas à Becket Driscoll. Within a week the white woman is dead from the effects of childbirth, leaving Roxana to nurse the heir to the Driscoll estate as well as her own slave child. She soon notices that the two blonde blue-eyed children look very much alike. Partly through fear of having her son sold down the river,[7] partly to give him the privileges of being white, Roxana changes the children's clothes and places her own part-black seven-month-old child in the cradle of the descendant of one of the first families of Virginia. The mulatto Chambers thus grows to manhood as the aristocrat, Tom Driscoll, while the real Tom Driscoll becomes the all-white slave, Chambers. The "mistake" is not discovered for twenty-three years—when the title character, David Wilson, a college-educated New Englander, uses his fingerprinting hobby to bring the story to a close by exposing Tom Driscoll as both the murderer of Judge Driscoll and a mulatto slave.

From the beginning this novel is a chronicle of interracial crime and punishment. The true *Tragedy of Pudd'nhead Wilson* is not the lawyer David Wilson's quarter-century of social exile in Dawson's Landing,[8] but the two centuries of white exploitation of black—the South's great self-inflicted wound. By the end of the story one harmless aristocrat, Judge York Leicester Driscoll, has been killed by the mulatto Tom Driscoll. Roxana, after two decades of sacrifice to protect her son from exposure, is condemned by a court of law for enslaving a white aristocrat in order to free a mulatto slave. And the all-white aristocrat Chambers is so bent and stifled from shuffling around the slave quarters all those years that he can be "liberated" only into a life of genteel misery: "He could neither read nor write, and his speech was the basest dialect of the negro quarter. His gait, his attitudes, his gestures, his bearing, his laugh—all were vulgar and uncouth; his manners were the manners of a slave. . . . The poor fellow could not endure the terrors of the white man's parlor, and felt at home and at peace nowhere but in the kitchen. The family pew was a misery to him, yet he could nevermore enter into the solacing refuge of the 'nigger gallery.' "[9]

The most eloquent commentary on Southern chauvinism over interracial intercourse comes from its least sympathetic victim. Coward, thief, and murderer though he is, the mulatto Tom Driscoll reaches a more profound understanding of the tragedy of racial mixture in a racially unequal society than any other character in Mark Twain's writing. When this villain learns that the mammy who wet-nursed him as a child is actually his mother, the shock almost destroys him. For the next quarter of the novel Driscoll suffers through an excruciating crisis of identity: he too is one of the despised race. In his person he gives the lie to white distaste for black and reveals the philistinism of a society that privately tolerates miscegenation, then publicly punishes its victims.

In an unpublished portion of the manuscript Driscoll asks himself which in fact is the higher or the lower in him, the white or the black, and has the perception to see that "the high is either color, when undegraded by slavery." In the published version of the novel he pursues the agonizing inquiry farther: "Why were niggers *and* whites made? What crime did the uncreated first nigger commit that the curse of birth was decreed for him? And why is this awful difference made between white and black? . . . How hard the nigger's fate seems [now]."[10]

Yet, for all his perception, Tom Driscoll's insight is wasted on a scoundrel. The reader who comes to this novel expecting to learn how a part-black man, given the privileges of passing as a white, will prove himself worthy of this rare opportunity is in for a surprise: Driscoll proves thoroughly unregenerate. Although Mark Twain implies that the mulatto may have been warped by six generations of decadent FFV blood rather than by his drop of Negro blood, Driscoll's mother Roxana is convinced that her son's wickedness flows from his invisible mark of blackness—a color irony which is compounded when we compare *Pudd'nhead Wilson* to *Huckleberry Finn*. Huck believes that Nigger Jim must be "white inside"; but Tom Driscoll is white on the *outside*. His whiteness thoroughly conceals both his wickedness *and* his blackness, until his bad behavior exposes them both.[11]

For all his heartfelt ruminations on the plight of niggers, Tom Driscoll's insight leads not to reformation but to recovery of his old vicious self. Self-pity soon gives way to more typical trains of thought, including future villainies which are directly spawned by his discovery that he is not who he thought he was. Before the revelation of his race Driscoll was a liar, gambler, and petty thief. He continues these activities but now expands his evil doings to include selling his mother Roxana down the river and murdering his foster father,[12] thus becoming Mark Twain's first, but not his last, mulatto avenger.[13] Although Driscoll gets his comeuppance by being sold down the river himself into the same slave fate he had decreed for his mother,[14] this facile ending of the story is not very satisfying, for it reminds us that the main problems posed by the novel have not been resolved. The defeat of the mulatto criminal at the hands of a depraved white society seems deliberately to extenuate rather than to lessen the larger crimes of slavery and of color discrimination. By declaring Tom Driscoll to be a black slave and hence a valuable piece of property to be sold rather than jailed, the court of Dawson's Landing denies Driscoll the dignity of human punishment and acts as the instrument of an avenging justice which ought itself to be punished. Blackguard though he is, Tom Driscoll's fate is more disturbing than gratifying, for it leaves us with the suspicion that the worse offender is not the mulatto avenger, but the white South.

That the innocent Judge Driscoll must bear the full white burden of "black" revenge in *Pudd'nhead Wilson*, while the aristocrat who started the trouble, Essex, dies unpunished, compounds the irony. There is, Mark Twain implies, no such thing as a "free" Southerner. All Southerners, innocent and guilty, will suffer for the sins of slavery and concubinage. And the suffering will go on until emancipation from both slavery *and* the stigma of miscegenation brings remission to black and white alike.

More than any character in the novel Roxana embodies this suffering and gives it enormous power and poignancy. Herself a fourth-generation product of interracial union, she adds one more. And more than any character in Mark Twain's writing she suffers the consequences.

Unlike her son, who is accepted as white and free until proven otherwise, Roxana is a slave. She too, however, has a color problem, though a very different one. Dawson's Landing had no difficulty deciding she was a mulatto, but her creator did. Mark Twain in effect wound up with two Roxanas: a near-white one, carefully adjusted to the proper shade for white readers, and a much darker Roxana who may have figured more prominently in Mark Twain's imagination. The public Roxana is, for all intents and purposes, an all-white Southern belle: "Only one-sixteenth of her was black, and that sixteenth did not show. She was of majestic form and stature, her attitudes were imposing and statuesque, and her gestures and movements distinguished by a noble and stately grace. Her complexion was very fair . . . her eyes were brown and liquid, and she had a heavy suit of fine soft hair which was also brown. . . . Her face was shapely, intelligent, and comely—even beautiful."[15]

Roxana's drop of blackness seems important at first only as a reminder that miscegenation did in fact take place in the South and to explain why this lovely white woman is a slave. For Roxana, however, it has always been disastrous. It dictates her mudsill position in white society and it explains why she despises all niggers, who remind her of her own invisible mark. Indeed much of Roxana's credibility is based on prejudice and hatred. Rejected by one race and hardly wishing to be embraced by the other, she resorts to almost any means of redress for the vast injustice that is her life. She lies, steals,[16] cajoles, threatens, and flatters. She never questions slavery, except as it applies to herself and her son; and she repeatedly attempts to catapult herself into the highest order of whites. When Tom Driscoll first learns he is tainted and timidly asks who his father was, Roxana launches into the sort of trumped-up family genealogy we customarily associate with white Southerners: "You ain't got no 'casion to be shame' o' yo' father, *I* kin tell you. He wuz the highest quality in dis whole town—ole Virginny stock. Fust famblies, he wuz. . . . Does you 'member Cunnel Cecil Burleigh Essex. . . . Dat's de man. . . . Dey ain't another nigger in dis town dat's as high-bawn as you is."[17]

As with Nigger Jim before her, much of Roxana's credibility is founded on her fallibility, especially the extent to which she has picked up white prejudices. When her son refuses to challenge a white man to a duel for a petty insult, Roxana denounces him by way of one of the more confusing family pedigrees in American literature. The passage is a fine piece of irony, and it momentarily places this mulatto woman in company with the poor-white Huck as a naive, and therefore merciless, reporter of bloated Southern notions of ancestry. In one spasm of specious reasoning Roxana manages not only to make a sharp distinction between superior African blacks and loathsome New World niggers, but to parrot one of the white South's favorite clichés about the desirability of mixing a smidgen of *red* with white:

"You has disgraced yo' birth. What would yo' pa think o' you? . . . Yo' great-great-great-great-gran'father was Ole Cap'n John Smith, de highest blood dat Ole Virginny ever turned out, en his great-great-gran'mother or somers along back dah, was Pocahontas de Injun queen, en her husbun' was a nigger king outen Africa—en yit here you is, a-slinkin' outen a duel en disgracin' our whole line like a ornery low-down hound! Yes, it's de nigger in you! . . . Ain't nigger enough in [you] . . . to show in [your] . . . finger-nails . . . yit dey's enough to paint [your] . . . soul."[18]

Yet for all her efforts to bolster her whiteness with nigger prejudices and genealogical fantasies, Roxana is a good deal darker than her physical appearance would lead us to believe. In the course of the story her whiteness is the one thing about her that we tend to ignore or to forget: her speech and manners, strength and endurance, shrewdness and passion are qualities that Mark Twain usually reserved for black women. In every characteristic except color Roxana is an exact duplicate of the female slaves and servants Clemens knew as a boy in Missouri and as a wealthy Yankee employer of black domestic help. Like Aunt Hanner of Quarles Farm, the Clemens's slave girl Jenny in Hannibal, Aunty Cord in Elmira who became Aunt Rachel in "A True Story," and Aunty Phyllis in "Refuge of the Derelicts," Roxana is statuesque, good-looking, courageous, arrogant, strong, and smart.[19] First introduced as a new mother, back on her feet caring for her white mistress's newborn child a few hours after giving birth to her own, Roxana is the archetypal black matriarchal figure—the combination of mistress and wet nurse who rears the white man's legitimate children and bears his bastards.

The one thing wrong with Roxana is that she is neither black nor white long enough at a stretch to be entirely convincing. The problem is not that she is, literally, a mulatto but that Mark Twain had trouble deciding which Roxana is the real one: the one who looks white or the one who acts black. Even *as* a black Roxana changes roles with bewildering speed. At times she is a loving, warm-hearted, pious and simple Black Mammy. At other times she is just as black but cunning and ruthless. When she meets her son for the first time in several years, Roxana first behaves like a doting mammy. Then, with incredible swiftness, she turns herself into a vengeful bitch, exulting over the "fine nice young gen'l'man kneelin' down to a nigger wench" and taking swigs from a whiskey bottle more in the manner of a black shrew than the tragic mother figure Mark Twain had carefully constructed up to this point.

The problem with this woman is not that she lacks qualities of character but that she has too many of them. Wandering back and forth between comedy and tragedy, between all-white Southern belle and all-black mammy, Roxana is the victim of Mark Twain's own color confusion. When obviously black, she is a creature of rare beauty and passion, courage and dignity, vitality and fertility, with an immense capacity to love, hate, and forgive. When near-white she is tepid. Alternately bleached and blackened too often and too haphazardly, Roxana ultimately fails to transcend the sentimentality she evokes and loses much of her identity and, therefore, much of her credibility.

Mark Twain's color confusion over Roxana was in part the result of a collision between his attraction to persons of dark skin and his bondage to white social and sexual values. Indeed it is not too much to say that he consciously used blacks and mulattoes to express sexual feelings that were prohibited by white standards of propriety, especially feelings about miscegenation. Concubinage was, after all, an accepted part of the social system of the ante-bellum South;[20] and Mark Twain, who was quite reticent about sexual relations between whites,[21] never tried to conceal the obvious fact of Southern interracial intercourse. There were a number of mulattoes in Hannibal and even in St. Petersburg white, mulatto, and Negro children patronize the town pump to which Tom flees from his whitewashing job. In his *Autobiography* Mark Twain remembered that Wales McCormick, a fellow newspaper apprentice in Hannibal, "was constantly and persistently and loudly and elaborately making love" to a mulatto girl and that "by the customs of slaveholding communities it was Wales's right to make love to that girl if he wanted to." Four years after he left Hannibal, while working on a Cincinnati paper, young Clemens placed one of his first fictional characters, Thomas Jefferson Snodgrass, in an embarrassing predicament. Snodgrass is approached on the street by a fashionably dressed white woman, who asks him to hold a basket for her for a moment, then disappears. When the lady does not return Snodgrass opens the basket and finds he has become foster father to a mulatto child. Then there was the furor in Virginia City launched by Mark Twain's ill-considered suggestion that some local charity funds had been turned over to a miscegenation society in the East; and as late as 1872 Clemens told Howells that he was so uplifted by Howells's favorable review of *Roughing It* that he felt like "a mother who has given birth to a white baby when she was awfully afraid it was going to be a mulatto."[22]

Neither serious nor malicious, these early remarks about miscegenation are playful flights of fancy by a humorist who liked to test the limits of public tolerance and of private taste. The same can be said for the commonplace jokes about black sexuality that Clemens set down in his notebooks. In 1882, on his trip down the river, he recorded a dialogue he supposedly overheard on board the *Gold Dust* between two black laundresses, who chit-chat about wayward nigger employees who "takes up with everybody and anybody that comes along." One laundress explains that if she were young again she would change her habits and refuse to sleep with strangers. While Clemens listened (or so he made it appear in his notebook), the laundress illustrated her technique by withstanding the advances of a brash "young colored chap" who happened along at that moment. Though she permitted the man to come "pretty close to it," the laundress made it clear that that was "just as close as I allows one of them young fellows to go." If she was going to go farther at her age, she was going to go with "a *man*."[23]

Given Clemens's imaginative and vernacular powers, this "conversation" is at least as suspect as the "dialogue" between the two black deckhands about God being responsible for man's sins—recorded on board the same boat, in the same river notebook, and on the same journey. At the very least the part pertaining to the young colored chap probably gained in elaborateness as Clemens warmed to his subject. Other notebook jottings, especially those made after Livy died, are almost certainly fictitious:

She. I cain't dance wid you. I don't know who you is.
He. Plenty knows me en dey kin tell you. My name's Clapp.
She. Oh yes. Is you de genlmn dat start de epidermic in de Babtis' chu'ch?

After this entry Clemens added a telephone conversation, in which a black woman accepts a proposition with, "Yas—but who *is* you, anyhow?"[24]

Taken separately these jokes are not compelling evidence of preoccupation with black sex. Clemens's notebooks are sprinkled with mild smut about animal copulation, masturbation, scatology, and heterosexual intercourse, most of it set down after Livy died.[25] Moreover, since it was taboo to write about white female sexuality, it was taken for granted by many whites that black females gave an extra excitement to sex jokes—a common prejudice which Clemens was willing to foster. Yet when taken together these "jokes" suggest that Clemens may have been sexually troubled in his late years, and that race came into it as an expression of his repression. The most revealing example is a dream Clemens said had been bothering him for a long time before he finally set it down in 1897:

In my dream last night I was suddenly in the presence of a negro wench who was sitting in grassy open country, with her left arm resting on the arm of one of those long park-sofas that are made of broad slats with cracks between, & a curve-over back. She was very vivid to me— round black face, shiny black eyes, thick lips, very white regular teeth showing through her smile. She was about 22, & plump—not fleshy, not fat, merely rounded & plump; & good-natured & not at all bad-looking. She had but one garment on—a coarse tow-linen shirt that reached from her neck to her ankles without a break. She sold me a pie; a mushy apple pie—hot. She was eating one herself with a tin teaspoon. She made a disgusting proposition to me. Although it was disgusting it did not surprise me—for I was young (I was never old in a dream yet) & it seemed quite natural that it should come from her. It was disgusting, but I did not say so; I merely made a chaffing remark, brushing aside the matter—a little jeeringly—& this embarrassed her & she made an awkward pretence that I had misunderstood her. I made a sarcastic remark about this pretence, & asked for a spoon to eat my pie with. She had but the one, & she took it out of her mouth, in a quite matter-of-course way, & offered it to me. My stomach rose—there everything vanished.[26]

The sixty-one-year-old man who dreamed this dream had grown up in a slaveholding society which had among its commonest institutions black wet nurses and black concubinage. The dream is open to numerous interpretations, but the least farfetched is the possibility that Clemens found the woman, who was "not at all bad-looking," less repulsive than the proposition itself, which was disgusting because it violated Clemens's code of *conduct,* not of color. The woman's blackness simply made her sexuality possible. Being nonwhite, she could behave in a manner that, for black women, was "quite natural." Being white, Clemens could not behave in such a manner, and he went to considerable pains to dissociate himself from this woman. Since most of his dreams, by his own admission, were shaped by guilt[27] and since he was rarely able or willing to untangle the dream from the reality, Clemens sought release from the haunting mystery of the black woman by insisting that the rational and responsible wide-awake Clemens had no physical or psychological resemblance whatever to the self of his dreams. By denying emphatically that the one had any knowl-edge of the other, he could disown any disturbing symbolic mean-ings he may have seen in his dreams. If the two Clemenses were wholly unknown and wholly unrelated, then how on earth could the real Clemens be held accountable for the actions or thoughts of his dream self?

This is precisely where Mark Twain boxed himself into a corner with Roxana in *Pudd'nhead Wilson.* For here, in full consciousness, is a near-*white* hussy: acting provocatively when seemingly black, yet white on the outside nonetheless. By combining disguised blackness with surface whiteness, Mark Twain managed to endow Roxana with the uninhibited mannerisms of his black dream woman, while at the same time satisfying the popular demand for the Tragic Mulatto who must appear to be white.

Always his own most rigid censor, Mark Twain approached Roxana's sexual behavior with great caution and delicacy. In her first appearance in the novel this off-white woman does not actually "appear" at all; instead she is introduced offstage as an invisible, seemingly all-black voice which exchanges a series of sexual sallies with a coal-black slave named Jasper, who plans to court her as soon as she has recovered from childbirth. Though Roxana makes it clear that she does not mix "wid niggers as black as you is," she teases Jasper ("how does *you* come on, Jasper? . . . Is ole Miss Cooper's Nancy done give you de mitten?") and comes off as a "high and sassy," plainly provocative woman. Only *after* this scene do we learn that Roxana looks white: Mark Twain's careful description of Roxana's physical appearance comes only after we have been led to believe she is black.

It is the invisible black mark that gives Roxana her marvelously uninhibited manner. White women simply do not behave this way in Mark Twain's writing, either because he was unwilling to break the bonds of convention or because he was constitutionally unable, until late in life, even to imagine the possibility of white women behaving in an overtly sexual manner.[28] The pity is that he failed to maintain the color dichotomy consistently. When obviously all-white, Roxana is anemic. When obviously part-black, she is a fascinating mixture of white pathos and black boldness. Indeed in her finest moments Roxana transcends the prototypical heroine of the age to become that rarest of nineteenth-century creatures, a white woman who acts "black." For all the color confusion that ultimately crippled her credibility, this woman, at her "blackest," is the one convincing female character in Mark Twain's writing who is not an adolescent, a widow, or a middle-aged aunt. Although Mark Twain failed to stick to a single image of Roxana, the very *idea* of such a woman, capable of running the full range of human passions, was a far more original and daring experiment than either the all-white Tragic Mulatto she finally turned out to be or the predictably disgusting and hardly original black wench who haunted Clemens in his dreams.

Roxana is more than a bewildering mixture of black and white, however. She is also the most poignant example in Mark Twain's writing of his conviction that the greater crime of the South was not miscegenation but the white Southerners' unwillingness to admit that mulattoes were, after all, the products of their own lust.[29] Since mulattoes offered visible evidence of a covert bond between the races, that bond had to be overtly denied at all costs. The price of such deceit was bound to be paid by Southerners of every hue: all-white aristocrats like Chambers, mistaken for black; supposedly all-white Southerners who must worry whether the stigmata might not turn out to be theirs also; mulattoes like Roxana who are recognized as contaminated; mulattoes like Tom Driscoll who pass the color line only to be brought back across into slavery and blackness. No amount of deceit or dissimulation can guarantee permanent protection from discovery. After twenty-three years of indoctrination into white manners, speech, and decorum, the fair-skinned Tom Driscoll can still be declared tainted. And, conversely, after twenty-three years of indoctrination into black manners, speech, and decorum, the fair-skinned Chambers is beyond redemption. Neither environment *nor* heredity can match Southern prejudice.[30]

In its exposure of the Southern racial trauma, *Pudd'nhead Wilson* anticipates one of the obsessive themes of Southern writing in the twentieth century. The legacy of slavery and concubinage is one of fear, suspicion, false accusation, hypocritical exoneration, and guilt—a legacy that can be wiped out only by putting an end not to miscegenation but to discrimination. In a society of mixed blood in which the central preoccupation is with purity of blood, denial of the dignity and worth of blacks and mulattoes becomes, inevitably, a denial of the self. If some blacks are partly white, then some whites must be partly black. If some whites are slaves, then some blacks must be free. Who are they? And how many? And how long is this self-defeating denial going to go on? The fear and the hypocrisy seem endless: by rejecting blackness by day and embracing it by night, white Southerners have planted a lie in the soul of their progeny, cut themselves off from a vital part of their past, and locked themselves into a dilemma which will last as long as the blood curse itself.

For Mark Twain this was the central tragedy of the Southern experience—the curse of blood. The problem was not one of racial mixture, but the destructive emphasis on purity of blood of *any* sort. Injustice toward blacks springs from intraracial as well as interracial discrimination. The whole business of "born a gentleman, always a gentleman," or Marshall Clemens's efforts to compensate for poverty by assuring his family they were "blood-pure," or the blood feud of the Grangerfords, or Pap Finn's hatred of black skin when his own was "a white to make a body's flesh crawl," or Roxana bragging to her mulatto son about his FFV blood—all this adds up to an intolerable burden imposed by white on black, white on white, and black on black. Tainted blood goes far beyond color; indeed it may have nothing whatever to do with race. But from blood consciousness springs the stultifying pride of those who believe they are pure and the paralyzing fear of those who believe they are not. Southern pride in blood and Southern fear of miscegenation are two sides of the same sword and the sword cuts black and white alike. More than any nineteenth-century novel except Cable's *The Grandissimes, The Tragedy of Pudd'nhead Wilson* implies that the greater tragedy of the South is not miscegenation but the curse that white Southerners have placed upon it; and, therefore, upon themselves.

11

From Stage Nigger to Mulatto Superman: The End of Nigger Jim & the Rise of Jasper

---

We took turns and spelled him, and he was
as thankful as he could be, and would set on the
gunnel and swab the sweat, and heave and pant,
and say how good we was to a poor old nigger,
and he wouldn't ever forgit us. He was always
the gratefulest nigger I ever see, for any little thing
you done for him. He was only nigger outside;
inside he was as white as you be.
Tom Sawyer Abroad (1892)

"You's a slave! . . . en I lay I'll learn you de paces!
I been one . . . but it's my turn, now;
dey's a long bill agin de lowdown ornery white
race, en you's a-gwyneter *settle* it."
"Which Was It?" (1902)[1]

THE LAST two decades of Mark Twain's life brought him international acclaim, loneliness, and despair. Always subject to seizures of remorse[2] and self-recrimination, his sense of guilt and paroxysms of rage grew in the 1890s to the point where he began to question his sanity. Beneath the public image of the crotchety, crusty old sage, parading in his white suit, walrus mustache, and black cigar, lay a bitter and neurotic cynic who believed, he said, in nothing. Life had no dignity or meaning. The mass of men were cowards, and he was in the front row, carrying a banner. Man was a slave of circumstance, his mind a mere machine, his body a mangy museum of diseases rotting in the intestine of God. The human race began as dirt, departed as stench, and was useful in between as a breeding place for bacteria, a repository for worms, and a urinal for dogs. The world, "the true one," was odious and horrible. It would have been better if Noah had missed the boat. If sheep had been created first, man would be a plagiarism.[3]

Much of Clemens's despair grew out of the crushing financial and family misfortunes that struck him soon after he finished *Pudd'nhead Wilson*. In 1894 his publishing company was shut down, its capital too quickly siphoned off to feed the Paige typesetting machine, that "baby with a Gargantuan appetite" that devoured $200,000 of Clemens's earnings and Livy's inheritance for nine long years. The diabolical typesetter finally failed, and Clemens declared bankruptcy in 1894, with his wife as largest creditor.[4] The house in Hartford, symbol of the distance Clemens had traveled from Hannibal, was closed down, then rented, then sold. The family idyll was destroyed. In London, on the last leg of his global debt-paying tour, Clemens received word that his favorite daughter Susy, aged twenty-four, had died in delirium at home, slowly and painfully, from meningitis. Stunned with grief and blaming himself for her death ("My crimes made her a pauper and an exile"), Clemens went on to compound the guilt he felt over Susy's death by talking his wife to death. Livy's steady eight-year decline into invalidism and death at the age of fifty-eight may have been hastened by her husband's dreaded monologues of gloom.[5] His youngest daughter Jean, an epileptic, died on Christmas Eve 1909. Of the five members of the family only one daughter, Clara, married and living in Europe, survived Clemens.

In the midst of personal tragedy there was public triumph.

159

The popular figure Mark Twain remained much the same, emerging from seclusion to receive the accolades of a doting public, dictating his memoirs, reading his fan mail, sending a notice to the *New York Journal* that the report of his death was an exaggeration, recouping his fortune, and building a less eccentric mansion at Stormfield in Connecticut. Inwardly, however, he changed a good deal. Fearing madness if he became enslaved by guilt, he worked, as he said, like a madman. Aware that he had reached the age when he could no longer afford to be prodigal, he also found that the literary luck he had always counted on had finally run out. He began to complain of psychosomatic pains in his writing arm, which started at the thought of taking up the pen and went away when he decided not to write. Nonetheless the mounting pile of skimpy manuscripts shows how often Mark Twain did take up the pen in pain and how quickly he laid the result aside.

Unfinished manuscript after unfinished manuscript piled up in his trunk of "posthumous stuff," finally exceeding in quantity all his published work. These pitiful scribblings reveal a man poisoned with self-loathing and consumed with a well-grounded fear that he was losing his creative powers. Driven to desperation, Clemens played a final and profitable joke on the public, spreading rumors that Mark Twain had so many wondrous truths to tell that the human race must wait a hundred years before it could bear to see them with the naked eye. Still the final condemnation of the vile race that he kept promising the public never came off. When the time seemed ripe to speak what Howells called the black heart's-truth, to lay his soul bare, it was too late. Like the derelict steamboats he had seen rotting on Southern docks twenty years before, his spark was quenched, his fire out.[6]

Unable to move in a new direction, he fell back on the three characters who had served him best before. As early as 1884, close on the heels of the triumph of *Huckleberry Finn*, Mark Twain tried to uproot Huck, Tom, and Nigger Jim and transplant them to virgin territory out West in "Huck Finn and Tom Sawyer among the Indians."[7] But the roots did not take hold. Jim, who mourned so convincingly for his wife and children on the river and planned to buy them as soon as he was free, is free now but he has forgotten all about his family and tags along to the territory with the white boys for the fun of it—something which would never have entered his head before. As always when Tom Sawyer is present, Jim is a dim-witted darky who contributes nothing to the story. When Indians capture him on the plains, they perform a service for which we are grateful. Mark Twain is relieved of a character about whom he no longer cares and Jim is relieved of the burden of a story which promised only to reduce him still further. Before we learn whether he was killed or rescued, Mark Twain gave the story up literally in mid-sentence, thus saving Jim for a fate worse than scalping in *Tom Sawyer Abroad*.

The idea of sending three Missourians around the world in a balloon, to hover above the wicked human race while Mark Twain pronounced his own judgments, was not promising. The three do not go around the world (the journey ends abruptly in mid-air), and the story borrows too much from Jules Verne. Although Huck frequently sides with Jim in arguments, their relationship never approaches the level of compassion and understanding reached on the river. For Huck Jim is still white inside,[8] but the expression no longer means the same thing. In *Huckleberry Finn* Huck called Jim white after Jim refused to abandon Tom when the boy was shot in the evasion. However melodramatic Jim's loyalty to Tom may appear in retrospect, Huck's compliment was sincere. Now, high in the air over the Sahara Desert, Jim receives this ultimate flattery only after he has been tricked by the white boys into shoveling their share of a sandstorm out of the balloon. When told by Tom to "shut" his head and stop arguing, he does so.[9]

Throughout the story Jim responds in the manner expected of a sideshow darky who finds himself up in the air with two venturesome white boys. He groans, faints, pouts, and prays. When Tom suggests that the three of them should try to overpower the insane professor who has captured them and is holding them prisoner, the noble black man of the river begs to be excused:

> And Jim—well, Jim was kind o' gasping, he was so scared. He says:
> "Oh, Mars Tom, *don't!* Ef you teches him, we's gone—we's gone sho'! I ain't gwine anear him, not for nothin' in dis worl'."[10]

Though Jim does make an attempt to seize the professor *after* he attacks Tom, the gesture is tardy and futile; and he returns to tears, prayer, and inaction. Finally, when the heroic Tom is wrestled overboard by the professor, only to seize the balloon's dangling ladder in the nick of time, yank the professor himself into the Atlantic Ocean, and reappear over the gunwale, Jim takes him for a ghost, screams, flings his arms about, and faints. Huck, who once believed in ghosts too, shows no comparable emotion.[11]

In a long series of similar incidents the terror-stricken darky begs, moans, weeps, and whimpers his way through one hundred pages of airborne misery. Lions attack the ship twice, so Jim goes through the same minstrel act twice, without variation. Each time the lions charge the ship on the ground Jim happens to be at the balloon's controls. Each time he loses his head "straight off" and forgets everything the white boys have patiently taught him about how to maneuver the vessel. Twice he leaves Huck dangling helplessly from the ladder, forcing Tom to risk his life by completing his own dangerous climb in order to lift the balloon, and Huck, to safety. Indeed if Tom, the sentimental and absent-minded white boy who endangered the lives of both Jim and Huck in the evasion episode in Arkansas, had not come to the rescue twice within a few days, theoretically Nigger Jim would have killed Huck twice.[12]

This frantic and bewildered black man is on the verge of mental collapse: Huck suggests that he is "crazy," insane, and "out of his mind." When Jim sees his first "*my*ridge," he trembles uncontrollably, his eyes white with terror, unable to speak. As soon as he finds his tongue he uses the same words to express his fright that he used at the height of his physical and mental torture in prison in Arkansas: "Mars Tom, *please* . . . I can't *stan'* it." The two white boys, who have also never traveled in a balloon, or killed a deranged professor, or seen a mirage, manage to keep their heads and to contain their emotions. Of the three skyborne "Erronorts" Jim is the only one who cries, and he does so four times. When he believes Tom has fallen overboard into the ocean, Jim kneels "with his arms on the locker and his face buried in them" and weeps for "po' Mars Tom!" Huck simply waits for Tom to reappear over the gunwale. When Tom shows up, Jim responds in the same manner in which he greeted Huck in the Grangerford swamp: he cries for the second time, groans with joy, hugs and kisses Tom, and calls him "all sorts of loving names." Tom returns the affection as cooly as Huck did at the Grangerford house. Later, after a long dry spell, the two white boys are just as happy to find water as Jim, but Jim is the only one who "*did* cry, and rip and dance and carry on, he was so thankful and out of his mind for joy." On approaching Egypt he breaks down for his fourth and final cry.[13]

The deterioration of Jim's mental faculties is more shocking. When Tom launches into long theoretical disquisitions, Jim rarely interrupts the way he used to except to interject typical Rastus expressions: "Mars Tom, is dat so?"; "Well, dat do beat me"; "Mars Tom, you ain't jokin', en it's *so*?"; "Why, Mars Tom, sholy you can't mean"; "My lan', Mars Tom, I never knowed." Each time he tries to argue with the white boy he goes down to defeat, but only after an agonizing intellectual struggle. He shakes his head, mutters to himself, "works his mind," and "studies" problems until he is prostrated, then sinks into a deep state of depression or falls asleep, exhausted:

> Jim begun to snore—soft and blubbery at first, then a long rasp, then a stronger one, then a half a dozen horrible ones, like the last water sucking down the plug-hole of a bath-tub . . . and some big coughs and snorts flung in, the way a cow does that is choking to death; . . . alarming the whole desert, and yanking the animals out, for miles and miles around, to see what in the nation was going on up there. . . .
> Jim said he hadn't been asleep; he just shut his eyes so he could listen better.[14]

And so it goes for a hundred pages. The most humiliating episode occurs when Tom and Huck divide the task of shoveling sand out of the balloon according to their version of the three-fifths compromise: two-fifths for themselves and three-fifths for Jim, "according to fairness and strength." Jim objects and insists that the white boys ought to shovel at least one-tenth apiece, which causes Tom to "smole a smile that spread around and covered the whole Sahara." On seeing the eight-tenths left to him, Jim is "powerful glad now that he . . . spoke up in time and got the first arrangement altered." Tom and Huck take turns with their share, "but there warn't nobody to spell poor old Jim, and he made all that part of Africa damp, he sweated so."[15]

Toward the end of Jim's ordeal he is left on top of the sphinx with an American flag and told to keep himself visible in whatever manner he chooses, while Tom and Huck circle in the balloon to gain artistic perspective. Jim complies by standing on his head and kicking his legs around in the air "the way a frog does," then begins to dodge real bullets fired by outraged Egyptian soldiers and to cry for help. Though the white boys return at once to scatter the astonished soldiers and to rescue Jim, it is too late to rescue his dignity.[16] The noble black man of the river has become a middle-aged clown.

After *Tom Sawyer Abroad* Mark Twain tried once more to synthesize the marvelous chemistry of the original Huck, Nigger Jim, and Tom. He made a step in the right direction by bringing them down to earth and back to St. Petersburg, Missouri.

"Tom Sawyer's Conspiracy," started in 1897 and dropped probably in 1900, begins promisingly enough with the capture of a white man who is thought to be a runaway slave. But the story soon bogs down in the same jailbreak shenanigans that ruined the last part of *Huckleberry Finn*. The King and the Duke are back, murderers now; but the greatest similarity between *Huckleberry Finn* and "Tom Sawyer's Conspiracy" is the deterioration of Nigger Jim. As in *Huckleberry Finn* his best lines occur early in the story, followed by the same pattern of gradual withdrawal, reenslavement, and final imprisonment. As in *Tom Sawyer Abroad* Jim labors exhaustingly over abstract problems in a futile attempt to reach the intellectual level of the white boys. Each surrender is expressed in the same minstrel medium he used in his donjon in *Huckleberry Finn* and in the balloon in *Tom Sawyer Abroad* ("Yessah—'deed he do"; "W'y sutt'nly, Mars Tom, dat's . . . right"). As in *Tom Sawyer Abroad* Jim fusses over his density, "mumbling to himself, the way a nigger does," to the point that Huck is compelled to remind us that when children and niggers behave in this fashion the best thing to do is to "let a nigger or a child go on and grumble in that kind of pitiful way a nigger has that is feeling ignorant and distressed," until he grows tired of listening to himself and "shuts up."[17]

As in *Huckleberry Finn* Jim is captured and put back into both slavery and prison, this time for the alleged murder of a white man. This time, however, he does not escape. Though Tom plans to go through the same game of freeing Jim again, he gets distracted by more and more elaborate ways to liberate Jim and never gets around to it. Jim for his part goes along even more willingly than before, responding in a manner that almost makes us wish he were back in that prison on Phelps's farm: "'By jim-minies, I don't mo'n git outer one scrape tell I gits in a wuss one.' But when he see how downhearted it made Tom to hear him say that, he was sorry, and put his old black hand on Tom's head and says, 'but I don't mine, I don't mine, honey, don't you worry; I knows you's gwyne to do de bes' you kin, en it don't make no diffunce what it is, ole Jim ain't gwyne to complain.' "[18]

Jim lives up to his word. He does not complain, as he wisely prepares himself to go through an experience comparable to the evasion episode in *Huckleberry Finn*. Tom's plan is to sell him back to the King and the Duke (who were of course responsible for reenslaving Jim toward the end of *Huckleberry Finn*), then rescue him from the two confidence men and ship him off to England, to work in the queen's kitchen. Jim is not certain he will enjoy separation from his family and his home, but he endures enough emotional turmoil in prison to make Tom's plan to pack him abroad seem merciful. When first put in jail Jim is "scared most to death" for ten minutes. As soon as he learns he is in Tom's hands he becomes cheerful and "comfortable" and sheds tears over his good fortune. When Tom decides to enter a first-degree murder charge against Jim for the "glory" of it, Jim is horrified ("Why, Marse Tom—why, bless yo' heart, honey"), but quickly recovers and celebrates by doing a prison hoedown: "Jim was all right, now, and joyful, and his mournfulness all went away, and took his banjo, and 'stead of singing 'Ain't got long to stay here,' the way he done since he got into jail, he sung 'Jinny git de hoecake done,' and the gayest songs he knowed; and laughed and laughed . . . til he 'most died; . . . and then danced a nigger breakdown, and said he hadn't been so young in his heart since he was a boy."[19]

At the end of his career Jim has become a banjo-plucking, cakewalk nigger, virtually indistinguishable from the slaphappy slaves of James Kirke Paulding's antebellum novels, who are "the very prototypes of children in their joys, their sorrows, their forgetfulness of the past, their indifference to the future."[20] It is almost as if Mark Twain deliberately took the half-man, half-buffoon he had created in *Huckleberry Finn*, split him down the middle, and saved only the slapstick darky half. We may deplore the decline and fall of Nigger Jim, but surely it was just as well that the man's career came to a close when it did. For each time Mark Twain tried to recapture the happy-go-lucky niggers and carefree white boys of *Tom Sawyer* and the first part of *Huckleberry Finn* the idyll became dimmer, the reality grimmer, and his attempts more feeble. As early as 1891 he sounded the grim note that rang with increasing shrillness through the last two decades. Huck returns to Hannibal for a midnight reunion on Holliday's Hill with his old playmates, and while he and Tom call the roll Old Jim answers for all the absent ones:

Huck comes back, 60 years old, from nobody knows where—& crazy. Thinks he is a boy again, & scans always every face for Tom & Becky etc. Tom comes, at last, 60 from wandering the world & tends Huck, & together they talk of old times; both are desolate, life has been a failure, all that was lovable, all that was beautiful is under the mold. They die together.[21]

For all the dismal soundings of doom in these late notes, Mark Twain was not yet ready to give Tom and Huck up. Six years later the two boys are still very much alive, though they might be better off dead. In one of his last efforts to recall the pristine South of *Tom Sawyer* Mark Twain had Huck and Tom try to pass themselves off as black boys:

Have Huck tell how one white brother shaved his head, put on a wool wig & was blackened & sold as a negro. . . . Tom sells Huck for a slave. . . . Tom [Huck] is disguised as a negro & sold in Ark for $10. . . . (Tom mesmerized, chased the nigger with pistol). . . . Killing the negro man with a chunk of coal. . . . Negro [brought] smuggled from Va in featherbed when lynchers were after him. In Mo he raped a girl of 13 & killed her & her brother in the woods & before being hanged confessed to many rapes of white married women who kept it quiet partly from fear of him & partly to escape the scandal.
    Whites seized the slave nurse & hanged her for poisoning the baby while another party were scouring the woods & discovered the baby's uncle in suspicious circumstance, hiding something, & charged him (Tom or Huck discovered him) & he confessed; & he arrived in custody just after the innocent slave girl had been lynched.[22]

In his last efforts to call up the bygone South, Mark Twain kept coming up with nightmare images of violence, sex, and hypocrisy, white and black alike. The business about "killing the negro man with a chunk of coal" shows how vividly he remembered the slave who was struck and killed with a slag of coal on the main street of Hannibal when Sam Clemens was nine years old.[23] And the notes about black rape—and about polluted white women who keep quiet "to escape the scandal"—imply that Mark Twain was interested in exploring a subject which would haunt the generation of Southern writers who followed him.[24] Five years later, in 1902, he made a start in that direction himself by recording a traumatic incident that was probably true. The boy in the following sketch, John Briggs, was one of Clemens's Hannibal playmates and appears here under his real name, rather than the fictional alias of Joe Harper that Mark Twain gave him in *Tom Sawyer*. But the boy's real-life companions, Tom Blankenship and Sam Clemens, appear under their fictional names, Huck Finn and Tom Sawyer. Whether this mixture of fact and fiction was accidental or intentional, it suggests that by 1902 Mark Twain was no longer making a clear distinction between fantasy and reality:

The time John Briggs's nigger-boy woke his anger and got a cuffing (which wounded the lad's heart, because of his love and animal-like devotion to John (it is two or 3 years gone by—a life-time to a boy, yet John still grieves and speaks to Huck and Tom about it and they even meditate a flight south to find him)—John went, hearing his father coming, for he had done something so shameful that he could never bring himself to confess to the boys what it was; no one knew but the negro lad, John's father is in a fury, and accuses the lad, who doesn't deny it; <Beebe comes along> no corporeal punishment is half severe enough—he sells him down the river. John aghast when he sneaks home next day and learns it. "What did you sell him for, father?" Tells him. John is speechless,—can't confess.

The lad, very old, comes back in '02 and he and John meet, with the others left alive.[25]

This passage was written by a man in the grip of a monomania over forbidden and therefore unclean actions or thoughts, possibly involving some kind of sexual experience.[26] Discovered by a black boy in the midst of a shameful act, John Briggs (perhaps Sam Clemens) not only cuffs the black boy (perhaps Marshall Clemens's slave boy Lewis), but is unable to confess his own guilt, even when the boy is unjustly accused of the shameful act and sold. Apparently the slave returns to Hannibal a half-century later and forgives Briggs. (Forgiveness was a crucial part of these late stories and notes.) Whatever the vagaries of the plot, one thing is clear: Mark Twain's Southern Arcadia has become so contaminated with slavery, prejudice, and guilt that it can no longer maintain the insouciance he had given it in *Tom Sawyer*. St. Petersburg lies buried beneath Bricksville and a host of other wretched and murderous villages where violent black men and timid white boys commit shameful acts and go unpunished. If the best he could dream was to be a boy again in a world of bigotry, violence, and sin where blacks get lynched, white women get raped, and white boys trick black boys into taking their punishment and then relieve their guilt by playing burnt-cork nigger, small wonder that Mark Twain's last efforts to call up the spirit of the South are more akin to nightmare than to nostalgia.

Even more nightmarish than white guilt over mistreatment of blacks was the possibility that blacks themselves might eventually turn the South upside down and seize control of the whites. Mark Twain had long thought about this possibility. In 1884, the year he had those long talks with Cable about a "deep subject," Clemens had made a terse entry in his notebook: "America in 1985. (Negro supremacy—the whites under foot.)" Four years later he moved the date closer; to the year, it turned out, that he died, 1910:

In the South, whites of both sexes have to ride in the smoking car (& pay full fare,) the populous & dominant colored man will not ride with them.

The colored brother has succeeded in having severe laws against miscegenation passed.

There is no such thing as a free ballot. The whites have to vote as they are told, or be visited by masked men & shot or whipped, & house burned & wife & d[aughter] [stripped] turned out in their night clothes.[27]

Mark Twain grew impatient and refused to wait for the real thing to happen in 1910. In 1899, in his last long piece of fiction about the South, he came up with a superhuman mulatto who, in his small limited way, begins to collect on what he calls the "long bill agin de lowdown ornery white race." Before he put the unfinished manuscript called "Which Was It?" into his bulging trunk of posthumous stuff in 1902 he had written more than a hundred pages on the one subject guaranteed to unravel white Southerners more quickly than miscegenation: the overthrow of the white race by the black.

The setting for this grim story is the antebellum village of Indiantown, Missouri—a bleak, squalid, snowbound Hannibal. The part of the story that concerns us is restricted to two characters: a white aristocrat named George Harrison and a free mulatto named Jasper. Harrison is a weak and sensitive young man, probably patterned after Orion Clemens (dead by the time the story was written) and clearly modeled after the nineteenth-century Hamlet stock of indecisive, guilt-plagued Southerners.[28] His father is a feeble and ruined aristocrat who owes money to the leading citizen of Indiantown, Squire Fairfax. To save his father from bankruptcy George Harrison tries to steal some money from Fairfax himself, so as to have something to pay him off. Caught in the act by a farmer, Jake Bleeker, Harrison strikes Bleeker an unintentionally fatal blow and flees. Fairfax, seen standing over the body, is accused of the murder and jailed; and Harrison takes his place as the leading village aristocrat. Memory of the homicide, however, keeps him from enjoying his new position. Hounded by guilt and by fear of discovery, Harrison is one of several characters in Mark Twain's late stories whose financial and family problems resemble Clemens's own and who lead double lives of public adulation and private agony.

The story breaks off before the crime is solved. Fairfax is still in jail and Harrison is still publicly unpunished. Privately, however, he has been punished a thousandfold by a disaster far greater, for him, than murder—the loss of his presumed superiority as a white man. Halfway through the manuscript the mulatto Jasper seizes control of both the story and Harrison. This tall, powerful "darkish mulatto"—one character calls him a "yaller-belly"—is a very different kind of Tragic Mulatto from the mild, self-pitying stereotype. Although his early life is calamitous, Jasper eventually manages to pass his calamities on to others. We learn his history from a white female thief named Mrs. Gunning, who once served as housekeeper for a wealthy aristocrat in Memphis who turns out to be both George Harrison's uncle and Jasper's father. Her rendering shows that Jasper indeed had a "long bill agin de lowdown ornery white race." Sired and then enslaved by his father, Jasper proves indomitable from the beginning. As an upright young man he purchases his freedom from his father on credit, loses the bill of sale in a fire, and is denied a new one by his father, who shouts "Out of my presence, you bastard, and keep mum, or I'll sell you South, as I did your sniveling mother!" Undaunted and still honest and "good," Jasper buys his way to freedom a second time and then makes the mistake of lending some money to the white housekeeper, Mrs. Gunning, who pockets it and runs off. Jasper is reenslaved as a pauper and jailed for a year. This is too much. Forced to purchase his freedom for the third time, he finally becomes crafty and cruel.[29]

Once committed to revenge, Jasper is merciless. For years he tracks and trails Mrs. Gunning and her grown son, Templeton, from town to town. When he finds them he enslaves them, living off Templeton's earnings and dictating each move his "family" of three makes. Learning that his father has died in Memphis and willed his fortune to an Indiantown nephew named George Harrison, Jasper brings the Gunnings to Indiantown, where he plans to seize the fortune and to add his cousin to his family of enslaved whites. This is the state of affairs when Jasper finally appears in the story. His meeting with Templeton Gunning in a dark room at midnight is unforgettable. The young white man sits, stands, and stutters at Jasper's command: he lights the mulatto's pipe, serves him whiskey, waits on him hand and foot. At the end of their conversation Jasper helps himself to more whiskey, indicates his hat with a nod, demands a five-dollar bill, and leaves. Within two blocks he is driven back across the color line. Captured by the constable for being out late without a pass, he is jailed for the night and given his "forty-save-one, frightfully laid on" at dawn: "With his swollen back streaming blood and caking his clothes to his body, he staggered his way homeward through the fleecy snowdrifts, brooding vengeance and cursing all the white race without reserve, out of the deepest deeps of his heart, and rejoicing that in fifteen years he had spared no member of it a pain or a shame when he could safely inflict it."[30]

The climax of the story comes with Jasper's complete conquest of George Harrison. Just prior to their first meeting Harrison has decided to stop blaming himself for the murder of Squire Fairfax and to accept his position as first citizen of Indiantown without further self-punishment. Little does he know that a free mulatto whom he has never met already knows that he, Harrison, is a murderer. (Jasper knows this because he saw Harrison fleeing from the scene of the crime.) When Jasper knocks at the front door Harrison, unaware that they are related, acts the role of severe white master and Jasper plays along:

"Kin I see you a minute, seh?" . . .
"Where are your manners, you dog? Take yourself to the back door. . . ."
"I wanted to ast you, seh—"
"Take your hat off!"
"I begs yo' pahdon, seh—I fo'got, deed I did, seh, I's in sich trouble en so worrited."

Jasper is worried that he is going to be lynched by citizens of Indiantown who don't like free niggers. Dropping to his knees, he begs Harrison to protect him. Harrison replies that it is his Christian duty to bow to the majority will and not to "obstruct the law in its course." Jasper puts his hat back on, grabs Harrison by the shoulders, shoves him in front of a mirror, and proclaims him the murderer.[31]

From this point on the mulatto makes Harrison's life a nightmare, threatening to seize the fortune and to have him hanged for murder. But these threats are calculated primarily to add to Harrison's discomfort. Jasper shows little interest in the money and no interest whatever in getting rid of Harrison by turning him over to the law. The important matter is to get down immediately to reversing the position of white over black. In a long soliloquy Jasper makes it clear that Harrison represents, for him, the entire white race:

"You's a slave! . . . en I lay I'll learn you de paces! I been one . . . slave to de meanest white man dat ever walked—en he 'uz *my father;* . . . en he sold my mother down de river, po' young thing, en she a cryin' en a beggin' him to let her hug me jist once mo' . . . en he hit her on de mouf, God damn his soul!—but it's my turn, now; dey's a long bill agin de lowdown ornery white race, en you's a-gwyneter *settle* it."[32]

As a start Jasper orders "Hahson" to "fetch yo' marster a dram," props his muddy boots up on Harrison's furniture, lectures him about his "lack o' manners," and revels in his triumph, "studying it, weighing it, measuring it." He installs himself as Harrison's new household servant, and informs him of their two-sided relationship. "When dey's anybody aroun'," Jasper explains, "I's yo' servant, en pow'ful polite, en waits on you . . . en runs arrants, en sleeps over yo' stable, en gits ten dollars a week; en when dey ain't nobody aroun' but me en you, you's *my* . . . *meat!*"[33] At dawn each day the mulatto flunky builds the fire, grinds the coffee, plunks "Camptown Races" on the banjo, and flirts with the black cook who is twice his age and size ("I's gwyneter cote you—dat I is, honey"). Later, alone with Harrison, he eats the white man's breakfast, while Harrison stands by his chair. When someone knocks on the door, Jasper orders the white man to take his place at the table and to beat and insult him ("'buse me, 'buse me, Hahson—keep it up!"). Harrison quickly becomes a terrified and beaten man; Jasper, strong from the beginning, becomes a mulatto superman:

He was visibly a changed man. The meek slouch of the slave was gone from him, and he stood straight, the exultation of victory burning in his eyes; and not even his rags and tatters could rob his great figure of a certain state and dignity. . . . He *looked* the master; but that which had gone from him was not lost, for his discarded droop and humble mien had passed to his white serf, and already they seemed not out of place there, but fit, and congruous, and pathetically proper and at home.[34]

Although these reversals finally grow tiresome, Harrison's ordeal as a white slave, shuffling constantly between master and servant, is haunting and convincing. And Jasper's performance as part-time lord of manor and part-time servant drives home the point that slavishness results from slavery, not from racial inferiority, and that each race and each man is a potential master and a potential slave.[35] When Jasper orders Harrison to "stop dat whinin' en blubberin'" and adds that he ought to be ashamed of himself, the shame transcends Harrison to take in the entire white race. We may question whether a weak murderer is a fair specimen of the race he represents; for Mark Twain, by 1902, Harrison comes close. This white Southerner pays for the sins of his fathers not only because he is white and guilty but because he is weak.

Jasper was the logical extension of Clemens's dire notebook warnings about violent confrontation between black and white. This "black" man is far more convincing than Nigger Jim or Roxana for two reasons: he lacks compassion, and he is capable of forceful action. No superstitions mar his judgment, no feelings of pity or loyalty stay his hand. Of all Mark Twain's late preachers of destruction Jasper is the most convincing. By comparison the man that corrupted Hadleyburg, or Little Satan in *The Mysterious Stranger*, or "Doangiveadam" in an unpublished manuscript are either curiously detached from the rest of the human race, or literally superhuman. Jasper alone shuns the temptation of striving for a cosmic snuffing out of the entire human race that mars the credibility of Mark Twain's other Satanic strangers. This man's plot to "s'rivel" up as many members of the white race as he can through a step-by-step process of intrigue, intimidation, and brute force has a jarring note of reality to it.

From Stage Nigger to Mulatto Superman

For Mark Twain by the opening of the twentieth century, Jasper *was* black power. Nigger Jim may have been blacker,[36] but the mulatto Jasper, wandering through the wind and snow of nighttime Indiantown plotting revenge, is the white man's very image of a black Satan. If we put this man of mixed blood together with Clemens's dire notebook predictions about the future overthrow of the white race, we come up with a South turned on its ear. To take Jasper seriously as a symbol is to hear Mark Twain saying there will be no reconciliation of black and white. There will be nothing but bigotry, hatred, and violence.

12

No Peace,
No Brotherhood

And let me say it. Dispossessed of Eden.
Dispossessed of Canaan.
William Faulkner,
"The Bear"

"I've seed de first en de last," Dilsey said. . . .
"First en last whut?" Frony said.
"Never you mind," Dilsey said,
"I seed de beginnin, en now I sees de ending."
Faulkner,
The Sound and the Fury[1]

"WHICH WAS IT?" was Mark Twain's last ambitious attempt to write about the South and the relationship between the two races. Although he tried to recall Huck, Tom, and Nigger Jim for more stories, each attempt was vitiated by the fact that his childhood Eden was part of the South. And that South was not, and probably never had been, the happy valley of his youth. Instead it was, and probably always had been, a wasteland of the soul. There had been no Southern Eden and there was to be no Southern Canaan.

Becoming fully aware at last that his sunlit South would always be haunted by his gothic South, Mark Twain felt a great loss. He had once given a full measure of artistic devotion to the South, but it had been misplaced. The vision of the South as the great good place of his youth had gone sour, along with the dream of Samuel Clemens as happy family man and of Mark Twain as prodigious author. For more than thirty years he had relied upon the South for inspiration. When the South failed him, he took that failure at once as a betrayal and an omen. Acutely aware of the South's historical decline, he associated that decline with his own: his final journeys into the South were, more than ever, journeys into the self. Clutched by turn-of-the-century anxiety, he felt that time and history were passing him by. The new century was no more a part of him than it was a part of the Old South. Both Mark Twain and the South were outmoded, misunderstood, vexed, and enigmatic.

In moments of self-deception Mark Twain tried to render the South bearable by reconstructing it. In defiance of what he had learned through forty years of experience, he would start a story about the South as ethereal and remote as anything in *Tom Sawyer*, only to run out of anecdotal material almost at once. Compelled to work himself into a kind of trance to bring the South back to life at all, he recorded the images and fragments that crossed his mind while in it and wound up with more than he could handle. Fiction and fact, romance and reality, nostalgia and polemic piled up one upon the other and became hopelessly entangled. The accumulated dreams and experiences of a lifetime came flooding in over him with such a rush and volume that he was rarely able to give them voice or shape. The last narratives are short in invention not because the South lacked substance, but because

Mark Twain's hallucinating memory of it suggested so much more than he could bring under control that he was immobilized amidst an incredible tangle of material—material at once vivid and unreliable, iridescent and evanescent. No sooner would he start a story of the South as a lost Arcadia, with the Mississippi River shining in the summer sun, than the currents of his mind would veer toward some dark vortex of horror—toward caves, tombs, dried-up oceans, pitch-black Antarctic wastelands, or the icebound villages that dominate Mark Twain's vision of the South after *Huckleberry Finn.* Even the river froze on him.

Whatever the metaphor these late visions have in common utter darkness. In the end the caverns of Mark Twain's mind were as closed to the light as was McDougal's Cave for Injun Joe. In the end, in fact, his dark thoughts had more in common with the thoughts and actions of his two men of color, Injun Joe and Jasper, than with Huck and Tom. Jasper especially was the final turning point in Mark Twain's image of the South—a frightful prediction of the angry Negroes and vengeful mulattoes who, in the twentieth century, began to call down what Faulkner would soon term the "curse of the South." But while Faulkner would stress that the curse and the burden were both black and white,[2] Mark Twain implied that the burden was black, the curse white. Thirty years before Faulkner called for forgiveness of white sins, Mark Twain was calling for punishment for white sins.

By the turn of the century the idea of interracial brotherhood, first championed and then rejected in *Huckleberry Finn,* was entirely out of the question. To compare Huck and Jim floating down the river on the summer flood to Jasper wandering alone through wintry Indiantown, plotting revenge, is to plot the great shift in Mark Twain's view of race relations. The very fact that Nigger Jim winds up a stage darky indicates the fragility of Mark Twain's hope for respect between the races. Instead he turned to a mulatto who wastes no time waiting for the white man's respect or speculating on the hope of reconciliation. Like Aaron the Moor and Cable's Bras Coupé, Jasper touches the bare nerve of a time other than his own. Fully two decades before racial theorists began to replace the Malicious Mulattoes and Tragic Halfbreeds of the nineteenth century with the Superior Mulatto, forged in adversity and inheriting the highest faculties of each race,[3] Mark Twain had already done so. Twenty years before there was currency to the notion that dark-skinned races were destined to overthrow the white, he had given us a fearsome example of just that.

Yet Mark Twain's gain in vision about the South (as he saw it) was won at frightful cost to his conscience and to his career as a writer. Caught between love and hate, he could neither completely forgive nor completely forget the South, black *or* white. He could not forgive the South for what he felt she had done to him; and, scourge himself as he would, he could not forget or disown the South and remain a writer. To the end he continued to be pulled back and forth between pride and shame for his native land.

Inevitably his confusion over the South was tied to his despair over the rest of the country and the world. As his own time ran short, Mark Twain urgently felt the need for some kind of personal atonement, some kind of approach to man and the universe that would relieve him of the deep remorse and bereavement he felt about almost everything—his family, his public life, the books he had censored, the ideas he had suppressed. Driven by the need to seek remission and to impose some form of order on a sprawling and chaotic life, he found an answer of sorts in his obituary to the human race at the end of *The Mysterious Stranger*. If things are as bad as Satan says they are—if there is "no God, no universe, no human race, no earthly life"—then no human being can be blamed for all the countless things that go wrong. If human existence is a grotesque and foolish dream, then there is, indeed, no hope. Nor is there any need to feel guilt or to try to rectify ancient injustices, including, presumably, racial injustices.[4]

What was really gone at the end of Mark Twain's life was any alternative to total despair—and this is what kept pulling him back to his self-awareness as a Southerner, however reconstructed. More than any other writer before the twentieth century, Mark Twain was torn and tormented by the South.[5] His sense of the past as pathos and calamity ("It's so damned humiliating"), his fascination with time and place,[6] his excruciating sense of racial conflict, and his inability to do anything about it—all this prefigures what we now call Southern writing. The very duality of his vision of the South—and the ambivalence of his feelings toward her—is the strongest indication of his lasting Southernness. It accounted for his reconstruction, and it also accounted for his guilt and for his feeling of profound loss and complete helplessness. To take serious-

179

ly Mark Twain's last writings about the South is to realize that for this Southerner there would be no Canaan, no new Jerusalem, no catharsis of the white conscience, no final purging of white guilt, and no notion that black and white might ever live in equality and brotherhood. With this message Mark Twain ended his career as commentator on the South and the black race. Like Faulkner's Quentin Compson he cursed the South and in doing so decried a part of himself, and remained a Southerner to the end.

Appendix:
"The Private History of a
Campaign That Failed"

———————

"THE PRIVATE History of a Campaign that Failed," published a comfortable twenty-four years after Clemens's two weeks in the Confederate army, depends upon myth for its success. As an apology for Clemens's brief flirtation with treason—or more accurately with twice treason—it stands alone in Mark Twain's writing, an unusual literary confession and the high point in his deliberate attempt to alter, if he could not abolish, his war experience. It was so successful as comedy and fiction that he never felt the need to publish the touchy subject again.

By the late 1870s the public reputation of Mark Twain made the private past of S. L. Clemens, converted Connecticut Yankee, a matter of national interest which was open for national inspection. Mark Twain had already filled the country in with an almost year-by-year account of his experiences on the Continent, in the Holy Land, in the West, and on the river. Yet he had surreptitiously left out his war experience. If he was to maintain his Northern popularity in the era of vote-as-you-shot and the bloody shirt, he somehow had to convert the campaign that failed into one that succeeded.

In 1864, more than twenty years before he wrote "The Campaign that Failed," Mark Twain hit upon one of the three strategies that eventually turned the trick—burlesque: "I was troubled in my conscience a little, for I had enlisted, and was not clear as to my lawful right to disenlist. But I remembered that one of the conditions of joining was that the members of the Guard would not be required to leave their homes except in cases of an invasion of the State by an enemy. The Confederate forces had invaded southwest Missouri. I saw at once that in accordance with the terms of enlistment I was required to leave the State, and I left at once by the overland route for Nevada."[1]

In 1877, when he accepted an invitation from the citizens of Hartford, Connecticut, to address the visiting "Ancient and Honorable Artillery Company" from Boston, Mark Twain was ready to put the finishing touches to the burlesque part of his war defense and to add a second and crucial ingredient—innocence. He was not, he assured his Hartford audience, a mere civilian guest. On the contrary he was a distinguished veteran of a stirring campaign unequaled in the annals of warfare and excluded from the "history of the United States of the Southern Confederacy" only by the "envy and malignity" of historians. In 1861 he had been a well-meaning though comic bungler who was elected "Chief Mogul" of a motely assortment of eleven "boys" (all in their late twenties and early thirties) only because none of them knew anything about war. Such naiveté naturally led to disobedience: when Clemens told an inferior officer to shut up and go relieve the night guard, the officer told Clemens to go get another nigger servant. After several retreats, however, a genuine crisis arose. Clemens's company ran out of Worcestershire sauce. Clemens requested that they be assigned another district where they could obtain some, and when this request was denied, he gave up altogether: "I hung up my sword and returned to the arts of peace, and there were people who said I hadn't been absent from them yet. We were the first men that went into the service in Missouri; we were the first that went out of it anywhere."[2]

By 1885, the year he published "The Private History of a Campaign that Failed," Mark Twain had honed to perfection two of the three tactics he would use in the essay: burlesque and innocence. The third defensive maneuver, the use of mock tragedy, enters only at the end of the story, when Mark Twain symbolically kills his chief postbellum competitor, General Ulysses S. Grant.

Innocence and the loss of it control the entire story. First we are asked to believe that these two weeks in the Confederate army were nothing less than Clemens's personal rite of passage, the weeks in which a twenty-four-year-old ex-tramp printer and river pilot suddenly ceased to be an adolescent and became an adult. As in "Old Times on the Mississippi" and the first twenty chapters of *Life on the Mississippi* Mark Twain sliced six or seven years off the age of Sam Clemens, paring him down to a slightly overgrown Tom Sawyer who cavorts in the woods with a wild "herd" of like-minded irresponsible teenagers. By night the boys sleep in comfortable corncribs; by day they divide their time between retreating, fishing, swimming, frolicking with farmer's daughters,[3] and filling up at tables groaning with the fruits of country life. Although they are uncertain at first about which side they should be on, a local rebel farmer feeds them a Missouri breakfast and, while the company is in a satiated mood, enlists them in the Southern cause. By night they retreat; by daylight the war is once again offstage. Cannons boom in the distance, but nearer at hand is the smell of corncob pipes and campfires. Since the whole affair is a holiday, the performance of these skylarking "Rangers" ("good name, by gosh") is both predictable and excusable. "What could you expect of them?" Mark Twain asks, carefully detaching himself through his persona. "Nothing, I should say." With considerable justice, "The Campaign that Failed" heads one section of Mark Twain's works entitled "Merry Tales."[4]

The neophytes finally lose their innocence toward the close of the merry tale, where the mock-tragic theme enters by way of Mark Twain's personal campaign against Ulysses S. Grant.

Clemens worshipped Grant. He also felt the need to compete with him, to measure his own greatness against Grant's. In November 1879, at the Grand Reunion of the Army of the Tennessee in Chicago, Mark Twain used his position as the lone ex-Confederate in an allstar cast of Yankee veterans to pit his own popularity against Grant's. When he accidentally "sauntered" onto a "dreadfully conspicuous" flag-draped rostrum high above a parade of 80,000 veterans marching through Chicago in honor of Grant, Mark Twain was delighted that the masses below mistook him for the general. When the crowd did recognize him and broke into "volcanic explosions and cheers," he modestly stepped back a few paces so as not to "interrupt Grant's speech by calling attention to myself." Grant graciously told him to stay where he was. Later Mark Twain sat "elbow to elbow" with "nearly all of the surviving great generals of the war" on the Union side and was introduced to Grant as "a man almost as great as yourself." Still later, when a theatre crowd discovered that both Mark Twain and General Grant were seated in a balcony above them, they kept up such "a determined and persistent call for me" (as Clemens wrote Livy) that Grant bowed toward Mark Twain and magnanimously turned the applause in his direction. That night, Grant-intoxicated, Clemens slept without the help of his usual whiskey toddies.[5]

The crowning event of the Chicago drama came with the final banquet at the Palmer House. In a feverish, 5 A.M. letter to his wife about the "night of my life," Clemens wrote that the high point of the evening came when he himself rose at two o'clock in the morning to give the fifteenth and final speech. Passing up motherhood in favor of a toast to "Babies," Mark Twain brought the male audience lurching to its feet by depicting General Grant as an infant with one of his toes in his mouth. In his early-morning letter to Livy, and in others to brother Orion and to Howells, Clemens resorted to aggressive terminology to describe the event: his speech brought the house down "with a crash," "shook" Grant "up like dynamite," "licked" the hero of the Civil War, "wracked all the bones of his body apart," and "broke" and "tore" Grant into "good-sized pieces." Following this performance Mark Twain shook hands for two and a half hours with Northern heroes of the war and was told he could "*command*" the Army of the Tennessee any time he wanted to. Six years later, in the same year that he published "The Campaign that Failed" (which he originally titled "My Campaign against Grant"), Clemens's own publishing company "captured" and published Grant's *Memoirs*, which became a best-seller. The victory (as he called it) over Grant and other Northern war celebrities became, in a sense, a victory over Clemens's own past.[6]

Up to this point Mark Twain had only "used" Grant in burlesque. But in several subsequent conversations with the general shortly before Grant died on July 23, 1885, Clemens learned that in 1861 he had come within a few miles and a few weeks of being captured by Grant in the Missouri woods.[7] Clemens soon cut the few weeks down to "a day or two" and finally "a few hours" and shortened the distance from several miles to the same spot. Grant, so to speak, had stumbled upon the smoldering campfires of the re-treating rangers.[8]

And Mark Twain had stumbled upon an opportune way to drag Grant into "The Campaign that Failed." In the most melo-dramatic episode of the story, Sam Clemens and other rangers "murder" a stranger who is riding through the woods at night. The boy Clemens, terrified and remorseful, walks to the body lying "splashed with blood" in the moonlight and strokes the man's face. As Justin Kaplan has pointed out, the stranger resembles Grant, who was in Missouri at the time and, like the murdered man, wore civilian clothes during his Missouri campaign.[9] The death scene is an eloquent appeal to the reader to accept a fabricated murder as the reason why young Clemens deserted the Confed-eracy. By shifting the emphasis at the close of the story from skylarking to killing, Mark Twain disposed of any remaining cavils about his war conduct. If murder is part of war, then how can a disillusioned Confederate be blamed for refusing to commit more "murder"?[10] If war itself, as Clemens believed by the 1880s, is unjust, then the cause for which Clemens had fought was also

unjust and it should not be too difficult for reasonable Northerners to forgive desertion from an unjust cause. With this adroit
maneuver—a maneuver far more successful and decisive than any
executed by the Ralls County Rangers—Mark Twain, ex-Confederate, was vindicated.

Notes

1. Samuel Butler, *The Way of All Flesh* (New York, 1936), p. 89; La Rochefoucauld's famous maxim is applied specifically to Mark Twain by Justin Kaplan in his introduction to *Mark Twain: A Profile*, ed. Justin Kaplan (New York, 1967), p. x.

2. See, for instance, C. Vann Woodward's "The Irony of Southern History," in *The Burden of Southern History*, rev. ed. (Baton Rouge, 1960); David M. Potter, "The Enigma of the South," *Yale Review* 61 (1961):141-42; David L. Smiley, "The Quest for the Central Theme in Southern History," paper delivered to the Southern Historical Association, Miami Beach, Florida, November 8, 1962.

3. Almost a quarter-century ago in his seminal study of the American West, *Virgin Land: The American West as Symbol and Myth* (Cambridge, Mass., 1950), p. v, Henry Nash Smith cautioned his readers about his use of the terms "myth" and "symbol." A similar warning is in order here. Smith spoke of the two words as "an intellectual construction that fuses concept and emotion into an image" that may have practical consequences in the conduct of men. As products of the imagination, myths and symbols may not qualify as facts, but it cannot be denied that they generate facts, that facts in turn feed myths, and that they may both constitute what we call "reality." In this study I have juxtaposed myths, symbols, and "historical facts" with a view to rendering Mark Twain's ideas about the South in their full complexity and confusion.

4. Clemens kept a "hate list" that grew steadily with the years and which he rarely trimmed. Whitelaw ("Outlaw") Reid of the *New York Tribune* was a "skunk," "idiot," "eunuch," and "missing link"; a lawyer, William Hammersley, had the sex of a tapeworm; Clemens's nephew and business manager, Charles Webster, was "not a man but a hog." For other examples see Justin Kaplan, *Mr. Clemens and Mark Twain* (New York, 1966), pp. 241, 283, 291.

5. Clemens considered manufacturing scissors, bed clamps, and fire-extinguishers that worked like hand grenades, and almost marketed a concoction of kerosene and cheap perfume under the trademark, "Swift Death to Chilblains." He debated getting a concession from the Sultan of Turkey to build a railroad between Constantinople and the Persian Gulf and invested in an engraving company, a publishing company, an insurance house, a watch factory, a carpet manufacturing firm, a health food called Plasmon, a new kind of cash register, a spiral hatpin, and the typesetter that ruined him.

6. Kaplan, *Mr. Clemens and Mark Twain*, pp. 150-51, 233, 236, 251-53, 257, 262, 373-74.

7. I have tried to maintain the distinction, usually insisted upon by Clemens, between Clemens the private man and his published creation, Mark Twain. This effort has not been very successful, for although Mark Twain sometimes wrote without reference to Samuel Clemens, more often the *persona* was either covering up something in the creator, or disclosing things about Clemens that his sense of privacy would not allow him to say on his own responsibility. The most illuminating examples of Clemens's own recognition of the possibilities

and problems of his *persona* are contained in several notebook entries made
in the late 1890s about having "S.L.C. interview M.T." See, for example,
Typescript Notebook 32a, p. 24, on file in the Mark Twain Papers (hereafter
cited as MTP), General Library, University of California, Berkeley.

8. *Mark Twain's Autobiography*, ed. Albert Bigelow Paine, Stormfield
edition, 2 vols. (New York, 1929), 1:5, 120. (Except where otherwise stated
I have used the 1929 Stormfield edition of Mark Twain's works.) See also
Mark Twain in Eruption, ed. Bernard DeVoto (New York, 1922), pp. 232, 235.

CHAPTER 1

1. William Faulkner, *Light in August* (New York, 1932), p. 239; Mark
Twain, *A Connecticut Yankee in King Arthur's Court* (New York, 1889), p. 65.

2. In his *Autobiography* Mark Twain thought he remembered hearing about
several Clemenses who were "pirates and slavers in Elizabeth's time," because
piracy and the slave trade were "respectable" professions (1:82-84).

3. *Autobiography*, 1:120-21; 2:90-91; Mark Twain, *In Defense of Harriet
Shelley and Other Essays* (New York, 1929), p. 272.

4. The original Clemens ancestor in the New World claimed a business
connection with the original Fairfax family in colonial Maryland. By 1688
several landed and slaveowning Clemenses were living in Lancaster and Norfolk
counties in Virginia. In 1727 Samuel Clemens, a planter, lived in Surry County;
in 1728 the name appeared in Northampton County; in 1751 in Accomac
County. Clemens's great, great uncle, Micajah Moorman, helped to establish the
town of Lynchburg, Virginia, and became one of the largest landowners and
slaveholders in Campbell County. Other Clemenses later settled in that county,
and in the neighboring county of Bedford. See A. V. Goodpasture, "Mark
Twain, Southerner," *Tennessee Historical Magazine* (1931): 253-60; William
Dean Howells, *My Mark Twain* (Boston, 1910), p. 134; Charles O. Paullin,
"Mark Twain's Virginia Kin," *William and Mary Quarterly* 15 (1935): 294-98;
Dixon Wecter, *Sam Clemens of Hannibal* (Boston, 1952), pp. 1-15. Clemens's
oldest daughter, Susy, had heard enough of the family tree by 1886, at the
age of thirteen, to begin her biographical sketch of her father with the notation
that "Grandpa Clemens was of the F.F.V.'s of Virginia."

5. Mark Twain especially remembered one incident from his childhood
which he thought epitomized his father's character. When two rowdy Missourians tried to kill each other in front of Marshall Clemens's undersized (and
largely unused) law office in Hannibal, the judge struck one of them with a
stonecutter's mallet, dragged both into his court next door, fined them, and
collected the fee. Later, according to Marshall Clemens's testimony in court,
one of these men tried to kill another distinguished resident of Hannibal, a
Southerner named Colonel Elgin, because he mistook the colonel for the
judge. See Return I. Holcombe, *History of Marion County, Missouri* (St. Louis,
1884), pp. 914-15; Mark Twain, *Following the Equator*, 2 vols. (New York,
1929), 2:18; Mark Twain, *The $30,000 Bequest and Other Stories* (New York,
1929), p. 277; Mark Twain, *Life on the Mississippi* (New York, 1929), p. 383;
S. L. Clemens, "Villagers of 1840–43," autobiographical reminiscence of Hannibal's citizens written in 1897, typescript on file in MTP under DeVoto
(hereafter DV) 47, p. 16, published for the first time in *Mark Twain's Hannibal,
Huck & Tom*, ed. Walter Blair (Berkeley, 1969), pp. 28-40. See also Albert
Bigelow Paine, *Mark Twain: A Biography*, 4 vols. (New York, 1929), 1:6, 45.

6. The land in Fentress County, Tennessee, was said to hold secret deposits
of coal, copper, and iron which might be discovered at any time. Jane Clemens
and her son Orion and daughter Pamela occupied themselves with such
chimeras long after Sam Clemens forswore the whole business.

7. *Mark Twain's Speeches,* ed. Albert Bigelow Paine (New York, 1929), pp. 254-55; Paine, *Biography,* 1:11, 19-20; *Autobiography,* 1:7-8. In 1835, the year Clemens was born, St. Charles County numbered 1,500 blacks, one quarter of the total population; Pike County numbered 2,000 in a population of 7,000; Marion County had 1,500 in a population of 10,000. By 1861 Monroe County, in which Clemens was born, claimed 672 slaveholders and 2,687 slaves. See the report on slavery in Monroe County by George Peage, "Centennial Edition," *Monroe County Appeal* (Paris, Mo.), pt. 2, August 13, 1931, p. 3. I am grateful to Ralph Gregory, curator of the Mark Twain Memorial in Florida, Missouri, for these figures.

8. Wecter, *Hannibal,* p. 60; Donald Welch, "Sam Clemens' Hannibal: 1836–48," *Midcontinent American Studies Journal* 3 (1962):28-43.

9. In *A Connecticut Yankee* Hank Morgan compares nineteenth-century Southern slavery to Arthurian slavery and talks about slavery "ossifying what one may call the superior lobe of human feeling" (p. 189).

10. "Since the social prestige and monetary rewards [for overseers] were seldom commensurate with the responsibilities, the profession did not attract many of the South's most talented men." Kenneth M. Stampp, *The Peculiar Institution: Slavery in the Ante-Bellum South* (New York, 1956), p. 39. "The low social status accorded to slave traders . . . when by normal southern canons of prestige their intimate relation with the peculiar institution . . . should have given them a relatively high rank" suggests that other Southerners used them to create "scapegoats on whom it could discharge the guilt feelings arising from the necessity of treating human beings as property." Charles G. Sellers, "The Travail of Slavery," in *The Southerner as American,* ed. Sellers (New York, 1960), pp. 60-61. Marshall Clemens and Beebe eventually took their business differences to court in 1843, and Beebe appears as a thinly disguised villain in Mark Twain's "Mysterious Stranger in Hannibal," DV 306, MTP, recently published in *Mark Twain's Mysterious Stranger Manuscripts,* ed. William M. Gibson (Berkeley, 1969).

11. *Autobiography,* 1:101-2, 123; Paine, *Biography,* 1:41. See also the ten-page manuscript regarding God and morality as depicted in the Bible, written in the 1880s, DV 129, p. 6, MTP.

12. Paine, *Biography,* 1:17, 48; Typescript Notebook 28b, pp. 22-23, MTP.

13. *Following the Equator,* 2:18. In *A Connecticut Yankee* Hank Morgan recalls that antebellum Southern slavery seemed so common and natural that it made no "particular impression upon me" (p. 351).

14. Paine, *Biography,* 1:63-64; Wecter, *Hannibal,* pp. 148, 298. For a summary of legal treatment and moral attitudes toward slaves in Illinois, see Norman Dwight Harris, *History of Negro Slavery in Illinois and of the Anti-Slavery Agitation in that State* (Chicago, 1906), pp. 112-15. There is no record showing if Benson Blankenship was punished or what happened to him.

15. Holcombe, *Marion County,* pp. 214-15, 298-99.

16. In 1897 Clemens made two separate entries in his notebook about the hanging in 1849: "Negro [brought] smuggled from Va in featherbed when lynchers were after him. In Mo he raped a girl of 13 & killed her & her brother in the woods & before being hanged confessed to many rapes of white married women who kept it quiet partly from fear of him & partly to escape the scandal." Typescript Notebook 31 (I), p. 22, MTP. The same year, in his nightmarish reminiscence of Hannibal, he added: *"The Hanged Nigger.* He raped and murdered a girl of 13 in the woods. He confessed to forcing three young women in Va., and was brought away in a feather bed to save his life— . . . was a valuable property." "Villagers of 1840–43," p. 9, MTP. The incident is examined in more detail in Chapter 11.

17. Stampp, *Peculiar Institution,* pp. 30-31. The average number of slaves

owned by the 12 percent of Missourians who owned any at all was 7.7; Marshall Clemens usually averaged about one-third that many. Ultimately he was forced to sell them all.

18. For the idea that Jane Clemens would not permit the word nigger in her house, see Rachel M. Varble, *Jane Clemens: The Story of Mark Twain's Mother* (New York, 1964), pp. 137-39. For examples of her own use of nigger, see the correspondence between Jane Clemens and Sam Clemens from 1853, when Clemens left Hannibal, to 1861, when he left for the West. MTP, Letter File.

19. *Autobiography*, 1:101; Paine, *Biography*, 1:17, 41; Typescript Notebook 28b, p. 23, MTP. In his last notebook, kept between 1905 and 1908, Clemens still remembered Jenny: "We sold slave to Beebe & he sold her down the river. We saw her several times afterward. She was the only slave we ever owned in my time." Typescript Notebook 38, p. 10, MTP. In his *Autobiography*, however, he was sure he also remembered the slave boy Lewis.

20. John M. Clemens to Messrs. Coleman and Johnson, November 2, 1844, published in part in Wecter, *Hannibal*, p. 75; John M. Clemens to Jane Clemens January 1842, MTP, Letter File, published in part in Paine, *Biography*, 1:43.

21. DV 206, pp. 13-2 through 13-5, MTP, quoted in part in Wecter, *Hannibal*, pp. 74-75; Daniel Morely McKeithan, *The Morgan Manuscript of Mark Twain's "Pudd'nhead Wilson"* (Cambridge, Mass., 1961), pp. 20-21.

22. Marion County Circuit Court Record No. 2685, *State of Missouri* v. *George Thompson, Alanson Work, and James Burr*, published in Holcombe, *History of Marion County*, pp. 256-59. Governor Edwards pardoned the three abolitionists five years later, and Thompson wrote a book about his years in prison. In response to a letter from R. I. Holcombe of Palmyra, Missouri, on August 29, 1883 requesting information about Marshall Clemens's role in the case, Clemens characteristically asked his brother Orion to attend to answering Holcombe. In "The George Harrison Story," formerly DV 302, now Box 24, MTP, and published in *Mark Twain's "Which Was the Dream?"* ed. John S. Tuckey (Berkeley, 1967), pp. 177-429, Mark Twain had a judge permit the prosecution in a court case to enter the evidence of a black man on behalf of a white.

23. Ralph Gregory, curator of the Mark Twain Memorial in Florida, Missouri, believes that Mark Twain's estimation in the *Autobiography* that Quarles owned fifteen or twenty slaves is excessive. The census of 1840 shows that Quarles owned, or at least recorded, only six: five females, two under age ten, one between ten and twenty-four, one between twenty-four and thirty-six, who would be Daniel's wife Maria, one between fifty-five and one hundred, presumably Aunt Hannah; and only one male, Daniel. The 1850 census shows that Quarles owned eleven slaves: six females, two aged three, one each ages six, eight, and twelve, one twenty-two, one thirty-five, and Daniel, forty-six. Daniel was probably the father of all the children. I am indebted to Mr. Gregory for these figures.

24. *Autobiography*, 1:99-100; Typescript Notebook 4, p. 41, MTP; Mark Twain, *Adventures of Huckleberry Finn* (New York, 1929), pp. 8, 327. In dictating his autobiography, Mark Twain confused Aunt Hanner, another character who will appear elsewhere in this study, with Aunt Hannah, but made the correct distinction in a working note for *Huckleberry Finn*, when he reminded himself to "Describe aunt Patsy's house. & Uncle Dan, aunt Hanner, & the 90-year blind negress," the latter being Aunt Hannah. Bernard DeVoto, ed., *Mark Twain at Work* (Cambridge, Mass., 1942), p. 66.

25. Ralph Gregory recently discovered that John Quarles, perhaps through the persuasion of his new bride, Sarah A. Stickley, who originally came from

Rhode Island, freed Daniel on November 14, 1855. Quarles's remarriage on January 27, 1852 is shown in Marriage Record No. 3, Pike County, Missouri, p. 3, and the freeing of Daniel is recorded in the *Monroe County Recorder's Deed Record,* 1:499-500.

26. *Autobiography,* 1:112-13; *Mark Twain's Letters,* ed. Albert Bigelow Paine, 2 vols. (New York, 1929), 1:403. According to Orion Clemens, ten years older than Sam, the original ghost-teller was not Daniel but the Clemens's own Hannibal slave, Uncle Ned.

27. Wecter, *Hannibal,* p. 75; *Autobiography,* 1:100; Mark Twain, "Corn-Pone Opinions," *Europe and Elsewhere* (New York, 1929), p. 399.

28. Orion Clemens was one of three signers of an "Address of the Whig Central Committee of Muscatine County," Iowa, in July 1854, denouncing the recent repeal of the Missouri Compromise of 1820 as "THE FIRST ATTEMPT OF CONGRESS TO ESTABLISH SLAVERY" legally in any state or territory. See Scrapbook 4 (1864):26-28, MTP.

CHAPTER 2

1. S. L. Clemens (hereafter SLC) to J. H. Burrough, November 1, 1876, *Letters,* 1:289.

2. SLC to Jane Lampton Clemens, August 24 and 31, 1853, MTP, Letter File. Both letters were published by Orion Clemens in the *Hannibal Daily Journal,* September 8 and 10, 1853, and the latter was reprinted in *Contributions to the Galaxy, 1868–1871, by Mark Twain,* ed. Bruce McElderry, Jr. (New York, 1961), p. 81.

3. *Autobiography,* 2:289; *New Orleans Daily Crescent,* May 8, 1859; Paine, *Biography,* 4:1594-96.

4. SLC to J. H. Burrough, November 1, 1876, *Letters,* 1:289-91; *Mark Twain, Business Man,* ed. Samuel C. Webster (Boston, 1946), p. 47.

5. Typescript Notebook 38, pp. 8-9, MTP; SLC to Orion Clemens, February 6, 1861, *Letters,* 1:48-51; *Mark Twain, Business Man,* pp. 60-62.

6. Typescript Notebooks 16, p. 17; 16a, p. 38, MTP; Paine, *Biography,* 1:162; James M. Cox, "Whitman, Twain, and the Civil War," *Sewanee Review* 59 (1961):185; John Gerber, "Mark Twain's 'Private Campaign,'" *Civil War History* 1 (March 1955):37-60; Fred W. Lorch, "Mark Twain and the 'Campaign That Failed,'" *American Literature* 12 (1941):454-70.

7. SLC to an unknown person, 1891, *Letters,* 2:541.

8. After his marriage Clemens was apparently circumspect in speaking of his war experience to his family. In her biography of her father, Susy Clemens omitted this experience entirely, carrying Clemens directly from the pilot house to the Nevada Territory. See the Appendix for an analysis of Mark Twain's fictional defense of his Confederate career.

9. Of 6,857 persons in the Nevada Territory in 1860, only 464 were from states that joined the Confederacy, and only 964 from states that permitted slavery. See Eighth Census, *Population of the United States in 1860,* published in William Hanchett, "Yankee Law and the Negro in Nevada, 1861–1869," *Western Humanities Review* 10 (1956):241-49.

10. Paul Fatout, *Mark Twain in Virginia City* (Bloomington, 1961), pp. 61-72, 147-48.

11. *The Twainian* (July-August 1956) p. 1, MTP; SLC to William Clagett, March 8, 1862, in C. Waller Barrett Collection, University of Virginia. Photocopy in MTP, Letter File, published in part in Kenneth S. Lynn, *Mark Twain and Southwestern Humor* (Boston, 1959), pp. 142, 144.

12. SLC to Jane Clemens, August 19, 1863, *Letters,* 1:92.

13. SLC to William Clagett, September 9, 1862, C. Waller Barrett Collection; photocopy in MTP, Letter File.

14. *Nevada Daily Independent,* June 4, 1864, preserved by Clemens in Scrapbook 3:147, MTP.

15. Paine, *Biography,* 1:238. After he shed his Southern convictions, Clemens continued to show some uneasiness throughout the Western years, especially over financial difficulties. One night early in 1866, in San Francisco and out of work, he put a pistol to his head. His most explicit reference to the suicide attempt is a marginal comment, April 21, 1909, in his copy of J. R. Lowell's *Letters.* See Kaplan, *Mr. Clemens and Mark Twain,* p. 15.

16. SLC to Pamela Clemens Moffett, March 1864, MTP, Letter File; Clemens, Scrapbook 1:31, 80; 2:5, 10, MTP.

17. "Mark Twain" sprang into being, if not full-blown at least with full potential, on February 3, 1863, in the offices of the *Virginia City Territorial Enterprise,* when the pseudonym was first used.

18. Effie Mack, "Mark Twain in Nevada: A Leaf from the Civil War History," *Oakland* (California) *Tribune,* November 16, 1958; Mark Twain, *Roughing It,* 2 vols. (New York, 1929), 2:122-23.

19. Mark Twain, "Answer to Correspondents," *Daily Californian,* June 24, 1865; Clemens, Scrapbook 3:148, MTP.

20. SLC to Jane Clemens, August 24, 1853, MTP, Letter File; Edgar M. Branch, "Samuel Clemens and the Copperheads of 1864," *Mad River Review* 2 (Winter-Spring 1967):11-16, 18.

21. Mark Twain, "How Is It?" (not extant) and "Miscegenation," *Virginia City Territorial Enterprise,* May 17 (possibly May 18), May 24, 1864, the latter published in *Mark Twain of the "Enterprise,"* ed. Henry Nash Smith and Frederick Anderson (Berkeley, 1957), pp. 197-98; Clemens, Scrapbook 3:146-47, MTP; SLC to Mollie Clemens, May 20, 1864, *Mark Twain of the "Enterprise,"* pp. 90-91.

22. *Mark Twain of the "Enterprise,"* pp. 191-96; Mark Twain, "Journalism in Tennessee," *Sketches New and Old* (New York, 1929), pp. 35-43; *Autobiography,* 1:272, 350, 354; DeLancy Ferguson, "Mark Twain's Comstock Duel: The Birth of a Legend," *American Literature* 14 (1942):66-70. Cyril Clemens's effort to refute Ferguson, in " 'The Birth of a Legend' Again," *American Literature* 15 (1943):64-65, is not convincing. For an account of Clemens's drinking habits in the West, see Paul Fatout, "Mark Twain's Nom de Plume," *American Literature* 34 (1962):1-7.

23. SLC to Mollie Clemens, May 20, 1864, and to Orion Clemens, May 25, 1864, *Mark Twain of the "Enterprise,"* pp. 190-91.

24. Albert S. Evans ("Amigo") in *Gold Hill News,* February 12 and 19, 1866, quoted in *Mark Twain, San Francisco Correspondent,* ed. Henry Nash Smith and Frederick Anderson (San Francisco, 1957), pp. 39-40. In a letter to Clemens, January 1864, Artemus Ward said: "Why would you make a good artillery man? Because you are familiar with Gonorrhea (gunnery)," quoted in Kaplan, *Mr. Clemens and Mark Twain,* p. 15.

25. See, for example, "Curing a Cold" (1864), *Sketches New and Old,* p. 368.

26. Typescript Notebooks 4, p. 13; 5, p. 44, MTP.

27. *Roughing It,* 2:251; Kaplan, *Mr. Clemens and Mark Twain,* p. 44. Though *Roughing It* was not published until 1872, the Sandwich Islands portion of the book was taken directly from Mark Twain's *Sacramento Union* letters.

28. James M. Cox, in *Mark Twain: The Fate of Humor* (Princeton, 1966), p. 196, notes that "the discovery of 'Mark Twain' in the Nevada Territory . . . had quite literally been a way of escaping the Civil War."

29. I am deeply indebted to James Cox's discussion of the distinction between the seriousness of Clemens and the humor of Mark Twain in *Mark Twain: The Fate of Humor.*

30. His most powerful ambitions, Clemens wrote Orion in October 1865, had been to be a preacher or a river pilot. He had given up on the first because he lacked "the necessary stock in trade—*i.e.*, religion." He had succeeded at the second, and it was the outbreak of war, not his choice, that cut his piloting career short. Now he felt he had "a 'call' to literature, of a low order—*i.e.*, humorous." SLC to Orion and Mollie Clemens, October 19, 1865, quoted in Kaplan, *Mr. Clemens and Mark Twain*, p. 14.

31. Except for a brief business trip six months later Clemens never returned to Nevada or to California. Not until twenty-seven years later, when he was lecturing his way out of bankruptcy, did he even see the Pacific again.

CHAPTER 3

1. *Speeches*, p. 316.

2. *Life on the Mississippi*, p. 185. Neighboring "rocks of New England" were Francis Gillette, U.S. senator and former abolitionist; Joseph Hawley, major general of Union volunteers in the war and former Connecticut governor; Thomas Hooker; Charles Dudley Warner; and Harriet Beecher Stowe—all distinguished Yankee company. Clemens's Hartford house and grounds cost $122,000 in all. Although Olivia Langdon's inheritance from her father did not come in the form of a dowry, it did give definiteness and amplitude to Clemens's plans and successes in the 1870s.

3. *Mark Twain's Notebook*, ed. Albert Bigelow Paine (New York, 1935), pp. 40-41, 43.

4. Orion had passed the zenith of his career as secretary of the Nevada Territory and was embarked on thirty years of drift and failure.

5. Mark Twain's first book, *The Celebrated Jumping Frog of Calaveras County and Other Sketches,* was published in April 1867 and had a small circulation.

6. Clemens's lobbying activities included petitioning for a clerkship for the hapless Orion and for the postmastership of San Francisco for himself, which he turned down because the pay did not come up to the prestige.

7. At sixteen Olivia Langdon slipped on the ice and lay in bed partially paralyzed for two years with a mysterious spinal ailment. When she was eighteen a mind-healing quack prayed over her and told her to get up, which she did. Though she had four children and lived to be fifty-eight, Livy suffered during her last years from asthma, hyperthyroidism, "nervous prostration," and a heart condition.

8. "Pudd'nhead Wilson's New Calendar," *Following the Equator*, 1:80.

9. "The White House Funeral," *New York Tribune*, March 4, 1869, published in part in Louis J. Budd, *Mark Twain: Social Philosopher* (Bloomington, Ind., 1962), p. 36.

10. *Buffalo Express*, July 26, August 19, September 23, 1869; "The 'Tournament' in A.D. 1870," *Galaxy*, July 1870, pp. 135-36. Mark Twain contributed monthly columns to the *Galaxy* from March 1870 to April 1871.

11. Marshall Clemens's long-tailed frock coat is worn by the Tennessee editor, by Squire Hawkins in *The Gilded Age*, by Judge Griswold in *Simon Wheeler, Detective,* and by Colonel Grangerford in *Huckleberry Finn.*

12. "Journalism in Tennessee," *Sketches New and Old*, pp. 35-43.

13. Briefly, Marshall Clemens was postmaster in Jamestown, Tennessee, and was later called judge in consequence of brief service as justice of the peace in Missouri. Squire Hawkins is postmaster in Obedstown, Tennessee, and is

called squire because the chief citizens in the South "always must have titles of some sort." Both men come from a distant tidewaster past, and both feel out of place in the Southwest.

14. Mark Twain and Charles Dudley Warner, *The Gilded Age*, 2 vols. (New York, 1929), 1:3-5.

15. Edgar Branch, *The Literary Apprenticeship of Mark Twain* (Urbana, Ill., 1950), p. 20; Typescript Notebooks 4, p. 38; 6, p. 44, MTP; *Mark Twain's Travels with Mr. Brown*, ed. Franklin Walker and G. Ezra Dane (New York, 1940), p. 71; "About Smells," *Galaxy*, May 1870.

16. *Buffalo Express*, May 10, October 8, 1869; "Shocking Result of Miscegenation and Jealousy—Two Attempted Assassinations—Three Horrible Murders, and One Suicide!!" *Buffalo Express*, late May 1870, reprinted in *The Forgotten Writings of Mark Twain*, ed. Henry Duskis (New York, 1963), pp. 250-55.

17. Typescript Notebook 4, p. 20, MTP.

18. "Riley—Newspaper Correspondent," *Sketches New and Old*, pp. 177-82. Sent by Clemens in 1870 to South Africa to dig up diamonds for both of them, Riley died of food poisoning.

19. Mary Fairbanks, wife of the owner of the *Cleveland Herald*, was a middle-aged, midwestern custodian of middle-class values whom Clemens met on the Holy Land tour and whom he called mother for forty years.

20. SLC to Jervis Langdon, December 29, 1868, *The Love Letters of Mark Twain*, ed. Dixon Wecter (New York, 1949), p. 37.

21. In a January 6, 1867, letter to the *Alta California*, Mark Twain changed nigger to negro, and on March 15, in an article entitled "Female Suffrage" in the *St. Louis Daily Missouri Democrat*, he used nigs. for the last time in print. In the final proofs for *The Innocents Abroad* he carefully changed each nigger to negro, and in his editorials for the *Buffalo Express* he used negro consistently.

22. *Buffalo Express*, August 26, 1869, published in Philip S. Foner, *Mark Twain: Social Critic* (New York, 1958), p. 218, and in part in Budd, *Mark Twain: Social Philosopher*, p. 87.

23. "Life on the Isthmus," *Buffalo Express*, October 4, 1870, reprinted in Duskis, ed., *Forgotten Writings of Mark Twain*, pp. 309-10.

24. Mark Twain and William Dean Howells, "Colonel Sellers as [a] Scientist" [1886], typescript in Barrett Collection, University of Virginia, Act 2, Sc. 2, p. 63, published in *The Complete Plays of W. D. Howells*, ed. Walter J. Meserve (New York, 1960), p. 229; Mark Twain, "Colonel Sellers," play manuscript, Act 2, Sc. 1, p. 18, MTP.

25. *The Gilded Age*, 1:66.

26. Ibid., pp. 199-200, 11; "Colonel Sellers," play manuscript, Act 2, Sc. 1, p. 19, MTP. Chapter 20, in which Sellers's remarks on blacks occur, was supposedly written by Warner. However, I believe Mark Twain wrote the pages pertaining to Sellers's comments about blacks, for three reasons: each author contributed material to the other's chapters; Mark Twain was responsible for the entire character development of Sellers; and Sellers's remarks are the same in the play version (typescript, Act 1, Sc. 1, pp. 21-22, MTP), written entirely by Mark Twain.

27. *The Gilded Age*, 1:11; "Colonel Sellers," play manuscript, Act 2, Sc. 1, pp. 23-24, MTP. The idea of postbellum North-South conniving to exploit blacks is a tenacious theme in American literature. See, for example, Thomas Dixon's *The Leopard's Spots: A Romance of the White Man's Burden, 1865–1900* (New York, 1902).

28. *The Gilded Age*, 1:20-24; "Colonel Sellers," play manuscript, Act 1, Sc. 1, p. 10, MTP. In the cast of characters for the play Daniel is listed as "an old stammering Negro." Robert Rowlette, in *Twain's "Pudd'nhead Wilson"*:

The Development and Design (Bowling Green, Ohio, 1971), p. 6, sees in Dan'l's comic offer of self-sacrifice "an anticipation of Jim's heroic sacrifice of himself for the wounded Tom Sawyer in *Huck* and of Roxy's sacrifice of her freedom for Tom Driscoll in *Pudd'nhead Wilson.*"

29. Although Mark Twain revised *The American Claimant* extensively before publishing it in 1892, the portions in which Uncle Daniel appears were written in the 1870s and remained largely unchanged. They belong in this study in conjunction with *The Gilded Age* as a single character portrait.

30. Jinny's name is similar to that of both the slave woman Jenny owned by Marshall Clemens and the servant Jenny at Quarry Farm.

31. Budd, *Mark Twain: Social Philosopher,* p. 153; Mark Twain, *The American Claimant and Other Stories and Sketches* (New York, 1929), pp. 22-23, 63.

32. Quarry Farm was the Clemenses' summertime retreat outside of Elmira, New York, and was owned by Olivia's relatives.

33. *The American Claimant,* pp. 61, 63-64; "Mental Telegraphy," *Harriet Shelley,* p. 136.

34. I am not competent to speak on the complexity of humor, only to raise a warning about it. For excellent discussions of the critical problems of humor in general and Mark Twain's in particular, see Cox, *Mark Twain: The Fate of Humor;* Franklin R. Rogers, *Mark Twain's Burlesque Patterns* (Dallas, 1960); and Henry Nash Smith, *Mark Twain: The Development of a Writer* (Cambridge, Mass., 1962).

35. Clemens's dramatic statement to Howells that he was responsible for his son Langdon's death ("Yes, *I* killed him") by exposing the nineteen-month-old child to cold on a sleigh ride is not consistent with the medical facts. Langdon died of diphtheria, not pneumonia.

36. SLC to James Henry Riley, March 27, 1870, *American and English Literature: Selections from the Library of the Late Dr. Samuel Wyllis Bandler of New York,* 4 vols. (New York, 1904), 2:20.

CHAPTER 4

1. "Tom Sawyer: A Play," in Blair, *Hannibal, Huck & Tom,* pp. 265-66; Typescript Notebook 13, p. 29, MTP.

2. Henry Nash Smith, "Mark Twain's Images of Hannibal," University of Texas *Studies in English* 37 (1958):3-23. I am indebted to this article for matters pertaining to St. Petersburg in this chapter and for those pertaining to Bricksville in Chapter 6, below.

3. Howells to Clemens, September 8, 30, 1874, *Mark Twain-Howells Letters,* ed. Henry Nash Smith and William M. Gibson, 2 vols. (Cambridge, Mass., 1960, hereafter cited as MTHL), 1:24-25n, 32; Paine, *Biography,* 2:513-14, 552; *Letters,* 1:223.

4. Paine, *Biography,* 2:515; "Family Sketch," mostly unpublished, written in 1896 or shortly thereafter. Photocopy in DV 226, pp. 59-61, MTP.

5. *Mark Twain's Fables of Man,* ed. John S. Tuckey (Berkeley, 1972).

6. "A True Story," *Sketches New and Old,* pp. 240-47.

7. Beecher was acquitted, but Clemens suspected he was guilty. The incident was embarrassing because members of the Beecher family were neighbors of the Clemenses, and Beecher's brother, Thomas, was Livy's spiritual adviser until she lost the faith.

8. One month after Howells received the commission from the *New York Tribune* to review *The Prince and the Pauper* he proofed and critiqued the book for Mark Twain, which did not please Whitelaw Reid, editor of the *Tribune.* In the nineteenth century, however, it was not uncommon to have

friends and editors act as reviewers as well. See George Monteiro, "A Note on the Mark Twain–Whitelaw Reid Relationship," *Emerson Society Quarterly* 19 (Spring 1960):20-21.

9. Kaplan, *Mr. Clemens and Mark Twain*, pp. 156-59, 181-83, 214.

10. Mark Twain considered writing a scorching biography of Mayor Oakley Hall, puppet and patron of the Tweed ring.

11. Six years later, in 1876, Clemens reversed himself, telling Bowen that worship of the past was "simply mental and moral masturbation"; SLC to Will Bowen, February 6, 1870, *Mark Twain's Letters to Will Bowen*, ed. Theodore Hornberger (Austin, 1941), pp. 18-21, 23-24. I am indebted to Kaplan's discussion in *Mr. Clemens and Mark Twain* of the effect of Clemens's marriage on his writing, and to James Cox's analysis of Livy's influence on Clemens in "The Muse of Samuel Clemens," *Massachusetts Review* 5 (Autumn 1963):127-41.

12. Mark Twain repeated the word delectable in describing Hannibal twenty-eight years later (*Speeches*, p. 249).

13. *The Adventures of Tom Sawyer* (New York, 1929), p. 243. The Welshman believes Huck at once when the boy tells him that Injun Joe plans to mutilate the widow, "because white men don't take that sort of revenge."

14. "Tom Sawyer: A Play," pp. 243-324. In 1874 Mark Twain published a long and tedious sketch about a ten-year-old black boy named Sociable Jimmy, whose one reference to his position in white society is an offhand admission that he is not permitted to attend white church services. His essential qualities are superlative ignorance and gullibility. "Some folks," he tells Mark Twain, "say dis town would be considerable bigger if it wa'n't on account of so much lan' all roun' it dat ain't got no houses on it." Mark Twain, "Sociable Jimmy," *New York Times*, November 29, 1874, reprinted in *The Twainian* 2 (February 1943):3-5. Since the Tom Sawyer play was started in 1872 (though not completed until 1883), "Little Jim" was quite possibly the model for Sociable Jimmy.

15. "Tom Sawyer: A Play," p. 251. Nigger was changed to negro when the manuscript was typed.

16. *Tom Sawyer*, pp. 13, 56.

17. Ibid., p. 228.

18. Typescript Notebook 28a, p. 34, MTP.

19. *Simon Wheeler, Detective* was published in part in 1963, edited by Franklin R. Rogers (New York, 1963); and in full in Rogers, ed., *Mark Twain's Satires & Burlesques* (Berkeley, 1967), pp. 307-454. Hereafter I cite the 1963 edition.

20. *Simon Wheeler*, pp. 46-51.

21. Ibid., pp. 4-5.

22. See also Mark Twain, *Pudd'nhead Wilson* (New York, 1929), p. 3.

23. *Simon Wheeler*, pp. 8-9, 29-30, 34, 183. I am indebted to Franklin Rogers's discussion of Mark Twain's burlesque of the Dexter-Burnside feud.

CHAPTER 5

1. SLC to Mrs. Boardman, daughter of a Hannibal jeweler, March 25, 1887, cited in Lynn, *Mark Twain and Southwestern Humor*, p. 262; Typescript Notebook 15, p. 7, MTP, cited in Roger B. Salomon, *Twain and the Image of History* (New Haven, 1961), p. 78.

2. SLC to Howells, October 24, 1874, MTHL, 1:34; Paine, *Biography*, 2:531; *Letters*, 1:229-30. Clemens had thought of writing a Mississippi River book but not necessarily from the pilot's viewpoint.

3. SLC to Wattie Bowser, a Dallas schoolboy, March 20, 1880, published

in the *Dallas Sun,* December 16, 1939, and the *Houston Post,* February 7, 1960.

4. Typescript Notebook 16, pp. 29, 33, MTP; *Life on the Mississippi,* p. 337. (The 1929 edition is hereafter cited as LOM.)

5. In some working notes for *Huckleberry Finn,* written shortly after returning from the Mississippi trip, Mark Twain considered including a scene about "an overflowed Arkansaw town," in which the "river booms up in the night" and creates havoc and destruction (DeVoto, ed., *Mark Twain at Work,* p. 66).

6. Typescript Notebooks 16a, pp. 2, 6; 16, p. 31, MTP; LOM, p. 340.

7. Typescript Notebooks 16a, pp. 1, 20, MTP; LOM, pp. 187-88, 191.

8. Typescript Notebooks 16, pp. 22, 38, 47; 16a, pp. 16, 34, MTP; LOM, pp. 222-23, 358-60, 363-64.

9. *Journals of Ralph Waldo Emerson,* ed. Edward Waldo Emerson and Waldo Emerson Forbes, 2 vols. (Boston, 1910), 1:275.

10. Typescript Notebook 16a, pp. 48, 20-21, MTP; LOM, pp. 219-22, 255.

11. Typescript Notebook 16a, pp. 13-16, 21, MTP; LOM, pp. 209, 260.

12. LOM, pp. 461, 250, 327, 288, 190.

13. Ibid., pp. 332-34, 340, 373-74; Typescript Notebook 16, p. 35, MTP.

14. LOM, pp. 375-78; Typescript Notebook 16, p. 35, MTP.

15. LOM, pp. 375-76. Maurice Hewlett, in "Mark on Sir Walter," *Sewanee Review* 29 (1921):130-33, thought that Mark Twain, after trying to flatten Scott, lay "far flatter" himself. Grace Warren Landrum, "Sir Walter Scott and His Literary Rivals in the Old South," *American Literature* 2 (1930):256-76; and G. Harrison Orians, "Walter Scott, Mark Twain and the Civil War," *South Atlantic Quarterly* (1941), pp. 342-59, both refute the charge that Scott exercised a baneful effect on the South.

16. *Life on the Mississippi,* ed. Willis Wagner (New York: Heritage edition, 1933), pp. 391-92, 399-401, 412-14; Mark Twain, *Life As I Find It,* ed. Charles Neider (New York, 1961), pp. 299-300, 303.

17. Walter Blair, in *Mark Twain & Huck Finn* (Berkeley, 1960), pp. 300-301, and "When Was *Huckleberry Finn* Written?" *American Literature* 30 (March 1958):1-25, states that Mark Twain probably wrote chapter 21 and the first part of 22, through Sherburn's repulse of the mob, within a year after returning from the Mississippi trip. I agree with Guy A. Cardwell, "Mark Twain, James R. Osgood, and those 'Suppressed' Passages," *New England Quarterly* 46 (1973):163-88, that the anti-Southern portions of chapter 48 are not very important and that their exclusion is more indicative of slapdash editing than a conscious intention on the part of either author or publisher to exclude them.

18. *Life on the Mississippi* (Heritage ed.), pp. 413-15; Typescript Notebooks 16a, pp. 48, 20-21, 34; 16, p. 36, MTP. In *What Is Man? and Other Essays* (New York, 1929), p. 21, Mark Twain has the Old Man tell about a Kentuckian whose "training made it a duty" to kill a stranger, but that he "neglected his duty—kept dodging it, shirking it, putting it off, and his unrelenting conscience kept persecuting him for this conduct. At last, to get ease of mind, comfort, self-approval, he hunted up the stranger and took his life."

19. In 1904 Clemens sought financial help for a woman whose husband had been "ruined" for declining to take part in a European "affair of honor" (*Letters,* 2:726-27).

20. Typescript Notebook 16, p. 33, MTP.

21. Typescript Notebook 16a, pp. 26-28, MTP.

22. Ibid., p. 51, MTP.

23. The Southern planter bears some resemblance to Harriet Stowe's Augustine St. Clare; the pretty young daughter who tries to protect the slave is similar to Little Eva.

24. About this time, at the top of a page in the second volume of Harriet

Martineau's *Society in America* that described the sale of a black woman into prostitution, Clemens scrawled "Horrible." Clemens's copy of the Martineau book is in MTP.

25. "Mr. Randall's Jew Story" and "Newhouse's Jew Story," DV 43 and 44, MTP.

26. Typescript Notebook 16a, pp. 24, 53; LOM, pp. 291-92.

27. Typescript Notebook 12, pp. 19-20, MTP; LOM, pp. 254-55, 121-22.

28. LOM, pp. 459-60.

29. Typescript Notebook 16, pp. 40-43, MTP.

30. The two books were by now symbiotic, and Mark Twain used one to jog the other; even his working notes for the two books overlapped. Almost the whole of chapter 3 of *Life on the Mississippi* about the raftsmen was pulled from *Huckleberry Finn,* and the period-piece description of the Granger-ford parlor shows the influence of the "House Beautiful" chapter in *Life on the Mississippi.* For one of several accounts questioning the deletion of the raft episode from *Huckleberry Finn,* see Peter G. Beidler, "The Raft Episode in *Huckleberry Finn,*" *Modern Fiction Studies* 14 (Spring 1968):11-20.

CHAPTER 6

1. Typescript Notebook 16, p. 49, MTP; Thomas Bangs Thorpe, *The Master's House; or, Scenes Descriptive of Southern Life* (New York, 1854), p. 152. The chapter title is from *Huckleberry Finn,* p. 275. Hereafter all page citations, through the end of chapter 8, without an accompanying source are from the 1929 Stormfield edition of the novel.

2. As a social historian I do not intend to engage in a critical discussion of *Huckleberry Finn.* However, I am especially persuaded by Leo Marx's recent remark that "sooner or later, criticism will be forced to consider the theoretical question raised by the book's special character: are the severe holistic standards by which we usually assess the novels of, say, Jane Austen and Henry James appropriate to the assessment of *Huckleberry Finn?*" *Adventures of Huckleberry Finn,* ed. Leo Marx (Indianapolis, 1967), p. xxxiv. In this chapter I confine my remarks to Mark Twain's treatment of the South in the novel; in chapter 8 I confine my remarks to the relationship between Huck and Nigger Jim. Recent critical discussions can be found in the Norton Critical Edition of the *Adventures of Huckleberry Finn,* ed. Sculley Bradley *et al.* (New York, 1961), and elsewhere.

3. Page 26.

4. The free "nigger p'fessor" visiting from Ohio had better return there within six months or he will be reenslaved.

5. Pages 36-38.

6. In a notebook entry dated January 30, 1865, from Angel's Camp, California, twenty-nine-year-old Clemens wrote: "W. Bilgewater, says she, Good God what a name." Typescript Notebook 3, p. 7, MTP. In *1601* Mark Twain introduced "ye Duchess of Bilgewater" as having the dubious distinction of being "roger'd by four lords before she had a husband."

7. Mark Twain suppressed E. W. Kemble's illustration of that "lecherous old rascal," the King, kissing the girl at the campmeeting. "It is powerful good, but it mustn't go in—don't forget it. Let's not make *any* pictures of the campmeeting. The subject won't *bear* illustrating. It is a disgusting thing, and pictures are sure to tell the truth about it too plainly" (Webster, *Mark Twain, Business Man,* p. 260).

8. The "Royal Nonesuch" was derived from "The Burning Shame" of Clemens's Western days, apparently a solo theatrical performance in which a

nude man pranced around the stage with a lighted candle in his anus. Type-script Notebook 13, p. 54, MTP.

9. Page 16.

10. Pages 78-80, 125-27, 225, 306-7.

11. Typescript Notebook 16, p. 49, MTP.

12. Pages 192-200.

13. Pages 197-99.

14. "Villagers of 1840-43," pp. 11-12, MTP; *Autobiography,* 1:131; Blair, *Mark Twain & Huck,* pp. 412, 306-8; Wecter, *Hannibal,* pp. 106-9.

15. See pp. 72-73 above regarding the cancelled chapter of *Life on the Mississippi.*

16. Smith, in *Mark Twain: The Development of a Writer,* p. 136, sees Sherburn as Mark Twain's first transcendent "mysterious stranger." As in chapter 4 I am indebted to Franklin Rogers's discussion of the difference between the Driscoll, Grangerford, and Sherburn variants of the code duello in his 1963 introduction to, and editing of, *Simon Wheeler, Detective.*

17. For comments on the meanings of the names Grangerford and Shep-herdson see Martha Banta, "Escape and Entry in *Huckleberry Finn," Modern Fiction Studies* 14 (Spring 1968):79-91.

18. Erratic clocks were one of Mark Twain's standard sources of humor. See "My Watch" (written about 1870), *Sketches New and Old,* pp. 1-5, and "The House Beautiful" chapter of *Life on the Mississippi,* pp. 316-23.

19. Pages 138-44. I am indebted to Walter Blair's fine discussion of the Grangerford parlor decor in *Mark Twain & Huck,* pp. 205-12.

20. Page 146.

21. Typescript Notebooks 16, pp. 13-14, 49; 16a, pp. 48-49, MTP, quoted in Blair, *Mark Twain & Huck,* pp. 283-84; LOM, pp. 221-22; Paine, *Biography,* p. 796. Louis Budd's "Southward Currents under Huck Finn's Raft," *Mississippi Valley Historical Review* 46 (September 1959):222-37, contains a thorough documentation of Clemens's sources of the feud.

22. Pages 136, 150.

23. Pages 150-52, 160.

CHAPTER 7

1. *Autobiography,* 1:263; "Wapping Alice," Autobiographical Dictation, April 9, 1907, typescript, DV 344a, p. 1951, MTP.

2. See chapter 1 and pp. 45-47 above, for remarks about Uncle Daniel. Scholars have customarily regarded Uncle Daniel as the chief, if not the sole, source of Nigger Jim, probably because of Mark Twain's inspired but vague recollections of Uncle Daniel in the *Autobiography.* Orion, ten years older than Sam, thought his brother confused Uncle Daniel of Quarles Farm with one of Marshall Clemens's Hannibal slaves (*Letters,* 2:403, n. 1).

3. Aside from Lewis's role as Uncle Rastus Timson in "Refuge of the Derelicts," I believe that the character of Dan'l in *The American Claimant* (published in 1892 but largely written in the 1870s) is a composite portrait of Uncle Daniel of *The Gilded Age* and John Lewis, especially in the kitchen squabbling episode between Daniel (Lewis) and Jinny (Aunty Cord).

4. SLC to Howells, August 9, 1876; August 25-27, 1877, MTHL, 1:144, 194-99. Mrs. Theodore Crane, Livy's foster-sister, owned the farm. Her brother Charles Langdon and his children were in the cart.

5. Off and on, the list included Anson Burlingame (later ambassador to China, whom Clemens met in the Sandwich Islands in 1866), Louis Napoleon III, Cecil Rhodes (for a while), Bert Harte (for a very short while), Ulysses

S. Grant, and Henry H. Rogers, the Standard Oil millionaire who rescued Clemens from bankruptcy in the 1890s and the only man whom Clemens consistently called "Mr."

6. SLC to Dr. John Brown, included by Rogers as an appendix to *Simon Wheeler, Detective,* pp. 169-75.

7. Paine thought Clemens's Southern upbringing gave him special understanding of black "humors" and of their "native emotions" (*Biography,* 2:515).

8. SLC to Joel Chandler Harris, December 12, 1881, *Letters,* 1:403; Paine, *Biography,* 2:599-600.

9. Mark Twain, "Refuge of the Derelicts," typescript, p. 156, MTP, published in Tuckey, ed., *Mark Twain's Fables of Man,* but not issued before this study was submitted for publication; hence I cite the typescript pages. In his notes for the story Mark Twain specifically identified Aunty Phyllis as "Cord" who told "the 'True Story,'" and Rastus as the man who "saved the Langdons, 28 yrs ago" (p. 3). There are at least four extant photos of Clemens and Lewis at Quarry Farm (one on the jacket of this book) but none to my knowledge of George Griffin.

10. "Refuge of the Derelicts," typescript, pp. 109-14, 116-17, 128, 135, 158, 171-76, 178-81, MTP. Mark Twain tried two more times to make the horse-jerking episode work—once in *Simon Wheeler, Detective,* where the hero of the deed is white, and once in a section deleted from *Pudd'nhead Wilson.*

11. Lewis lived until 1906 on a pension provided first by Clemens and then, when Clemens went bankrupt, by Henry H. Rogers (Paine, *Biography,* 2:600). When Lewis died, Clemens scribbled his usual obituary: "Poor Lewis is dead, & I am so glad he is set free" (SLC to Clara Clemens, July 27, 1906, MTP, Letter File).

12. *Autobiography,* 1:296; 2:60-61; Paine, *Biography,* 2:573; SLC to Professor Lounsbury, July 21, 1904, MTP, Letter File; *What Is Man?* p. 119. Unless otherwise cited, the information on Griffin in this chapter is taken from Clemens's "Family Sketch," typescript, pp. 7-32, MTP.

13. "Mental Telegraphy," *Harriet Shelley,* p. 136; SLC to Jean Clemens, January 11, 26, 1907, MTP, Letter File; SLC to Karl Gerhardt, May 13, 1891, MTP, Letter File; Paine, *Biography,* 2:778; 3:838; Mary Lawton, *A Lifetime with Mark Twain: Memories of Katy Leary* (New York, 1925), pp. 32, 99.

14. *Autobiography,* 1:298.

15. SLC to "Brer [Frank] Whitmore," August 4, 1889, MTP, Letter File; SLC to Howells, October 11, 1876, MTHL, 1:158; SLC to Livy Clemens, July 17, n.d., MTP, Letter File; Clara Clemens, *My Father Mark Twain* (New York, 1931), p. 211.

16. Typescript Notebook 15, p. 6, MTP; SLC to Joseph Twichell, October 2, 1879, MTP, Letter File.

17. Clara Clemens, *My Father Mark Twain,* pp. 27-28, 110, 212.

18. "Wapping Alice," Autobiographical Dictation, April 9, 1907, typescript, DV 344a, p. 1948, MTP.

19. Ibid., pp. 1951-52, 1954, MTP.

20. In "Those Extraordinary Twins" a "fool-hearted Negro wench" named Nancy reacts to her first sight of Siamese twins by paling to chocolate, then to off-orange, and finally to amber (*Pudd'nhead Wilson,* p. 279).

21. "Wapping Alice," pp. 1952-53, MTP.

22. Clara Clemens, *My Father Mark Twain,* pp. 110-12.

23. Typescript Notebook 28, p. 30, MTP. "Write Geo Griffin for Forum" and several other comparable entries can be found in Typescript Notebooks 32, p. 12; 32 (I), p. 8; 32a (I), p. 29; 32a (II), pp. 42, 46; and 32b (I), pp. 18, 21, MTP.

24. Paine, *Biography*, 2:573.

25. Griffin accompanied the Clemenses on an Atlantic voyage to England and the Continent in April 1878 (Kaplan, *Mr. Clemens and Mark Twain*, p. 212).

26. "Taming the Bicycle," *What Is Man?* p. 291.

27. "The Great Dark," Tuckey, *Which Was the Dream?* pp. 102-50.

CHAPTER 8

1. *Pudd'nhead Wilson's New Calendar; Huckleberry Finn*, pp. 294, 116.

2. James M. Cox, in "Remarks on the Sad Initiation of Huckleberry Finn," *Sewanee Review* 62 (1954):389-405, also sees Jim as the moral center of the novel.

3. From time to time the NAACP, the Urban League, and other black organizations have objected to the characterization of Nigger Jim, but more often to the use of the word nigger.

4. This chapter is not so much about Nigger Jim as it is about Huck's feelings about Jim. Chadwick Hansen's "The Character of Jim and the Ending of *Huckleberry Finn*," *Massachusetts Review* 5 (1963):45-66, remains the best analysis of Nigger Jim.

5. Pap, we recall, has returned to claim Huck's half of the twelve thousand dollars taken from the cave by Huck and Tom at the end of *Tom Sawyer*.

6. Pages 23-25. The usual equation between black as evil and white as good is repeated twice in the novel. The Pokeville sinners at the camp meeting are "black with sin" (p. 182), and Huck considers Jim to be a particularly "good nigger" because he is white inside (p. 381). But Mark Twain was careful not to maintain the color pattern consistently: Pap's face is "a white to make a body sick" (p. 26). In a later story, "Was It Heaven? Or Hell?," *The $30,000 Bequest*, pp. 65-98, a doctor pays two black nurses the ultimate compliment by calling them "white souls with black skins" (p. 78).

7. Pages 66, 89, 69, 63, 91; Robert L. Vales, "Thief and Theft in *Huckleberry Finn*," *American Literature* 37 (1966):420-29. Daniel Hoffman, in *Form and Fable in American Fiction* (New York, 1965), pp. 317-42, shows that all superstitions in *Huckleberry Finn* except the hairball are of European, not African, origin.

8. Pages 116, 128, 161, 73-74. J. Barchilon and J. S. Kovel, in "*Huckleberry Finn:* A Psychoanalytic Study," *Journal of the American Psychoanalytic Association* 14 (1966):775-815, see Jim as a substitute mother for Huck. Kenneth S. Lynn, in "Huck and Jim," *Yale Review* 47 (1958):421-31, develops the idea of Jim as surrogate father.

9. In a fine analysis of the moral meaning of the novel, Leo Marx, in "Mr. Eliot, Mr. Trilling, and *Huckleberry Finn*," *American Scholar* 22 (1953):423-40, calls attention to the full implications of "They're after us!"

10. Pages 100, 71. "Huck clings to Jim because the slave's companionship provides a bulwark against the forces of loneliness." Campbell Tatham, " 'Dismal and Lonesome': A New Look at *Huckleberry Finn*," *Modern Fiction Studies* 14 (1968):47-55.

11. Pages 106, 92, 128, 155.

12. There has been considerable difference of opinion on the authenticity of Nigger Jim's dialect, and whether it enhances or detracts from his character. Lee A. Pederson, "Negro Speech in the *Adventures of Huckleberry Finn*," *Mark Twain Journal* (Winter 1965-66), pp. 1-4, concludes that education, social class, and occupation are more relevant criteria for distinguishing dialect than race. James J. Kelley, in "They're Trying to Kill *Huckleberry Finn*," *Mark*

203

Twain Journal (Winter 1965–66), pp. 13-14, argues that the average black person did, and does, speak a "lower-vulgate English."

13. Pages 106-11.

14. Pages 215-16. Hansen, in "The Character of Jim," pp. 49, 54, argues that the deaf-and-dumb story, "one of the tritest popular themes" of Mark Twain's time, is made "effective and genuine by giving it to Jim." DeVoto, *Mark Twain at Work*, p. 67, shows that Mark Twain considered using the story early in the manuscript, but did not assign it to Jim until later.

15. Pages 116-20.

16. "By humbling himself [Huck] . . . did more than assuage a hypersensitive conscience. . . . [He] needed to do it *for himself.*" Sidney J. Krause, "Huck's First Moral Crisis," *Mississippi Quarterly* 18 (1965):70.

17. Both Huck and Jim are misinformed about how much freedom awaits Jim at Cairo. Southern Illinois was no haven for runaway slaves. It was settled largely by Southerners, and all residents of Illinois were legally required to capture and return runaways. Moreover Jim must still take a steamboat up the Ohio River, bordered on one side by the slave state of Kentucky, before he can make contact with the underground railway to Canada. Nevertheless, despite its dangers, the Ohio River Valley was certainly a better alternative than the deep South. See Harris, *History of Negro Slavery in Illinois,* pp. 22-23, 53, 109-10.

18. Pages 123-25. Walter Blair, in "Why Huck and Jim Went Downstream," *College English* 18 (1956):106-7, and Henry Nash Smith, in his introduction to the Riverside edition of the novel (1958), pp. vii-x, have explained that Huck and Jim miss Cairo in the fog because Mark Twain decided to switch the novel's emphasis from Jim's quest for freedom up the Ohio (which Clemens did not know and which would eliminate the anti-Southern theme) to a report of life in the deep South. As Smith explains, his device to allow the raft to float deeper into slave territory was to bring the King and the Duke on board.

19. Mark Twain was obsessed with the sum of forty dollars. The two slave hunters float forty dollars to Huck to save his "family" from the smallpox (p. 127); the King sells Jim for forty dollars (p. 294); and Tom gives Jim forty dollars at the end of the novel "for being prisoner for us so patient" (p. 403). Probably the figure became fixed in Mark Twain's mind through repetition, but it happens to coincide with the price Marshall Clemens got for selling his slave Charley in 1842. See Victor A. Doyno, "Over Twain's Shoulder: The Composition and Structure of *Huckleberry Finn,*" *Modern Fiction Studies* 14 (Spring 1968):3-6; and Thomas Werge, "Huck, Jim and Forty Dollars," *Mark Twain Journal* (Winter 1965–66), pp. 15-16.

20. Pages 294-95. I am indebted to Henry Nash Smith's analysis of the language structure Mark Twain used to dramatize Huck's predicament (*Huckleberry Finn,* Riverside edition, pp. xv-xvi).

21. Pages 296-97. This crucial passage is one of the few that received a thorough rewriting. Walter Blair has found evidence to suggest that Mark Twain first wrote the "go to hell" sequence as a burlesque. In revising the episode he expanded it by some 150 words and changed the tone, thus turning it into the moral climax of the novel (*Mark Twain & Huck,* p. 353).

22. Page 358; Blair, *Mark Twain & Huck,* p. 353.

23. The argument that Huck, as a child, cannot perceive Jim's deterioration is not convincing if viewed within the context of his thoughts (two chapters earlier) about going to hell for Jim. Either the chapter entitled "You Can't Pray A Lie" is indeed a lie and the evasion the "truth," or vice versa.

24. Earlier, when the King and the Duke invade the raft to "work" the villages downstream, Jim is tied and abandoned for hours at a time. When he complains about being bound for so long, he is painted blue, dressed in a

horse-hair wig, and displayed on the raft as a "Sick Arab—but harmless when not out of his head," in order to keep suspicious slave hunters from coming on board. But that's not all: if Mark Twain had not discarded some notes he intended to use in the novel Jim would have been ridden around Arkansas on an elephant, turned into a gorilla in a circus act, and "sawed in two, nearly" in a minstrel show (DeVoto, *Mark Twain at Work,* pp. 67, 75-79). Jim's deterioration at Phelps's Farm therefore is not unique; it happens whenever he encounters whites other than Huck. The uniqueness of the Phelps episode is that Huck, too, is involved in Jim's denegration.

25. In nineteenth-century Banjo-Bones minstrel productions darkies threw threats and pantomime punches but registered no pain—much as we laugh today at animated cartoon characters who are repeatedly "killed," only to rise again.

26. Far more than the raft, the cabin prison *is* a stage and Mark Twain put it to dramatic use: the evasion chapters were one of his favorite platform readings on his tour with George Washington Cable in 1884.

27. Pages 328-29, 369, 343, 360-65, 332. The argument that Jim is dependent upon the boys for his freedom and therefore must be submissive is not totally convincing. His relationship with Huck on the river suggests that he could have exerted some influence on the way he was treated in prison.

28. "All modern American literature comes from one book by Mark Twain called *Huckleberry Finn.* If you read it you must stop where the Nigger Jim is stolen from the boys. That is the real end. The rest is just cheating." *Green Hills of Africa* (New York, 1935), p. 2. Hemingway forgot that Jim was stolen from Huck only, not from "the boys." Robert Penn Warren, in "Mark Twain," *Southern Review* 8 (1972):459-92, is only the most recent of numerous critics who argue that the novel evolves unexpectedly into a series of moral problems that demand confrontation and resolution. Other critics minimize the importance of the quest for freedom and uphold the ending as fulfilling the artistic canons of the novel as a self-contained work of art.

29. Actually Jim is a burden to Huck in two ways: his role as teacher reveals him as a person to whom care and respect are owed, and the moral lessons he teaches Huck are constraining to a boy accustomed to having his way with blacks.

30. Page 404.

31. In one of the books he began and finished during the hiatus in the composition of *Huckleberry Finn* Mark Twain wrote that rafting on the Neckar in Germany was "gentle, and gliding, and smooth, and noiseless . . . a deep and tranquil ecstasy." Mark Twain, *A Tramp Abroad,* 2 vols. (New York, 1929), 1:107.

32. Page 399. Mark Twain thought so little of Miss Watson that he had difficulty remembering who she was: "Who is 'Miss Watson?' Ah, she's WD's sister.—old spinster" (DeVoto, *Mark Twain at Work,* p. 71).

CHAPTER 9

1. SLC to Howells, August 22, 1887, MTHL, 2:595. The chapter title is from Mark Twain, "American Authors and British Pirates," *New Princeton Review* 5 (January 1888):50-51.

2. We remember that it is Nigger Jim's remorseful mistreatment of his daughter, that is, his fallibility, that first draws Huck's sympathy.

3. SLC to Garfield, January 12, 1881, *Letters,* 1:393-94. I have not found any other evidence that Douglass was "a personal friend" of Clemens, though the two doubtless met socially.

4. The Rev. Joseph Chester (president of Lincoln University) to SLC,

August 16, 1882, MTP, Letter File; Paine, *Mark Twain's Notebook,* pp. 191-92; Philip Butcher, "Mark Twain's Installment on the National Debt," *Southern Literary Journal* 1 (1969):48-55.

5. Charles Porter to Samuel and Olivia Clemens, February 29, 1882, April 4, 1883; SLC to Karl and Josephine Gerhardt, May 1, 1883, MTP, Letter File.

6. Bret Harte, Dan Slote, James Osgood, Whitelaw Reid, Charles Webster, Ray Bliss, and James Paige are a few examples of men who suffered Clemens's wrath for real or alleged offenses.

7. Typescript Notebook 17, p. 42, MTP; SLC to Howells, September 17, 1884, MTHL, 2:509-10; Paine, *Biography,* 2:777.

8. SLC to Howells, February 27, 1881, MTHL, 1:356; Typescript Notebooks 23, p. 59; 24, p. 4, MTP.

9. SLC to Howells, September 19, 1877, MTHL, 1:202-4.

10. Typescript Notebooks 17, p. 42; 16, pp. 14-15, MTP. I am grateful to Fred Anderson and Bruce T. Hamilton, editor and editorial assistant for the Mark Twain Papers respectively, for pointing out to me that the Clara in the quotation was not Clara Clemens (who was eight at the time), but Clara Spaulding, a friend of Livy's.

11. SLC to James Osgood, March 4, 1882, in *Mark Twain's Letters to His Publishers, 1867–1894,* ed. Hamlin Hill (Berkeley, 1967), pp. 152-53.

12. Unpublished letter titled "In Mrs. Cleveland's Autograph book," June 5, 1888, MTP, Letter File.

13. "On Stanley and Livingstone," July 15, 1886, *Speeches,* p. 133; Typescript Notebooks 25, pp. 9-11; 26, p. 10, MTP. I have not found another instance in which Mark Twain used a form of *nigger* in print or speech between 1867 and the London incident in 1886.

14. There are unmistakable parallels between Arthur's England and the antebellum South: squalid villages, boorish manners, feudal estates, knight-errantry, and, above all, an explicit comparison of English servitude with Southern slavery: the "death march" and the sale of the girl on the road are taken, with some embellishment, from the autobiography of a South Carolina slave, Charles Ball, in *Fifty Years in Chains, or the Life of an American Slave* (New York, 1860), pp. 29-42. After writing an entire chapter on the "Southern" innuendos in *A Connecticut Yankee* I have chosen not to include it. Most of the comparisons between Hank Morgan and Arthurian England are as much Yankee versus the Old World as they are Yankee versus the South. For some of the comparisons see Henry Nash Smith, *Mark Twain's Fable of Progress: Political and Economic Ideas in "A Connecticut Yankee"* (New Brunswick, N.J., 1964), p. 36, and especially Louis D. Rubin, Jr., *The Writer in the South* (Athens, Ga., 1972), pp. 69-74.

15. In Cable's *The Grandissimes* (1882) the quadroon Palmyra Philosophe has the same "passion" and "barbaric and magnetic beauty" as Roxana in *Pudd'nhead Wilson.* For accounts of the relationship between Cable and Clemens see Guy A. Cardwell, *Twins of Genius* (Michigan State College, 1953), pp. 71-76; Arlin Turner, "Mark Twain in New Orleans," *McNeese Review* 7 (1954):10-13; and idem, *George W. Cable* (Durham, N.C., 1956), pp. 120-22, 175-93.

16. SLC to George Washington Cable, July 17, 1881, MTP, Letter File; Howells, *My Mark Twain,* p. 99; LOM, p. 380.

17. G. W. Cable, "The Freedman's Case in Equity," *Century Magazine* 29 (December 1884); Henry W. Grady, "In Plain Black and White," ibid., 29 (April 1885); Cable, "The Silent South," ibid., 30 (September 1885). See Arlin Turner, ed., *The Negro Question: A Selection of Writings on Civil Rights in the South* (Garden City, N.Y., 1958), for some of Cable's essays on blacks.

18. "Cable is a great man," Clemens wrote Livy during the tour; and if he continued his fight on behalf of the black race "his greatness will be recognized" (February 3, 1885, quoted in Kaplan, *Mr. Clemens and Mark Twain*, p. 265.) But Clemens also admired one of Cable's detractors, Grace King (1851–1932), the New Orleans author who combined patrician charm with a passionate loyalty to the South and who considered Cable's writing biased toward blacks. As Clemens soured on Cable, he found Grace King excellent company. The two exchanged speculation on whether "Providence was a darkey" and Grace King once observed that Clemens ate at the dinner table "like a corn-field darkey." See Robert Bush, "Grace King and Mark Twain," *American Literature* 44 (1972):31-51.

19. Cardwell, *Twins of Genius*, pp. 71-76. Cable expressed satisfaction that many letters praising his performance came from colored men.

20. In 1884, the year he had those talks with Cable on "a deep subject," Clemens wrote in his notebook: "America in 1985, Negro supremacy—the whites under foot" (Typescript Notebook 18, p. 19, MTP).

21. *Following the Equator*, 1:60-64, 190.

22. Typescript Notebook 28, p. 24, MTP; *Following the Equator*, 1:239.

23. *Following the Equator*, 2:319, 372-73.

24. Typescript Notebook 30 (II), p. 35, MTP.

25. Typescript Notebook 10, p. 30, MTP.

26. DeVoto, *Mark Twain in Eruption*, pp. 33-34, 49.

27. Foner, *Mark Twain: Social Critic*, pp. 295-303.

28. See James Elbert Cutler, *Lynch-Law* (New York, 1905), pp. 161-79. Blair, in *Mark Twain & Huck*, p. 314, cites 114 lynchings in 1882, the year Clemens revisited the South; 134 in 1883; more than 1,500 in the 1890s; 115 in 1900, the year Mark Twain began to gather data for "The U.S. of Lyncherdom"; and 130 in 1901, the year he wrote the article.

29. The *Monroe County* (Mo.) *Appeal* reported lynchings in the area where Clemens was born on the following dates: May 29, 1891; December 27, 1895; March 31, 1899; June 16, 1899; November 16 and 23, 1900; May 9 and 29, 1902; September 12, 1902; and October 3, 1902.

30. "The United States of Lyncherdom," *Europe and Elsewhere*, pp. 248-49.

31. Budd, *Mark Twain: Social Philosopher*, p. 201; SLC to Frank Bliss, August 26, 29, 1901, original at University of Texas, Austin, photocopy in MTP, Letter File.

32. Paine, *Biography*, 4:1273.

33. *Speeches*, pp. 276-80; Paine, *Biography*, 4:1272-73; *Autobiography*, 2:2-3. For Washington's high estimation of Mark Twain see "Tribute to Mark Twain," *North American Review* III (1910):828.

34. "The Rhodes Scholars' Club Address," unpublished autobiographical dictation made in 1907, pp. 2129-33, MTP.

35. August 22, 1897, *Letters*, 2:645-46.

36. See, for example, Typescript Notebooks 22 (II), pp. 37, 42; 32b (I), pp. 24-25, MTP.

37. Clara Clemens, *My Father Mark Twain*, p. 188.

CHAPTER 10

1. *Pudd'nhead Wilson*, pp. 71, 123; *Harriet Shelley*, p. 264; *Following the Equator*, 1:247; 2:51.

2. For an account of Malicious Mulattoes—variously called Guineas, Brass Ankles, Red Bones, Ramps, Issues, Red Legs, Melungeons, and Buckheads—see Brewton Berry, *Almost White* (New York, 1963), pp. 101-38, 185-245, 287-92.

For what is still an excellent account of the subject, see Sterling A. Brown, *The Negro in American Fiction* (Washington, D.C., 1937), pp. 1-115 passim.

3. For the similarities between Roxana and the mulatto slave woman Cassy in *Uncle Tom's Cabin,* see Lynn, *Mark Twain and Southwestern Humor,* pp. 265-66. Clemens read Cable's *The Grandissimes,* which deals in part with miscegenation, and may have borrowed part of the plot for *Pudd'nhead Wilson* from Cable's *Madame Delphine,* which deals with a quadroon mother who renounces her daughter so she may enter the white world. Howell's *Imperative Duty,* about a white man and a very white octoroon woman who have trouble deciding whether they should marry, was published one year before *Pudd'nhead Wilson.*

4. DV 128, MTP. Paine dates the story in the 1880s.

5. As with *Huckleberry Finn* I do not intend to summarize or to cite critical discussions of *Pudd'nhead Wilson.* Numerous listings are available.

6. *Pudd'nhead Wilson,* p. 17.

7. The novel is filled with ironic counterpoints, most having to do with the disparity between appearance and reality, or between speech and deed. One such counterpoint involves the phrase "down the river." Early in the book Roxana jokingly threatens to ask the owner of a black slave named Jasper to sell him down the river; a few pages later Percy Driscoll seriously threatens to sell Roxana herself down the river. Tom Driscoll, who sells his mother Roxana down the river, eventually gets sold there himself.

8. David Wilson is condemned to twenty-three years of social exile in Dawson's Landing for remarking on his arrival in the village that if he owned half of a dog that was yelping, he would kill his half. The villagers promptly label him a pudd'nhead ("What did he reckon would become of the other half if he killed his half?") and boycott his law practice. In his leisure Wilson takes fingerprints of most of the citizens, including the mulatto Tom Driscoll, whom he ultimately exposes as the murderer of Judge Driscoll.

9. *Pudd'nhead Wilson,* p. 202.

10. Ibid., pp. 70-72, 76-79.

11. Cox, *Mark Twain: The Fate of Humor,* p. 228.

12. In the working notes for the novel Mark Twain made Judge Driscoll himself the father of Tom. But in the finished work he shied from such intimacy, possibly because his own father, Marshall Clemens, resembled the aristocrats in the story. Marvin Fisher and Michael Elliott, in *"Pudd'nhead Wilson:* Half a Dog is Worse than None," *Southern Review* 8 (1972):544, point out that Percy Driscoll would have had "to vault out of one bed and leap into another in order to father sons born to different mothers on the same day."

13. The mulatto Jasper, discussed in the next chapter, is Mark Twain's superlative portrait of the black avenger.

14. Mark Twain originally had Tom Driscoll hang himself with his suspenders after David Wilson finds him guilty of murder. By changing Tom's fate to being sold down the river, Mark Twain completes the cycle of Tom earlier selling Roxana down the river.

15. *Pudd'nhead Wilson,* pp. 11-12.

16. Mark Twain made it clear that for slaves robbed of their freedom, stealing was not immoral. According to Kenneth M. Stampp, adult slaves "doubtless detected the element of hypocrisy in white criticism of their moral laxity" (*The Peculiar Institution,* p. 350).

17. *Pudd'nhead Wilson,* p. 75. Roxana's genealogical pretensions are strikingly similar to Aunt Rachel's in "A True Story," as Roxana herself is similar to Rachel in every detail but color.

18. Ibid., pp. 123-24. Thomas Jefferson, among others, elaborated on the desirability of mixing red with white as opposed to black with white in *Notes on the State of Virginia*, ed. William Peden (Chapel Hill, 1955), pp. 58-64, 100-102, 140. For an excellent account of Jefferson's racial feelings and fantasies, see Winthrop D. Jordan, *White Over Black: American Attitudes toward the Negro, 1550–1812* (Chapel Hill, 1968), pp. 475-81.

19. Jenny, Marshall Clemens's slave in Hannibal, is described by both Mark Twain and Paine as young, handsome, arrogant, stubborn, insolent, and statuesque. Later, like Roxana, she was sold down the river and became a chambermaid on a steamboat.

20. W. J. Cash wrote that black women, "taught an easy complaisance for commercial reasons," were "to be had for the taking" and that white boys "inevitably learned to use" them. *The Mind of the South* (New York, 1940), p. 87. Bernard DeVoto speaks sweepingly of the "forbidden world of slaves," with its black concubines ready to initiate "their quota of pubescent boys" into manhood, *Mark Twain's America* (Boston, 1932), pp. 64-65. Kenneth M. Stampp, using specific evidence, concludes that "sexual contacts between the races were not the rare aberrations of a small group of depraved whites but a frequent occurrence involving whites of all social and cultural levels." *The Peculiar Institution*, pp. 350-51.

21. The Beinecke Rare Book and Manuscript Library at Yale University has some verses by Mark Twain about lost virility, and his speech to the Stomach Club on "The Science of Onanism." There is of course *1601*, and Mark Twain's late remarks about white female sexuality in *Letters from the Earth*, ed. Bernard DeVoto (New York, 1962), pp. 16-17, 50-53.

22. *Autobiography*, 2:276-77; MTHL, 1:7. Dixon Wecter discusses Hannibal's brothels and prostitutes and concludes that Clemens, "with a taste for the 'low company' of the Blankenships, and tutelage in several newspaper offices," was probably well-acquainted with the town's "seamy side" (*Hannibal*, pp. 147, 174-75, 214-15).

23. Typescript Notebook 16a, pp. 26-28, MTP.

24. Typescript Notebook 38, p. 14, MTP.

25. Kaplan, *Mr. Clemens and Mark Twain*, pp. 222, 323, offers a few titillating examples of Mark Twain's sex jokes, but omits the more numerous and mild examples, such as a couple copulating under a bridge; a girl who goes to a doctor to be vaccinated, is raped, and asks "to be vaccinated again"; and a "procrastitute," who is defined as "a woman who promises & then fools along & doesn't perform." In the last notebook there is some very bad verse about lovers returning a buggy with "a grease-spot on the cushion/And I think there's been some pushing,/For there's boot-tracks on the dashboard upside down," and a comparison between Standard Oil being slapped with a heavy fine and the June bride who "expected it but didn't suppose it would be so big." Typescript Notebook 38, pp. 17-19, MTP.

26. Paine, *Mark Twain's Notebook*, pp. 348-52.

27. "I go to unnameable places. I do unprincipled things; and every vision is vivid, every sensation—physical as well as moral—is *real*" (Kaplan, *Mr. Clemens and Mark Twain*, pp. 340-46).

28. Joan of Arc was, for Clemens, an idealization of nonsexual and, as he understood it, constitutionally nonnubile young womanhood. In his copy of Jules Michelet's *Jeanne d'Arc* (1853), opposite a passage citing the testimony of Domrémy women that Joan had never menstruated, Clemens wrote: "The higher life absorbed her and suppressed her physical (sexual) development" (*Mr. Clemens and Mark Twain*, p. 315). In a courtship letter to Livy, Clemens described her "as pure as snow . . . untainted, untouched even by the impure

thoughts of others." March 1869, *Love Letters*, p. 76. Howells called Livy "heavenly white," and Mrs. James T. Fields described Livy as especially "white and delicate and tender." *Atlantic Monthly*, 130 (1922):342-48. When told of the alarming amount of venereal disease among British troops in India, Clemens wrote that clean native women "subject to rigid inspection ought to be kept for these soldiers," so the soldiers would not subsequently infect the "fresh young English girls" they married. Paine, *Mark Twain's Notebooks*, pp. 280, 286.

29. In 1906, in response to William Lecky's remarks in his *History of European Morals, from Augustus to Charlemagne*, 2 vols. (New York, 1903; Clemens's copy in MTP), that "the chastity of female slaves was sedulously guarded by the Church," Clemens scrawled in the margin: "This is better than the Southern Protestant Church of America ever did, *nicht wahr?*"

30. Robert Wiggins, in *Mark Twain: Jackleg Novelist* (Seattle, 1964), p. 107, points out that Mark Twain is inconsistent when he argues that environment (what he called training) determines human behavior exclusively. With Chambers, Mark Twain's deterministic theory is convincing: slavery ruins him. But Tom Driscoll is carefully shown to be wicked *before* his white training has the opportunity either to uplift or to damage him. With Chambers, environment is the determining factor; with Driscoll, both environment and heredity (including six generations of white blood) could be said to determine his behavior.

CHAPTER 11

1. Mark Twain, *Tom Sawyer Abroad, Tom Sawyer, Detective and Other Stories* (New York, 1929), p. 102; Tuckey, *Which Was the Dream?* p. 415.

2. "Remorse! remorse!" Mark Twain wrote as early as 1876 in "Carnival of Crime in Connecticut." "It seemed to me that it would eat the very heart out of me!" In 1903, after believing he was once again bankrupt only to find he had made an error in his arithmetic and multiplied his debts by two, Clemens wrote that "two or three nights like that [last] night of mine could drive a man to suicide" (*Letters*, 2:734).

3. Typescript Notebook 36, p. 20, MTP. "What a man sees in the human race is merely himself in the deep and honest privacy of his own heart. Byron despised the race because he despised himself. I feel as Byron did, and for the same reason" (Paine, *Biography*, 4:1539).

4. Henry Rogers, the Standard Oil millionaire who took charge of Clemens's financial affairs, insisted that Livy's $60,000, invested in Clemens's bankrupt publishing company, was the largest single claim on the firm and therefore entitled her to the status of a preferred creditor. This meant that all of Clemens's copyrights, and his stock in the Paige typesetter, would be assigned to her.

5. In Livy's last illness Clemens was singled out by her doctors as the chief external cause of the nervous collapse that accompanied her hyperthyroid heart disease. On December 30, 1902, he was permitted to see her for five minutes, the first time in three months; on their thirty-third wedding anniversary in February 1903 he was allowed five minutes with her. After Livy's death Clemens was not permitted to see, telephone, or write his daughter Clara for a year, because he might "upset" her.

6. Clemens was fond of metaphors about aging, most of them premature. As early as 1867, at the age of thirty-two, he informed "Mother" Mary Fairbanks on the *Quaker City* tour that he was "an old burned-out crater" and that "the fires of my life are all dead within me" (Kaplan, *Mr. Clemens and Mark Twain,* p. 45).

7. Blair, *Hannibal, Huck & Tom*, pp. 92-140.

8. Mark Twain, *Tom Sawyer Abroad*, p. 102.

9. Ibid., p. 112.

10. Ibid., p. 19. What Jim's performance lacks in quality is more than made up by quantity. In *Huckleberry Finn* he appears, in dialogue or action, in less than one-quarter of the novel, between long absences. In *Tom Sawyer Abroad* he is constantly present and participates actively in more than half the story.

11. Ibid., pp. 34-35.

12. Ibid., pp. 43-45, 70-71.

13. Ibid., pp. 34-35, 70, 105.

14. Ibid., pp. 39-40, 56, 86-87.

15. Ibid., pp. 100-102.

16. Ibid., pp. 108-09.

17. "Tom Sawyer's Conspiracy," published in Blair, *Hannibal, Huck & Tom*, pp. 170-71.

18. Ibid., pp. 213-16, 228.

19. Ibid., pp. 214, 216, 234.

20. James Kirke Paulding, *Westward Ho! A Tale* (New York, 1832), 1:57-58.

21. Typescript Notebook 25, p. 24, MTP, quoted in part in Paine, *Mark Twain's Notebook*, p. 212. Blair, *Hannibal, Huck & Tom*, p. 16, n. 35, notes that Mark Twain struck a similar tone of despair as early as 1882, after a recent visit to Hannibal recorded in Chapter 55 of *Life on the Mississippi*.

22. Typescript Notebooks 32a (II), pp. 34, 58; 31 (I), p. 22, MTP; "Villagers of 1840-43," p. 9, MTP; Wecter, *Hannibal*, p. 215.

23. *Autobiography*, 1:123-25.

24. Winthrop Jordan, in *White over Black*, pp. 136-78, traces the widespread white opinion, dating from the sixteenth century on, that the black man's genital organs were larger and thus posed a grave threat to white dominance and that miscegenation would cause widespread disease and "pollution" of the white race.

25. Typescript Notebook 35, p. 13, MTP, published in Blair, *Hannibal, Huck & Tom*, p. 16. "Beebe" was William Beebe, Hannibal's most conspicuous slave trader, discussed in chapter 1 of this study. The angle brackets in the quotation appear in the Blair citation.

26. R. B. Bowen, the son of Clemens's boyhood friend Will Bowen, wrote in 1940 that his father had told him a "naughty and unprintable story" about something that happened between a black man and "those 'bad boys' in Hannibal" (*Mark Twain's Letters to Will Bowen*, p. 41).

27. Typescript Notebooks 18, p. 19; 22, p. 46, MTP. Mark Twain was far from the first well-known white Southerner to consider the possible overthrow of white by black. In *Notes on the State of Virginia* Thomas Jefferson wrote that "deep-rooted prejudices entertained by the whites" for "blacks" (the term in vogue then) meant that black moves toward equality would be fought. In 1849 John C. Calhoun wrote that if blacks were ever permitted political equality they would eventually hold "the white race at the South in complete subjection." See Richard Hofstadter, *The American Political Tradition and the Men Who Made It* (New York, 1948), p. 80.

28. In 1861 William Gilmore Simms cautioned his son to avoid "that lack of firmness, that overcaution, always trembling at consequences, & calculating chances, which was the infirmity of Hamlet" and was also the curse of the South; quoted in William R. Taylor, *Cavalier and Yankee: The Old South and American National Character* (New York, 1961), pp. 273-74. George Harrison is one in a long line of introspective, conscious-stricken Southerners in Southern

literature, ranging from Poe's neurasthenic Roderick Usher through Simms's Porgy and Harriet Stowe's Augustine St. Clare to Faulkner's Quentin Compson III.

29. "Which Was It?" Tuckey, *Which Was the Dream?* pp. 318-39.

30. Ibid., pp. 311-16.

31. Ibid., pp. 407-10.

32. Ibid., p. 415. In Harper Lee's *To Kill a Mockingbird* (New York, 1960), p. 223, Atticus Finch, the white lawyer, says to his children: "Don't fool yourselves—it's all adding up and one of these days we're going to pay the bill for it."

33. "Which Was It?" pp. 408-19.

34. Ibid., p. 415.

35. "The skin of every human being contains a slave" (Paine, *Mark Twain's Notebook,* p. 393).

36. By making a mulatto superior in courage and intellect to his black characters, Mark Twain opened himself to the charge of "racism." But by making Jasper a mulatto, he also magnified the crime of the South: George Harrison is forced to pay for the sins of his race at the hands of a man who is his blood relation.

CHAPTER 12

1. Faulkner, "The Bear," *The Portable Faulkner,* ed. Malcolm Cowley (New York, 1949), pp. 292-93; idem, *The Sound and the Fury* (New York, 1929), p. 313.

2. Faulkner, *Light in August,* pp. 238-40.

3. See, for example, the Mexican writer José Vasconcelos, one of the first to reverse the traditional ideology of racial purity as the basis of racial superiority and to predict the future supremacy of dark-skinned races, in *La Raza Cósmica* (Paris: Agencia Mundial de Librería, 1920).

4. Mark Twain, *The Mysterious Stranger* (New York, 1929), p. 140. One version, written in 1897, is set in snowbound Hannibal.

5. "The essence of the art *is* the breaking away, and is constituted of the tension between the pull of the old community and that of the forces separating the individual from it. . . . [Mark Twain stands] in a relationship to the society he knew that anticipates that of the generation of writers who came to literary maturity after the first world war. Not for decades after his time would there be other southern writers who would find themselves both tied to and dissociated from the southern community in something like the way he had been." Rubin, *The Writer in the South,* pp. 66, 80.

6. Howells, *My Mark Twain,* p. 30. To Quentin Compson in *The Sound and the Fury* time is man's enemy. Ellen Glasgow wrote of the relentless passage of time as the source of decay and death, and that she "had been born with an intimate feeling for the spirit of the past, and the lingering poetry of time and place." Carson McCullers spoke of the South as a "clock with no hands." Katherine Anne Porter calls herself "a grandchild of a lost War." Robert Penn Warren has written repeatedly on the importance of time and place. Time was Thomas Wolfe's great "enemy," and Eudora Welty has written that she is "touched off" by time and place.

APPENDIX

1. Mark Twain to Tom Fitch (a writer for the *Virginia City Union*), 1864, reprinted in Fatout, *Mark Twain in Virginia City,* pp. 66-67.

2. *New York Times,* October 7, 1877, reprinted in *The Twainian* 13 (March–April 1954):1-2.

3. Clemens's niece recalled that Clemens "knew plenty of girls but he always . . . managed to be polite about it, Southern-style" (Webster, *Mark Twain, Business Man,* p. 51).

4. "The Private History of a Campaign that Failed," *The American Claimant,* pp. 261-62, 265-68. E. W. Kemble's illustrations for the essay, which Mark Twain endorsed enthusiastically, depict the soldiers as backwoods boys on a lark.

5. *Autobiography,* 1:32-33, 36-38, 40-42, 49-51, 53; SLC to Howells, November 17, 1879, MTHL, 1:278-81.

6. Paine, *Biography,* 2:654-57, 799-816. A few months after "capturing" Grant's *Memoirs,* Clemens completed negotiations for the publication of the memoirs of McClellan, Sherman, and Sheridan.

7. Ulysses S. Grant, *The Personal Memoirs of U. S. Grant,* 2 vols. (New York, 1885), 1:246-49.

8. Paine, *Mark Twain's Notebook,* p. 183; Howells to SLC, December 5, 1885, MTHL, 2:541; "The Campaign that Failed," *The American Claimant,* p. 281.

9. "The Campaign that Failed," *The American Claimant,* pp. 276-79. In *Mark Twain's "Which Was the Dream?"* pp. 33-75, Major General Tom "X" (Clemens) was Grant's commanding officer in the Mexican War (p. 51). Later in the story another character refers to Clemens ("X") as one "of the three or four men of towering eminence in the Union." One of the others, predictably, is Grant (p. 63).

10. J. Stanley Mattson, "Mark Twain on War and Peace: The Missouri Rebel and 'The Campaign That Failed,'" *American Quarterly* 20 (1968):783-94. Later Mark Twain turned the fictitious murder from tragedy back into burlesque. Addressing a banquet of Union veterans in Baltimore in 1887, he called the murder the "bloodiest battle ever fought in human history," because the enemy was totally annihilated. If things continued at this pace Mark Twain would exterminate the Union Army singlehandedly every two weeks, so the honorable thing to do was to retire and give the Union cause a chance ("Sumter Six and Twenty Years Ago," in Neider, *Life As I Find It,* pp. 216-18). In London on July 4, 1899, Mark Twain thanked the British for referring to his conduct in "the war profession, in which I distinguished myself, short as my career was" (*Speeches,* pp. 187-89). In 1901, joining his Southern cousin Henry Watterson in Carnegie Hall to celebrate Lincoln's birthday, Mark Twain declared: "It was my intention to drive General Grant into the Pacific . . . and I told Colonel Watterson to surround the Eastern armies and wait till I came. But he was insubordinate and . . . the Union was saved" (*Speeches,* p. 229). In 1909, in reply to a letter from General Oliver Howard asking him to preside over a meeting to raise funds for Lincoln Memorial University at Cumberland Gap, Tennessee, Mark Twain wrote: "You ought not to say sarcastic things about my 'fighting on the other side.' General Grant did not act like that. General Grant paid me compliments. . . . He said if all the confederate soldiers had followed my example and adopted my military arts he could never have caught enough of them in a bunch to inconvenience the Rebellion. General Grant was a fair man . . . but you are prejudiced, and you have hurt my feelings" (*Letters,* 2:825, 827).

Primary Sources

THIS bibliography is confined to primary sources; the most useful secondary sources are cited in the footnotes. Most of the collections of material used in this study are housed in the Mark Twain Papers in the General Library, University of California at Berkeley. Other collections include: the Grant Smith collection of papers dealing with Mark Twain in Nevada, Bancroft Library, University of California at Berkeley; private collections in Hannibal; microfilmed material in the Beinecke Rare Book and Manuscript Library, Yale University; the C. Waller Barrett Library of American Literature at the University of Virginia; the Henry W. and Albert A. Berg Collection at the New York Public Library; and the Mark Twain Library in Florida, Missouri, under the supervision of Ralph Gregory.

1

The most valuable unpublished manuscripts, sketches, and notes written by Clemens, all available in the Mark Twain Papers, were the following:
"Adam Monument" (1906). Box 24.
Autobiographical Dictations File.
"Battle Hymn of the Republic (Brought Down to Date)" (1903).
    DeVoto 74.
Berg Collection (typescripts of Clemens-Howells correspondence).
"Colonel Sellers, A Drama in Five Acts" (July 1874). Play File.
Documents and Clippings File.
"Family Sketch" (1906). DeVoto 226.
"The George Harrison Story," formerly DeVoto 302, now Box 24.
"Newhouse's Jew Story." DeVoto 43.
"The Quarrel in the Strong-Box" (probably late 1890s). Paine 52a.
"Mr. Randall's Jew Story." DeVoto 44.
"A Record of the Small Foolishnesses of Susie & 'Bay' Clemens (Infants)."
    DeVoto 6.
Scrapbooks.
"Tom Sawyer, Detective" (original manuscript). Box 9.
Typescript Notebooks 1-38.
Unfinished, unpublished, ten-page manuscript regarding God and morality as depicted in the Bible (probably written in the 1880s).
    DeVoto 129.
"Wapping Alice" (about 1898). DeVoto 344a.

2

All letters in the Mark Twain Papers written by and to Clemens and members of his family between 1850 and 1910 were consulted. Of these the most important were exchanges with Frank Bliss, publisher; Will Bowen, boyhood companion; George Washington Cable; William Clagett, a secessionist friend in Nevada; Olivia, Orion, Jane, Pamela, Clara, and Jean Clemens; Carl and Josephine Gerhardt, sculptor and wife; Joel Chandler Harris; William Dean Howells; James Laird, the Nevada editor with whom Clemens exchanged insults over the miscegenation affair; James Osgood, one of Clemens's publishers; Charles Porter, the black artist whom Clemens financed in Paris; Joseph Twichell, Congregational pastor, neighbor, and Clemens's closest friend; and Frank ("Brer") Whitmore, another neighbor and publisher.

3

The following newspapers were consulted in California, Connecticut, Iowa, Kansas, Missouri, and New York: *Boston Post, Buffalo Express, Chicago Republican, Chicago Times, Chicago Tribune, Gold Hill* (Calif.) *Daily News, Grass Valley* (Calif.) *National, Hannibal Courier, Hannibal Daily Journal, Hannibal Daily Messenger, Hannibal Gazette, Hannibal Western Union, Hannibal Whig Journal, Hartford Courant, Humboldt* (Nev.) *Register, Kansas City Star, Keokuk* (Iowa) *Gate City, Keokuk Saturday Post, Monroe County* (Paris, Mo.) *Appeal, Nevada Daily Independent, New Orleans Daily Crescent, New Orleans Times-Democrat, New York Daily Graphic, New York Herald, New York Independent, New York Times, New York Tribune, Oakland Tribune, Palmyra* (Mo.) *Whig, Paris* (Mo.) *Mercury, Richmond Examiner, Sacramento Daily Union, St. Louis Daily Missouri Democrat, St. Louis Missouri Republican, St. Louis Times, San Andreas Independent, San Francisco Alta California, San Francisco Call, San Francisco Chronicle, San Francisco Golden Era, Sonora Herald, Virginia City Evening Bulletin*, and *Virginia City Territorial Enterprise*.

4

The following articles by Mark Twain were especially pertinent:
[Clemens, S. L. (Thomas Jefferson Snodgrass)]. "Julius Caesar Localized." *Keokuk* (Iowa) *Saturday Post*, November 1, 1856.
"About Smells." *Galaxy*, May 1870.
"An Accumulation of Copperheads." *San Francisco Call*, August 11, 1864.
"American Authors and British Pirates." *New Princeton Review* 5 (January 1888): 50-51.

"Another Traitor—Hang Him." *Virginia City Evening Bulletin,* April 1, 1864.

"Answers to Correspondents." *Daily Californian,* June 24, 1865.

"Blind Tom." *San Francisco Alta California,* August 1, 1869. Published in *The Twainian* 8 (July–August 1949): 4-5.

"Democratic Meeting at Hayes' Park." *San Francisco Call,* August 3, 1864.

"Democratic Ratification Meeting." *San Francisco Call,* September 9, 1864.

"Demosthenes." *Buffalo Express,* May 10, 1869.

"Female Suffrage: The Iniquitous Crusade." *St. Louis Daily Missouri Democrat,* March 15, 1867.

"Greeley and Jeff." *San Francisco Alta California,* May 28, 1867.

"Home and Mrs. Byron." *Buffalo Express,* September 11, 1869.

"L' Homme Qui Rit." In *Mark Twain's Satires & Burlesques,* ed. Franklin R. Rogers (New York, 1963), pp. 40-48, 460-64.

"How Is It?" *Virginia City Territorial Enterprise,* May 17 (possibly May 18), 1864.

"Inspired Humor." *Buffalo Express,* August 19, 1869.

"Journalism in Tennessee." *Buffalo Express,* September 4, 1869.

"Key West." *San Francisco Alta California,* Letter VII, January 6, 1867. Published in *Mark Twain's Travels with Mr. Brown,* ed. Franklin Walker and G. Ezra Dane (New York, 1940), pp. 69-81.

"Letter from Nevada Territory." *Sacramento Union,* December 23, 1862.

"Life on the Isthmus." *Buffalo Express,* October 4, 1870. Reprinted in *The Forgotten Writings of Mark Twain,* ed. Henry Duskis (New York, 1963), pp. 309-10.

"Miscegenation." *Virginia City Territorial Enterprise,* May 24, 1864. Published in *Mark Twain of the "Enterprise,"* ed. Henry Nash Smith and Frederick Anderson (Berkeley, 1957), pp. 197-98.

"Notable Things in St. Louis." *San Francisco Alta California,* April 16, 1867. Published in *Mark Twain's Travels with Mr. Brown,* ed. Franklin Walker and G. Ezra Dane (New York, 1940), p. 142.

"Only a Nigger." *Buffalo Express,* August 26, 1869.

"River Intelligence." *St. Louis Times,* May 2, 1874. Clippings File, MTP.

"The Sandwich Island Legislature." *San Francisco Golden Era,* June 24, 1866.

"The Scandal against Judge Field." *Chicago Republican,* February 8, 1868. Microfilm 22, MTP.

"A Scrap of Curious History." *Harper's Weekly,* October 1914.

"The Sex in New York." *San Francisco Alta California,* Letter XXII, May 26, 1867.

"Shocking Result of Miscegenation and Jealousy—Two Attempted Assassinations—Three Horrible Murders, and One Suicide!!" *Buffalo*

Express, May 1870. Reprinted in *The Forgotten Writings of Mark Twain,* ed. Henry Duskis (New York, 1963), pp. 250-55.

"Sociable Jimmy." *The Twainian* 2 (February 1943): 3-5. [Written early 1870.]

"The 'Tournament' in A.D. 1870." *Galaxy,* July 1870, pp. 135-36.

"The Treaty with China." *New York Tribune,* August 4, 1868.

"A Tribute to Anson Burlingame." *Buffalo Express,* February 1870.

"The White House Funeral." *New York Tribune,* March 4, 1869. Clippings File, MTP.

"Ye Cuban Patriot: A Calm Inspection of Him." *Buffalo Express,* December 25, 1869.

5

The following books by Mark Twain were the most useful. For a near-complete listing to 1935, see Merle Johnson, *A Bibliography of the Works of Mark Twain* (New York, 1935). A more recent compilation is needed.

The Adventures of Colonel Sellers, ed. Charles Neider. New York, 1915.

Adventures of Thomas Jefferson Snodgrass, ed. Charles Honce. Chicago, 1928.

The Autobiography of Mark Twain, ed. Charles Neider. New York, 1959.

Contributions to "The Galaxy" 1868–1871 by Mark Twain (Samuel Langhorne Clemens), ed. Bruce R. McElderry. Gainesville, Fla., 1961.

Court Trials in Mark Twain, ed. Daniel McKeithan. The Hague, 1958.

The Forgotten Writings of Mark Twain, ed. Henry Duskis. New York, 1963.

King Leopold's Soliloquy; A Defense of his Congo Rule. Congo Reform Association, 1905.

Letters from the Earth, ed. Bernard DeVoto. New York, 1962.

Letters from the Sandwich Islands, ed. G. Ezra Dane. Stanford, 1938.

The Love Letters of Mark Twain, ed. Dixon Wecter. New York, 1949.

Mark Twain: Letters from Hawaii, ed. A. Grove Day. New York, 1966.

Mark Twain: Life As I Find It, ed. Charles Neider. Garden City, 1961.

Mark Twain and the Government, ed. Svend Petersen. Caldwell, Idaho, 1960.

Mark Twain at Work, ed. Bernard DeVoto. New York, 1942.

Mark Twain-Howells Letters, ed. Henry Nash Smith and William M. Gibson. 2 vols. Cambridge, 1960.

Mark Twain in Eruption, ed. Bernard DeVoto. New York, 1940.

Mark Twain in Three Moods, ed. Friends of the Huntington Library. San Marino, 1948.

Mark Twain of the "Enterprise," ed. Henry Nash Smith and Frederick Anderson. Berkeley, 1957.

Primary Sources

Mark Twain on the Damned Human Race, ed. Janet Smith. New York, 1962.

Mark Twain's Correspondence with Henry Huttleson Rogers, 1893–1909, ed. Lewis Leary. Berkeley, 1969.

Mark Twain's Hannibal, Huck & Tom, ed. Walter Blair. Berkeley, 1969. (Particularly "Tom Sawyer's Conspiracy" and "Villagers of 1840–43.")

Mark Twain's Letters in the Muscatine Journal, ed. Edgar Branch. Chicago, 1942.

Mark Twain's Letters to His Publishers, 1867–1894, ed. Hamlin Hill. Berkeley, 1967.

Mark Twain's Letters to Mary, ed. Lewis Leary. New York, 1961.

Mark Twain's Letters to Will Bowen, ed. Theodore Hornberger. Austin, 1941.

Mark Twain's Mysterious Stranger Manuscripts, ed. William M. Gibson. Berkeley, 1969.

Mark Twain's Notebook, ed. Albert Bigelow Paine. New York, 1935.

Mark Twain's San Francisco, ed. Bernard Taper. New York, 1963.

Mark Twain's Satires & Burlesques, ed. Franklin R. Rogers. Berkeley, 1967.

Mark Twain's Travels with Mr. Brown, ed. Franklin Walker and G. Ezra Dane. New York, 1940.

Mark Twain's "Which Was the Dream?" and Other Symbolic Writings of the Later Years, ed. John S. Tuckey. Berkeley, 1967. (Particularly "Indiantown" and "Which Was It?")

Mark Twain to Mrs. Fairbanks, ed. Dixon Wecter. San Marino, 1949.

Mark Twain to Uncle Remus, ed. Thomas H. English. Atlanta, 1953.

Republican Letters, ed. Cyril Clemens. Webster Grove, Missouri, 1941.

Simon Wheeler, Detective, ed. Franklin R. Rogers. New York, 1963.

Sketches of the Sixties. San Francisco, 1927.

Traveling with the Innocents Abroad, ed. Daniel M. McKeithan. Norman, Oklahoma, 1958.

Washington in 1868, ed. Cyril Clemens. Webster Grove, Missouri, 1943.

Washoe Giant in San Francisco, ed. Franklin Walker. San Francisco, 1938.

The Writings of Mark Twain. Stormfield Edition. 37 vols. New York, 1929.

Index

Index

Index

Index

This book has been typeset
in Linotype Caledonia with Garamond
Bold Italic used for display. Printing
by NAPCO Graphic Arts, Inc.
Design by Jonathan Greene